Culture and the State

CULTURE
AND THE
STATE

David Lloyd and Paul Thomas

Routledge   New York and London

Published in 1998

Routledge
29 West 35th Street
New York, NY 10001

Published in Great Britain by

Routledge
11 New Fetter Lane
London EC4P 4EE

This book is for our children, George, Sam, and Talia.
It is also dedicated to the memory of Richard Ashcraft, Eugene
Lunn and Gwylfa Roberts.

Library of Congress Cataloging-in-Publication Data

Lloyd, David, 1955–
    Culture and the state / by David Lloyd and Paul Thomas.
      p. cm.
    Includes index.
    ISBN 0-415-91102-8 (cloth). — ISBN 0-415-91103-6 (pbk.)
    1. Great Britain—Civilization—19th century. 2. Great Britain—
Politics and government—19th century. 3. Culture—Political aspects—
Great Britain. 4. Art and state—Great Britain—History.
I. Thomas, Paul, 1943– . II. Title.
941.081—dc21   97-29639
                                                            CIP

Contents

Acknowledgments

Our Epilogue first appeared under a different title in *Theory and Society*, no. 14 (1985), pp. 419–44. We are grateful to Karen Lukas for permission to reprint it here. Some material in Chapters 2–4 first saw print in an earlier version as "*Culture and Society* or Culture and the State?" in *Social Text*, no. 30 (1992), pp. 27–56, reprinted in Christopher Prendergast, ed., *Cultural Materialism. On Raymond Williams* (Minneapolis: University of Minnesota Press, 1995), pp. 268–304. Part of Chapter 1 appeared in another form in *Rethinking Germanistik: Canon and Culture*, ed. Robert Bledsoe et al. (New York: Peter Lang, 1991).

This book has been some years in the making. There are more people to whom our thanks are due—particularly our students—than can possibly be listed here. Even so, we would like to thank in particular Cecelia Cancellaro at Routledge (not least for her patience), and Blakey Vermeule, Michel Chaouli, Françoise Vergès, Melissa Perez, and Vanessa Poole for their invaluable research. To Celeste Langan and Shannon Stimson our thanks for their various contributions and responses at different stages of our work. To Lisa Lowe, David's thanks for enduring intellectual exchange and steady love.

Thanks also to Christopher Prendergast and to the *Social Text* Collective—a Collective much-maligned, though not by us—for giving our argument its trial run. Most particularly of all, our thanks go to Greg Forter, who was present at the inception of our project, and whose Herculean efforts were of invaluable help to us in bringing it to a conclusion. Thanks, Greg: the stock phrase "above and beyond the call of duty" doesn't capture the half of what you contributed.

Our thanks for institutional support are due to the Committee on Research at the University of California, Berkeley, the Center for Cultural Studies at the University of California, Santa Cruz, and the

Humanities Research Institute at the University of California, Irvine, all of which greatly aided our work. Thanks also to the American Political Science Association, the Humanities Institute at Scripps College, Claremont, and José Crisóstomo de Souza, of the Federal University, Salvador, Bahia, Brazil, for opportunities to present this work at various stages and to receive valuable feedback. Responsibility for drawbacks, omissions, flaws in argument, lapses in judgment, want of good taste, or just plain mistakes is, however, ours and ours alone.

Berkeley, August 1997

INTRODUCTION

Culture and Society *or* Culture and the State?

From the end of the eighteenth century to the late nineteenth century, a remarkable convergence takes place in Europe between theories of the modern state and theories of culture. By 1867, Matthew Arnold can state quite baldly that "Culture suggests the idea of the State."[1] *Culture and the State* explores this theoretical convergence in relation to the social functions of state and cultural institutions in an emergent modern society. Both are given the role of furnishing sites of reconciliation for a civil and political society that is seen to be riven by conflict and contradiction. Both are seen as the sites in which the highest expressions of human being and human freedom are realized. Both are seen as hedges against the potential anarchy of rapidly transforming societies. But there are more than conceptual parallels. *Culture and the State* elaborates the function that culture plays for the state, that is, the way in which, from the time of Friedrich Schiller to that of Matthew Arnold, cultural (or aesthetic) formation comes gradually to play the role of forming citizens for the modern state. By and large, the formative function of cultural or liberal education in modern society is taken for granted. Yet this ethical function of *cultural*, as opposed to technical, vocational or even civic, education is by no means self-evident. We seek to show why specifically culture is seen to provide the ground for political citizenship and how, on this foundation, the theoretical principles that inform the development of state educational institutions were elaborated.

We will develop our argument on culture more fully in following chapters, but, in order to avoid confusion from the outset, we will specify what we mean by culture here. Culture is a term that since the eighteenth century has accrued not only many meanings but multiple connotations. It emerges during that century in differentiation from its root meanings in agriculture and the cultivation of nature to become a concept-metaphor for the relations of human subjects to natural phenomena and human artifacts. It refers in part to the objects that constitute a "culture," in the sense of the ensemble of artifacts and aesthetic practices of a developed civilization rather than to any given "mode of living," but designates primarily the disposition of the human subject in relation to those objects and to nature. It thus extends the purview of the prior concept-metaphor, "Taste," and the philosophical elaboration of the "aesthetic" comes to consider culture as a process of cultivation, the gradual formation of an ethical human subject, characterized by disinterested reflection and universally valid judgments. Though some thinkers, notably Schiller, regard art objects as the proper instruments of cultivation, the dominant tradition of cultural thought emphasizes the disposition of the subject rather than the qualities of the objects of aesthetic judgment. Culture, accordingly, is not confined in its objects to the artistic, or, more narrowly, the literary, but aims rather at the harmonious cultivation of all the capacities of the human subject at a time when it was already apparent that the division of intellectual and manual labor was increasingly formative of specialized or partial individuals. Only in the slow but steady emergence of state institutions did literature and fine arts become the exemplary objects of pedagogy, a process which has to do no less with the increasing division of social spaces than with the gradual dissemination of cultural theory. In the discourses we are examining, culture includes but is not defined by such objects.[2]

In the same way, we would want to clarify in advance our conception of the state. Like culture, the term "state" has undergone multiple transformations, not least in the period of which we write. The first necessary distinction, which is at once genealogical and categorical, is between the autocratic state which dominated pre-enlightenment and enlightenment Europe and what we shall call the *modern* state. The autocratic state is embodied in the monarch—"L'état, c'est moi"—and appeals to no principle of identity between the state/monarch and its subjects. Its principle of organization is territorial rather than ethnic or national: Bretons, Languedocians, and Flemings, Hungarians, Italians and Germans, can all fall under the rule of the same monarch without for that reason needing to assimilate to a common culture, language or system of local administration. The state or monarch's legitimacy is founded in divine right and in blood line. With the conjoined emergence of the legitimating principles of democracy and nationhood, that is, of a state whose authority is derived from a *people*, a quite different conception of the state emerges. The state is no longer a machine functioning according to an arbitrary relation of ruling, but supposes a principle of *organization* in which the people and their institutions are expressed in and through the state.[3] At very different rates and with equally various emphases, modern states draw together notions of nationality and of popular sanction that have a far longer genealogy in the emergence of modernity. But that very process whereby the people and the nation become, in ways concretized by the American and French Revolutions, the foundations of the legitimate state leads to a major and irreversible shift in political theory. No longer is the state conceived of as being in an *arbitrary* relation to its population, but as the fully developed and unifying representative of a national people. The modern state is the expression of a popular will that has emerged historically from a kind of latent principle: its legitimacy is guaranteed less by the immediate assent or will of the people than by its historical development as the fullest expression of that will. For this reason, the state must be understood as representative in the fullest sense: it is at once an institution that derives from the people and one which expresses at a higher level the still developing essence of that people. Accordingly, the state is an exemplary institution of the people, ideally moving them towards the realization of their own essence and towards an ever greater approximation to universality.

For this reason, we distinguish our concept of the state from those which regard the state as a contingently linked assemblage of institutions which have emerged over time in *ad hoc* response to political and social pressures. Within such conceptions, the state is referred to no "organizing" principle, theoretically or practically, but appears rather as a collocation of often incompatible and conflicting institutions and apparatuses. The most articulate exposition of this conception of the state is Michel Foucault's influential analysis of "governmentality," a term he introduces to describe the process by which, in the general emergence of the "policing" of societies, a population becomes subject to bureaucratic regimes and disciplines. Such disciplines include modes of bodily discipline—hygiene, regulation of labor, incarceration or education—and the scientific disciplines—demography, criminology, medicine, and so forth—by which a population can be categorized and regulated in manageable groupings.[4] Although we concur with

Foucault's propositions on a descriptive level, and, indeed, analyze the practical emergence of governmental institutions in nineteenth-century England in subsequent chapters, it is important to note how easily his arguments veer towards a virtual positivism that lacks any real analytical capacity. Certainly, his analyses are of little help in broaching the questions that are crucial to *Culture and the State*: what is the nature of the fundamental nineteenth-century distinction between government and the state, and how are these two aspects of the political sphere coordinated? How do specific governmental institutions get formed and how are transfers and relations among them possible? How do these specific forms become dominant and established, as opposed to the potentially infinite variety of possible forms that "might have been"? To put this latter question another way, how does it come about that certain forms gain passive if not active assent to the point that they come to seem natural? How, in other words, do state institutions come to seem self-evident within the common sense of a population? And why, after a certain point, is it so hard to imagine alternatives to them even in the face of their repeated inadequacy to the work of the state or the needs of the population? How are subjects formed as citizens who by definition and for all practical purposes accept the forms and precepts of the state at least to the extent that alternatives become literally and figuratively the state's "unthinkable"?

What we will argue is that the effectivity of developments and transformations gathered under the concept of an emergent governmentality requires not only disciplinary institutions themselves, but a certain *idea* of the state. That idea, reproduced in state institutions of all kinds, is a regulative one which determines, in Raymond Williams's sense, the forms and ends of those institutions and, therefore, the possibility for subjects formed within them to transfer continually among them.[5] This idea of the state is a crucial concern of the line of thinkers whom we address here and it constantly implies, even where it does not always elaborate, a conception of the proper subject of the state. What is at issue for these thinkers, from Schiller to Arnold and Mill, is not simply the theorization of the state but the means to produce subjects who can "work by themselves," in Louis Althusser's sense, within its institutions and within the civil and political society the state as form presupposes.[6] Moreover, common conceptions of culture, in the larger sense defined above, inform a nineteenth-century consensus on the formation of the proper subject for the state among bureaucrats, politicians and reformers as well as cultural critics. These critics may be its theoreticians and disseminators, but our concern is not so much with their personalities or their direct influence, palpable as that sometimes is, as with the congruent forms of subject and state they theorize even as these gradually become embodied in institutions. What is instructive in all these domains is the continuing labor it has taken to make an idea attain the condition of common sense which permits its reproduction.

Marx famously comments on the French peasants who supported Louis Bonaparte: "They cannot represent themselves, they must be represented."[7] Our own formula for the reformist strategies of the liberal state would be: "They may not represent themselves, they must learn to be represented." It is within the concept of representation that we trace the manner in which an apparent parallelism between state and cultural theory gives way to a relationship of substitution or supplementation in which culture comes to mediate between a disenfranchised populace and a state to which they must in time be assimilated. As Mill put it in *Considerations on Representative Government* (1861), the "instructed minority" becomes a corrective to the unenlightened will of the majority, acting at once as tutors in citizenship and representatives of the state at the local level. This role of the "instructed" instantiates the ideological role which culture (cultivation, *Bildung*) perforce plays within the context of a state formation: the state must, for its legitimation, lay claim to universality, i.e., to the capacity to be truly *representative*, while at the same time allowing free play to the competing but nonetheless *representative* partial interests that find their expression in the sphere of politics. In one of those paradoxes which mask profounder contradictions, the bourgeois epoch that invents politics is equally one in which politics, the representation of and contest between irreconcilable group interests, is supposed to be sublated in the formal universality of its institutions. It is culture that resolves that paradox, not by dissolving it but by displacing it onto a temporal schema in which the subject is defined in terms of the development of its full human capacity.

From its inception, aesthetic culture defines a set of practices which at once define and moralize the bourgeois public sphere. For Kant, common sense, as the universal substrate of human reason, is the foundation equally of the aesthetic and the public sphere. For this reason, aesthetic judgments, which both develop in themselves as taste develops and ground the ethical disinterest of the public sphere, constitute a kind of precursor to any possible politics, insofar as any social contract which will assume the participation of autonomous (*mundig*) citizens demands equally their prior ethical formation.[8] Such thinking, still latent in Kant, becomes the explicit program of Schiller's letters on *The Aesthetic Education of Man* or Fichte's *Addresses to the German Nation.*[9] This genealogy of the theory of aesthetic culture in no way reduces the significance of the model as it gets adopted and adapted in the very different context of a reformist England in the nineteenth century and by figures as diverse as Wordsworth and Coleridge or Matthew Arnold. To trace this story is to grasp the reasons for the continuing importance of cultural institutions to the liberal state, as means to its maintenance in being, its reproduction, rather than its foundation.

In the first instance, the gradual consolidation of bourgeois gains and anxiety at the "Terror" of the French Revolution bring intellectuals like Schiller, Wordsworth or Coleridge to turn from the more radical elements of their former political associations to a form of cultural politics. That cultural politics, which is profoundly pedagogical in its aims, turns upon the exemplary person (Coleridge's "parson" or *persona exemplaris* and Wordsworth's poet) who comes to represent "man in general" by virtue of a painstakingly cultivated disinterest. As we argue in Chapter 2, the structure of representation here involved is strikingly congruent with the theory of the representative in political theory and succumbs to the same paradox, namely, that the representative is empowered in the name of certain specific interests (or passions) only in order that those interests may be sublated in the formal universality of culture or state. But if this paradox at one level merely reveals the logic of "alien politics,"[10] this perception should in no way obscure the remarkable internal consistencies in the theory of representation which underlies and connects distinct institutions of bourgeois political culture.

Indeed, representation operates as if in a series of concentric circles moving from the individual to society at large. For Wordsworth, an exemplary Romantic in this as in other respects, the individual experience becomes representative of human truths "general and operative" precisely in the process of meditative repetition or representation. The temporal or developmental model, by which a "raw" experience is converted through its reconception into an *aesthetic* experience of universal validity, is crucial here. Inscribed ineradicably in the Romantic lyric as a pattern of continuous ironic reevaluation of any experience, this model becomes, in the second circle, so to speak, the basis of a pedagogical imperative for which it is the *formal* identity of the experience of experiencing that permits the individual poem to become for its subsequent readers exemplary or representative of the universal human being. In turn, it is to such a cultural pedagogy that the task is granted of legitimating a structure of representative democracy for which participation is a purely formal expression of equality. A pedagogy based on aesthetic judgment furnishes, as it were, an ethical training devoted to the "educing" of the citizen from the human being. Aesthetic culture represents, therefore, the very form of bourgeois ideology, proffering on the one hand a purely formal space of reconciliation through identification while on the other containing, in transmuted forms, the constant deferral of autonomy that is the inevitable consequence of a substitution of political for human emancipation. For this reason, the aesthetic provides the theoretical rather than the instrumental articulation of the citizen-subject, whose education is aimed not so much at particular objects of knowledge as at forming an ethical disposition that is most clearly elaborated within the concept of culture.

As we argue in Chapter 3, it is in the work of Matthew Arnold that this model receives its most explicit and influential formulations, but with a turn which, under the pressure of events and developments, reveals a crisis of culture to be at once imminent and immanent. The imminence of that crisis is indicated in the first place by the predication of Arnold's most important work regarding these matters, *Culture and Anarchy,* upon a recognition of the phenomenon of class struggles in progress around the second Reform Bill. If Arnold's exceptional concentration, in however idiosyncratic a fashion, on class issues (issues by and large foreign to Wordsworth and Coleridge) lead him to an equally exceptional affirmation of the need in Britain for a strong state on continental models, it obliges him equally, if he is to avoid explicit statement of the class interest served by cultural institutions, to address in oblique form the "alien politics" which finds its expression in aesthetic culture. Standing outside their classes of origin as *Aliens,* the men of culture come to represent its disinterest as a perpetual deferral of ethical selfhood, and therefore of the reconciling state. But that deferral has become structural to the theory of culture in a way that differs markedly from the processive pedagogy of earlier Romantic cultural theories. That this is so is partially masked by Arnold's retention for most of *Culture and Anarchy* of a similar model based on the development of a "best (i.e., ethical) self" out of the anarchic desires and interests of the "ordinary self." Though we must recognize the enormous hegemonic force of the cultural thinking of Arnold and others, including Mill, and come to terms with its impact on working class assimilation to the state through its provision of education, it is nonetheless during reform agitation that the contradictions of the bourgeois state become thematized in ways which once again make room for a future radical class critique.

Although we insist on the hegemonic force of bourgeois ideas of culture by the 1860s, we will emphasize that the arguments for the cultural formation of citizens did not go unchallenged. Crucial to our argument has been the history of resistance in radical working-class circles to the emergence of state educational institutions as well as the gradual acceptance of state education by working-class movements later in the century. This resistant discourse had profound theoretical implications that may well have determined Marx's own consistent antagonism to separate educational institutions from *The Communist Manifesto* (1848) to his *Critique of the Gotha Program* (1875).[11] It becomes apparent that originally radical thinking resisted not only state education in itself, but the very division of social spheres—educational, political, economic—and the theories of representation on which the idea of cultural education is based. Only as working-class participation in reformist representative democracy prevails do these resistances lose their sway, though at the same time certain values of cooperation and self-organization remain embedded and in antagonism to the individualist and patronizing assumptions of bourgeois educational reform. Our conclusions will lead us to critique the way in which subsequent left thinking, through to contemporary cultural studies, has largely taken the concept of culture for granted and failed fully to critique the intrinsic relation of culture to the idea of the state. This will lead us to argue the necessity for a combined critique of the reification of cultural spaces and of contemporary political formations, suggesting the importance of contemporary social movements as a practical embodiment of long-standing but occluded alternatives.

The most influential work on recent thinking about politics and culture, and about the relation between cultural theory and social transformation, has been Raymond Williams's *Culture and Society, 1780–1950* (1958).[12] As Williams himself indicated in *Politics and Letters*, that work more or less archaeologically reconstructed an occulted tradition.[13] More importantly, it countered "the appropriation of a long line of thinking about culture to what were by now decisively reactionary positions."[14] At the present moment, in the context of a resurgent, militant cultural conservativism, such a venture might well seem not only relevant but to require an even more radical repetition. *Culture and Society* defined the canon of cultural thinking as being in opposition to the detrimental effects of industrialization and democratization. For Williams, of course, the emphasis fell on the former process; for contemporary conservatives the emphasis falls, more often than not, on the latter. Both appeal, neither without reason, to the tradition that, as Williams taught us, runs from Burke through Arnold to Orwell. The possibility of this dual appeal lies in the fact that this very tradition defines the terms by which culture is differentiated from the political, social, or economic spheres of society as a corrective supplement. The values to which the discourse of culture appeals and that it seeks to preserve are those by which it is defined: wholeness, disinterest, humanity, cultivation, reconciliation.

Our title, *Culture and the State,* signals both our debt to and our differences from Williams. We wish to address the tradition of culture that he first sketched but propose to do so not in connection with the concept of society which, for reasons we will analyze below, remains somewhat nebulous in *Culture and Society,* but rather with that of the state. We will argue that the under-theorization of the state in Williams's early work prevents him from adequately addressing either the striking parallels between state and cultural theory or the reasons for the gradual subordination of the institutions of culture to the work of the state that occurs in the period he analyzes.[15] In addition, we will show that his emphasis on an "intellectual history" or "history of ideas" concerning culture, rather than on debates around industry, politics, and culture, prevents Williams from grasping more radical possibilities that existed outside his chosen terrain. We hope to show that the discourse on representation always implicit in the theory of culture has to be understood in connection with debates concerning representation within the radical press and the emergent socialist or protosocialist movements of the period. Since our emphasis will fall precisely on the fact that what concerns us here are debates rather than *positions,* we will want to consider Williams's account of the critical values of culture in relation to other recent accounts and criticisms of emergent English socialism. We hope to show that in all these accounts an uncritical acceptance of a division of spheres—whose features were indeed crystallizing in the 1830s and 1840s, but which were not yet set in stone—leads to a foreclosure of the very open and still critical terms of debate about education, representation and exploitation in radical circles. Divisions such as culture and society, politics and economics, even theory and practice are taken for granted in a manner that assumes their self-evidence even at the moment of their emergence. For us, on the contrary, what is pointedly of interest in these moments is the fluidity, at times even the contradictoriness, of debates over representation, education and class at the moment (that of the first Reform Bill and its immediate aftermath) when representative democracy was an idea profoundly contested on both left and right. In these debates, and against much working-class critique, emerges the by now self-evident conjuncture of representation and democracy—concepts which, as Rousseau argued, formerly had had nothing to do with each other.[16]

More immediately at issue for us, in relation to the tradition isolated by Williams, is the place of culture in the formation of citizens and the legitimation of the state. For the debates around issues of representation and education that we discuss concern precisely the question of the legitimacy of representation and of the kind of subject to be formed for or against the emergent state and the economic relations that subtended it. In the tradition from Burke through Coleridge to Mill and Arnold that is ultimately most important to Williams, culture occupies the space between the individual and the state, forming the citizen as ethical "best self." But this process is precisely what was under contestation in working-class radical circles, as we show in Chapter 2. Contrary to the concerns that Williams is able to draw from the "high" tradition of culture (concern with the fragmentation of the human by the division of labor, concern with mechanization, deracination, and the cultural impoverishment as well as the exploitation of the mass of the population), our interest is in reading in that same tradition an account of the function of "culture" in its intersection with the state and in the foundation of what Althusser was to term "ideological state apparatuses." If our account differs from Williams's, the difference is in large part due to the different historical juncture at which we write. Our interest in reading back into the relatively occulted tradition of working-class discourse on education and representation is connected with a timely suspicion of the grand narrative of culture in which Williams's generosity was able to read a humane and still viable potential.

In order to clarify our differences from Williams, it is worth outlining our sense of his project, of its strengths and, from our perspective, its omissions. To do so demands also a sketch of two different institutional moments as a means of articulating the exigencies of Williams's project and our own. The title of a largely forgotten English journal, the *Universities and Left Review*, mentioned in Williams's Foreword, offers an illuminating epiphany of a cultural moment—*Culture and Society* was first published, by Chatto and Windus, in 1958—and its perceived possibilities. Easily overlooked at the beginning of *Culture and Society*, the title of this journal gains an effect of strangeness when one considers entitling a journal in this fashion at the present time. The title speaks to a moment in British intellectual socialism at which educational and other institutions seemed an available territory for hegemonic struggle and of which Williams's own trajectory is not untypical. It seemed possible that the institutions of education and communication at long last might be genuinely open to the reception and dissemination not only of working-class students and teachers but also to left-wing thought. Accordingly, *Universities and Left Review* was not the oxymoron it might now seem. At the same time, the possibility for such optimism rested in a relative confidence in the efficacy and value of state intervention when directed by more or less socialist policies. The long revolution of representative democracy could be seen to be leading gradually to the occupation of the institutions of the state at least by "representatives" of the people, and in the name of a left agenda.[17] Accordingly, it is necessary to read in *Culture and Society* a covert and revisionist institutional history. Although Williams is never very explicit about this, the canon of cultural thinkers that he effectively establishes is a canon of those thinkers who furnish the theoretical bases for educational institutions generally and for cultural education (especially literature) in particular. Williams was retrieving for the socialist tradition the cultural concepts that had by and large been appropriated by conservatives; in so doing he was regrounding the institutions themselves as a means of establishing them as sites with an increased potential for socialist inflection. Understood in this sense, *Culture and Society* is a counter-hegemonic work of considerable strategic value. At the same time, the desire to reoccupy cultural positions appropriated all too monolithically by reactionary elements necessarily involves Williams in what now seems a rather problematic overidentification with the positions themselves. For it is not simply that Williams rearticulates the historical logic of the discourse on culture so that it points towards a socialist community. He also attempts to insert himself into that tradition as a means of reappropriating its ethos as well as its institutions. For this reason, it is exactly the concept of *tradition* rather than, for example, ideology or discourse, that recurs throughout his discussion.

Williams's attempt leads him to incontestably significant transformations of the discourse on culture, but these transformations remain deeply problematic by virtue of what they cause him to overlook. We can isolate two distinct but related transformations in the discourse on culture that Williams undertakes. First, there is the reclamation of the idea of "wholeness" for the socialist tradition, a tradition from which, in a line of attack running back at least to Burke's assaults on Paine and on sundry heartless rationalizers, conservatism has sought to divorce socialism. Small wonder that his interlocutor in *Politics and Letters* is quick to note that Williams's sympathy often seems to be on the side of conservative "structures of feeling" as opposed to radical demystifications.[18] The tone is set early on and significantly through Arnold's praise of Burke:

> Arnold is himself one of the political heirs of Burke, but again this is less important than the kind of thinking which Arnold indicates by the verb "saturates." It is not "thought," in the common opposition to "feeling"; it is, rather, a special immediacy of experience, which works itself out, in depth, to a particular embodiment of ideas that become, in themselves, the whole man.[19]

Given the recurrence of such terms throughout *Culture and Society* and Williams's work as a whole, it is not enough to characterize it as a mere vestige of F. R. Leavis's here very evident stylistic and intellectual influence. Williams's understanding of socialism's utopian moment is always inseparable from a desire to overcome division and contradictions in the self (a desire doubtless accentuated by his own biographical displacements). Accordingly, it is the explicitly extrapolitical category of the "whole man" that determines Williams's selection of the canonical figures of the cultural tradition.

What is at stake in Williams's invocation of a concept of wholeness, a concept instantiated for him in Burke, is the adequacy of given persons to an idea of humanity itself. The divisions that are seen to characterize bourgeois society, either those between feeling and thought or those between politics and culture, are divisions within a prior concept of the human. Whether or not one accepts the notion of an organic wholeness of the human, what is crucial here is the manner in which the prepolitical concept of "the whole man" posits an undivided concept of humanity to which particular individuals are more or less adequate. In this concept Williams reproduces the regulative idea of the discourse of culture for which the representative human is he (principally he) who most adequately, though never entirely, approximates to wholeness. The concept is prepolitical precisely insofar as the political stands for a division of the human into partialities. The same, by analogy, applies to every other conceivable division by which the human is alienated from itself: the "whole man" of culture is by the same token above economics and above class, strictly indifferent. Williams thus well represents the tradition of culture but at the same time continually risks merely ventriloquizing that culture. *Culture and Society* establishes not only a canon of cultural texts by virtue of the importance of their individual propositions; it also establishes a canon in the stronger and proper sense of a body of texts that represent or embody their own ideal and accordingly stand for humanity as a whole. Williams's selected texts on culture thus come to have the status and all the self-evidence of Arnoldian touchstones, being exemplary in their form as in their content. Let us simply stress at this juncture a point to which we shall shortly return: that what governs the canonicity of culture's texts is their approximation not so much to reality as to a regulative *idea.*

The argument of *Culture and Society* indisputably seeks to pass beyond the purely formal definition of representativeness articulated in Coleridge, Mill, and Arnold, a definition that is devoted to determining and restricting the terms by which the capacity for either self-representation or consensual representation by others seems possible. Williams's argument proceeds, however, not by critiquing the manner in which "culture" is established as a distinct domain, devoted to the cultivation of the "whole man" over against the divisions of labor and politics. It proceeds by collapsing these distinctions. As *Culture and Society* progresses, it becomes increasingly difficult to differentiate "Culture" in the specialized sense that Coleridge or Arnold gave to it from "culture" in the anthropological sense of functionally integrated life-worlds. Clearly, this apparent confusion on Williams's part belongs with his large strategy, which is to establish, in the face of reactionary distinctions, the potential for wholeness in non-élite cultures. Accordingly, his conception of culture is increasingly articulated as tied to "an effective community of experience"[20] rather than to a canon of works to be absorbed. A "common culture" is recast not as the legacy of the best that has been known and thought and directed at the production of best selves, but as only possible "in a context of material community and by the full democratic process."[21]

With Williams's call for "material community" and "the full democratic process" we can only agree unreservedly. At the same time, however, the full context of that citation will serve to indicate the extent to which we must dissent from the terms by which the relation of culture to those conditions is presented:

The emphasis that we wish to place here is that this first difficulty—the compatibility of increasing specialization with a genuinely common culture—is only soluble in a context of material
community and by the full democratic process. A skill is only an
aspect of a man, and yet, at times, it can seem to comprehend that
man's whole being. This is one kind of crisis, and it can only be
overcome as a man becomes conscious that the value he places on
his skill, the differentiation he finds in it, can only ultimately be
confirmed by his constant effort not only to confirm and respect
the skills of others, but also to confirm and deepen the community
which is even larger than the skills. The mediation of this lies
deep in personal feeling, but enough is known to indicate that it is
possible.[22]

Consistent with Williams's general argument, the distinction maintained in the traditional discourse of culture between Culture and
other domains of practice tends to erode here. What remains of that
discourse, and remains as a powerful presence, is a vestigial conception of culture as representing the possibility of "the whole man"
against the division of labor. What is valued in Burke at the outset as a
representative individual is transposed here onto a collective, but the
form of the opposition remains. And though it would be difficult to
specify from here the contents of culture as opposed to any "specialization," it is precisely our principal contention that this form of
thinking is of crucial importance to understanding the historical role
of culture in relation to the state.

Indeed, the strength of Williams's desire to save the discourse of
culture by giving it a socialist direction prevents him from subjecting
its formal properties to sustained critical analysis. Yet it is exactly
from the distinction between the wholeness sought in culture and the
division of labor characteristic of society in general that Arnold and
others derive the notion that "culture suggests the idea of the State." If
we replace the slightly nebulous term *society* with the more technical
civil society the point may become clearer. Culture is to a civil society
conceived as the site of the war of all against all a domain of reconciliation, precisely as is the state. But while the function of the state is to
mediate conflicts among interest groups, it is the function of culture
to interpellate individuals into the disposition to disinterested reflection that makes the state's mediations possible. Culture produces the
consensual ground for the state form of representative democracy by

drawing the formal or representative disposition in every individual out of each person's concrete particularity. The ethical moment in each individual, which Arnold terms the "best self," suggests the state and the state is in turn the collective representation of the ethical disposition. The importance of the discourse on culture lies in its theorization of an extrapolitical, extraeconomic space in which "freedom" and "the harmonious development of the whole person" can be pursued as the very ground on which representational politics can be practiced. Culture mediates the shift from self-representation to being represented by developing in each that "indifferent" disposition of the Subject in which material differences are annulled. While allowing representational politics to take place by formalizing political subjects, it simultaneously allows that politics to take place as if material conditions were a matter of indifference.

Williams's fastidious and deprecatory comment on Arnold, that "[t]he State which for Burke was an actuality has become for Arnold an idea"[23] is not only misplaced with regard to the theoretical and *institutional* importance of Arnold's work. It expresses a critical position that logically prevents Williams from undertaking the critique of cultural discourse that will be a necessary prelude to making the transition from representative democracy to "material community and the full democratic process," to, that is, radical democracy. The differential position of culture with regard not to "industrialization" and "democracy," as Williams has it, but to the political and the economic, so deeply saturates the structure of bourgeois society that even the so-called aestheticization of daily life in the postmodern era has not fundamentally altered its significance. The structure of "recreationary space," whether defined as Arnoldian culture or the mass media, is, in relation to the specialization of the workplace or the interests of politics, fundamentally little changed and continues to provide the mechanisms by which the formal subject of the state is produced as *in this domain* undivided. Without a radical critique, not only of the terms but also of the conditions of possibility of such differentiation of spheres, the function of culture in the reproduction of the state and material social relations cannot adequately be addressed.

In view of the fact that it was written, as Williams points out, in the same moment as E. P. Thompson's *The Making of the English Working Class* and Richard Hoggart's *The Uses of Literacy*, it is perhaps surprising at first sight that *Culture and Society* turns so little to working-class writings on education, politics, society or culture. Williams's comments on "working-class culture" make clear why this is so. Pointing out that often enough what gets termed "working-class culture" is generally not produced by working-class people, he goes on to a more substantial point:

> To this negative definition we must add another: that "working class culture," in our society, is not to be understood as the small amount of "proletarian" writing and art which exists. The appearance of such work has been useful, not only in the more self-conscious forms, but also in such material as the post-Industrial ballads, which were worth collecting. We need to be aware of this work, but it is to be seen as a valuable dissident element rather than as a culture. The traditional popular culture of England was, if not annihilated, at least fragmented and weakened by the dislocations of the Industrial Revolution. What is left, with what in the new conditions has been newly made, is small in quantity and narrow in range. It exacts respect, but it is in no sense an alternative culture.[24]

We have no quarrel with the proposition that popular and working-class cultural forms have suffered damage, even fragmentation and annihilation, in the history of capitalism and exploitation that defines them as "working-class." Indeed, not to recognize this would be to remove a principal rationale from class struggle and would reduce—in a way now not hard to conceive—working-class culture to one more equivalent variation among the many cultures of a jagged pluralist postmodernity. But Williams's judgment of working-class culture from the perspective of a Culture devoted to supplying an alternative space to "industrialism" and "democracy" relegates the former to the status of a mere "dissident element," rather than reading in it the outline of terms for self-representation which refuse the differentiation of spheres imposed by the rationale of capitalist social forms. An alternative reading of radical and working-class discourse will show that, though it recognizes the damage inflicted by exploitation, it does not do so by confessing inadequacy to an imposed model of cultural fulfillment.[25] It is such a reading that we provide in the following chapters.

A far more stringent and elaborate critique of *Culture and Society* and of left critiques of education that derive from or accord with it is Ian Hunter's *Culture and Government*.[26] Hunter's aim is to show that, far from being the effect of the tradition of cultural thinking that Williams and others have outlined, literary pedagogy or "English" is in fact a "contraction" of the formative role of the nineteenth-century school into a specialized domain within schooling that is only retrospectively constructed as derivative of Arnold and others. The gradual emergence of government schooling was in fact the work of religious and bureaucratic initiatives which sought to produce a manageable population; that work already defines the function of the teacher as ethical tutor and as exemplary figure through whom the internalization of normative values in the child is facilitated. Only in the early twentieth century does literary teaching become seen as the ideal instrument of such an education.

Insofar as we have ourselves already argued that what is at stake in "culture" is not simply the subject's relation to art objects even as symbolic of a possible harmonious formation of the self, we would concur with the view that literary culture does not determine the form of institutionalized education. But our argument is that cultural theory presents more significantly an account of the very possibility of representational structures that found political process within the modern state. This account requires a specific model of subject formation and a specific division of social spaces such that formation and its generalization can take place. Hunter's eagerness to displace a tradition of historicizing "the rise of English," from Raymond Williams through Terry Eagleton to Chris Baldick and others, leads him finally to an untenable positivism that views the emergence of specific forms of educational institution as the result of merely contingent measures that is, as he puts it over and again, a "piecemeal" process:

> The ensemble of historical surfaces and forces which brought modern literary education into being is not, as I have described it, unified by either of the two figures of "man's" completion. Rather it takes the form of a purely contingent and provisional configuration or "programme", whose emergence is not governed by any overarching historical purpose or theoretical goal.[27]

There is no doubt that the specific institutions of education that emerged in the nineteenth century came about experimentally and gradually in a series of measures; nor is there any doubt that the measures taken were so taken in response to, not merely in anticipation of, an articulate working-class resistance to and contestation of governmental and capitalist measures in general. It was not possible at once to impose a coherent and unified national system of education given

the multiple and discordant positions involved in educational debates
—and indeed that goal remains to be achieved at the institutional
level. This does not, however, imply that a merely *ad hoc* and accidental formation of educational institutions took place. What strikes us in
all the literature on nineteenth-century education, whether historical
studies or contemporary documents, is the consistency of the subject
imagined as the product of the institutions and the regularity of the
spaces and pedagogical relations that form that subject. Even Hunter's
own examples bear this out, though he relies on detailed accounts of
only two figures, David Stow and James Kay, a religious reformer and a
government bureaucrat respectively. We will return to the "geography" of that subject's formation presently, seeking only to emphasize
at this point that Hunter's positivistic assumptions not only belie his
own empirical evidence but prevent him from asking the questions
stimulated by the fact that the concern of educationalists was with the
children's internalization of "the new social and moral norms" and
with the necessity for "a new 'sympathetic' relation between the children and a specially-trained teacher."[28] What are these new norms,
why do they involve a new pedagogical relationship and why do they
dominate middle-class reformism to the extent that they become the
very business of emerging and expanding state projects? And why is it
that their object is consistently and specifically the working classes
rather than what he loosely terms "the population"?[29]

A considerable labor of disavowal informs Hunter's work, not least
in his suppression of Kay's—and the state's—concern with social unrest during the whole period of his endeavors, an unrest that was
clearly and explicitly to do with emergent relations of production and
that called for an intensification of educational apparatuses in the city
and the country.[30] Lord Macaulay was not alone in demanding rhetor-
ically, "Can it be denied that the education of the common people is
the most effective means of protecting persons and property?"[31] This
was virtual orthodoxy among Whigs and Radicals and there was no
mystification of their purposes in parliamentary debates. The very
commissions of inquiry on which Kay worked that produced the
"series of statistical frequencies connecting the condition of streets
and housing, poverty, mortality, licentiousness, crime, numbers of
taverns and ginshops, church attendance, 'domestic economy' and literacy" were precisely, *pace* Hunter, generated by "the spectre of a
politically volatile working class."[32] This was self-evident to middle-
class reformers and, no less, to working-class radicals, as we show in
Chapters 2 and 3. Their fundamental purpose was to protect the rights

of property, meaning, as the working classes well knew, control of the means of production.

Hunter's claims, thinly based as they are, very deliberately fly in the face of the empirical evidence from which numerous historians of British education draw their claims that "the early Victorian obsession with the education of the poor is best understood as a concern about authority, about power, about the assertion (or the reassertion) of control."[33] There is no doubt, since both radicals and reformers were explicit about this, that the expanding system of education was understood at the time as an instrument of social control directed specifically at the working classes. Conservative opposition to educational and other reforms, usually on the grounds that an enlightened working class would be more troublesome than an ignorant and deferential one, marks the period as one that involved both a shift from aristocratic to bourgeois control of the state and a shift in the mode of that control that we will analyze as a shift from domination to hegemony. Only a peculiarly naive concept of ideology could regard any connection between the mode of production and the hegemonic apparatuses that allow for its reproduction as requiring, in Hunter's words, "a line of class domination running from the factory to the school."[34] Hegemony depends exactly, not on direct control (domination), but on dispersion. It is not a mode of mystification, producing "false consciousness" as opposed to scientific and political knowledge, but a disseminated form of self-evidence or "common sense" that regulates subjects across the differentiated domains of modern society.

Hegemony cannot depend on the repetition and inculcation of a given ideological content; it depends precisely on assent. Nor can it depend on an efficacy restricted to a particular domain of society; on the contrary, the differentiation of spheres in bourgeois society is a mechanism that contains the appearance of contradiction between, for example, exploitation and "universal rights," equality and patriarchy, but needs the possibility of transfer so that contradiction does not merely reemerge as the clash of incommensurable spaces. Accordingly hegemony demands at once the formation of subjects as *potentialities* (that is, capable of functioning across different spaces as one identity), and congruence among the forms of social spaces. In terms of the workings of hegemony, Hunter's examples are suggestive beyond the argument that he makes. What the exemplary Stow and Kay constitute in their model schools is a *form* rather than a content for education. They are little concerned with the actual materials of education, and closely focused on the spatial forms of the classroom and the

formal temporality of ethical subjectification. In fact, "the organization of pedagogical space"[35] embodies both a logic of social relations
embodied architecturally and the temporality through which the subject's disposition is assimilated to those social relations. Stow in effect
invents the modern classroom that Kay succeeds in generalizing and
does so in the form of the "gallery" whose architecture we recognize
as the contemporary lecture hall or "theater."[36] It permits the simultaneous surveillance of multiple subjects and, more importantly, their
simultaneous interpellation as individuals through their "training" on
the same elevated object, the teacher. The elevation of the teacher, and
his constitution as exemplary representative of ethical formation,
places him *before* the class in both temporal and spatial senses of the
word.[37] He represents the ethical to them as the single, spatially isolated common object of their regard as much as by the superior development that his position in the pyramidal structure of the classroom
instantiates. The very form of the classroom materializes the lesson
of subjectification that is the end of educational techniques—its architecture or geography constitutes what Althusser would call a
"material ideological apparatus" in which certain repeated "material
practices" constitute the subject of ideology.[38] The very formality of
what is held forth in the classroom—the exemplary abstract subject
that the teacher represents to and for the students—is permitted by
the materiality of that pedagogical space. That is why we regard the
classroom as a crucial space for the formation of the political subject
for whom being represented is self-evident: quite as much as the
teacher self-consciously assumes the place of the *pater familias* (*in
loco parentis*), adopting a combination of authority, remoteness and
intimacy, he prefigures the yet more abstract role of the state as ultimate representative of ethical subjectivity. The school, in other words
most effectively permits the transfer of the subject from the private
domain of the family into the public world of the political, not by
teaching civics but by representing representation.

   We will elaborate this function of cultural education further in the
following chapter, particularly in relation to the theater, which might
be another model for the classroom so closely are their architectures
related. But we are left with the question here as to what unifies or at
least relates and integrates the dispersed spheres of bourgeois society so
that they seem to function as a unity for the subject.[39] To this question
the concept of governmentality offers no satisfactory answer, precisely
because it cannot surmount its assumption of contingency. Far more
valuable to us throughout our work on this book has been Antonio

Gramsci's concept of the "ethical state." Not unlike Foucault, Gramsci recognizes the multiple institutions of the state and, moreover, their frequently contradictory operations. By invoking the state, however, as opposed to the "contingent" workings of government, Gramsci affirms the ultimate unity of the state formation as an instrument of class rule. The state operates, however, through multiple institutions and in different modes to achieve and maintain dominance. The first mode of its operations constitutes what Gramsci terms "the night-watchman state," the state as a repressive apparatus which comes into play whenever its borders or regulations are directly challenged. Its institutions are the army, the police and the law courts and prisons. The night-watchman state is set over against the ethical state which is altogether more complex as the instrument of hegemony. The institutions that compose it are various, including the Church, trade unions, political parties, as well as more evidently state-connected ones like schools. The state as a whole accordingly becomes for Gramsci "political society + civil society, in other words hegemony protected by the armour of coercion."[40] Gramsci's conception that the institutions of civil society that are usually conceived of as private are actually part of a general conception of the state turns on his understanding of the "educative and formative role of the state," of the hegemonic state as *educator*.[41] The function of the ethical as opposed to the night-watchman state is to form citizens and to gain consent, the two distinct projects being in fact the same: the subject is to be formed as one who consents to hegemony. The schools are of course crucial here, but the work of formation is continuous, taking place not only through pedagogy but through the work of intellectuals in all the spheres of civil society. Gramsci is somewhat vague here, but we would contend that the very possibility of the "ethical state" and its institutions requires the replication of the same forms across different institutions—as, for example, the trade union, the school and the political party come to share a common structure of representative activity. Their formal consistency guarantees that even where these institutions come into antagonism, they do so within the same fundamental paradigms. Hegemony, or ideology, is the process by which certain paradigms become so self-evident as to relegate alternatives to the spaces of the nonsensical and the unthinkable. It is not so much that hegemony represses as that the dominance of its "forms" of conceptualization renders other forms, other imaginaries, unreadable, inaudible and incomprehensible. The subject of ideology is formed not in "wholeness," but in the displacement and occlusion of its multiple possibilities.

The primary, though not the only, mechanism of that displacement is for us the classroom, its primary agent, the teacher. Again, we emphasize that this is not a question of the teacher's personal qualities, political opinions, or ethical disposition: it is an effect of the formal structures of pedagogy which are inseparable from the paradigms within which "sense" is constructed. This imbrication of the intellectual in the very structures of bourgeois institutions leads us to dissatisfaction with Gramsci's seminal and misleading distinction between the traditional and the organic intellectual.

To contextualize this troubled distinction, we have to take note of the centrality of the revolutionary intellectual in Gramsci's writings. Many of his arguments derive more or less directly from his meditations on this figure, and quickly come to involve a set of related questions. What is a revolutionary intellectual? What does this figure bring to the preconditions and processes of revolution? How is he or she to be recruited? How activated? What should his or her functions be? It is arguable that Gramsci's entire, original vocabulary is formulated around answers to these very questions, imbricated within his discussions of the relationship(s) of the state to civil society, and of domination to hegemony, his analyses of Italian history, his presentation of the Communist Party as the "modern Prince."[42]

Gramsci's central belief that bourgeois culture and values must of necessity be transformed from within if revolution is not to be stymied or still-born is, in particular, one that privileges the revolutionary intellectual in an original way. Only the intellectual, broadly conceived, can bridge the gap between civil society and political society, or the gaps between the polity, the economy, and society at large. To do this, the intellectual must not set him- or herself up over, against, or outside the proletariat, as in debased notions of Leninism. To the contrary, Gramsci insists, the intellectual is to be a constitutive part of the proletariat; no loss of class identity should be involved in being an "organic" intellectual in this sense—that criterion being, in fact, part of the definition of the organic intellectual. Such a loss of class identity can by contrast be involved in the formation of the "traditional" intellectual who, in creating consent, ceases to represent the interests of his own class—his class origin becomes irrelevant—and becomes the functionary or cohort of the ruling group. (Gramsci is presumably thinking of "traditional" intellectuals in the service of the Catholic Church in Italy who, overwhelmingly drawn as they were from the peasantry, nevertheless came in the end to perform "cosmopolitan" functions.)

Gramsci believed that the distinction between intellectual and material production cannot be maintained in absolute terms and is in general indefensible, since it is in the end nothing but an expression or exemplification of the capitalist division of labor. On the other hand, it can in principle be overcome by the "organic" intellectual of the proletarian class. Gramsci's ultimate target in advancing this view is the notion of the intellectuals as a distinct social category that is "free-floating" in Karl Mannheim's sense, somehow independent of, above or beyond class. This view can be shown to be a self-serving myth. The status of "traditional" intellectuals, literary, scientific, religious, philosophical, etc., people whose positions in the interstices of society give them an apparently classless aura, can be shown to be derived in the last analysis from past and present class relations; typically, the "traditional" intellectual will conceal his or her attachment to various historical class configurations, but this concealment can in principle be exposed for the falsehood it is.

While there is much here with which we can agree, the counterposition of the category of "traditional" to that of "organic" intellectuals raises nagging doubts—doubts that, we must say, are little allayed by the reluctance of commentators on Gramsci to interrogate critically the distinction in question.[43] In view of this reluctance it might be helpful to paraphrase briefly how the English-language editors of the *Selections from the Prison Notebooks* characterize the "organic" intellectuals by way of pointing up what is at issue in our doubts. "Organic" intellectuals, on Quintin Hoare and Geoffrey Nowell-Smith's account, are "the thinking and organizing elements" of a particular "fundamental" social class, i.e., the proletariat.[44] They are distinguished less by their occupations—which may be jobs characteristic of their class—than by their function in directing the ideals and aspirations of the class to which they perforce belong. (The implied model here, as Gramsci's discussion eventually makes clear, is that of the Jacobins during the French Revolution, all of whom started life as "traditional" intellectuals, and ended it as anything but.)

Hoare and Nowell-Smith characterize the centrality of the distinction between the "traditional" and the "organic" intellectual along the following lines: (1) it connects with the proposition that "all men are philosophers,"[45] and with Gramsci's discussions of the dissemination of philosophical ideas and ideology throughout a culture; (2) it relates to Gramsci's thoughts on education[46] through his emphasis on the class character of the formation of the intellectual through schooling; (3) it underlies his thoughts on Italian history (intellectuals during the Risorgimento performed an essential mediating function in the struggle of class forces); and (4) it provides a refutation of Kautsky, who had seen the relationship between workers and intellectuals in formal, mechanistic terms. According to Kautsky, intellectuals of bourgeois origin—like Marx, Engels and Kautsky himself—magnanimously dispense the fruits of an expensive education, theory, leadership and direction to an otherwise inert and rudderless mass of resolutely nonintellectual (or even anti-intellectual) workers.

It is precisely an earlier version of a Kautskian position, adopted at first by middle-class radicals and elaborated by Mill, Arnold and others, that we will see the radical working classes of the 1830s rejecting on the grounds not only of its patronizing assumptions but of its evident falsity: the autonomy of working-class institutions and the self-direction of their movements were fundamental principles, threatened as they constantly were. Even in the more reformist 1860s, working-class arguments retained some vestige of these principles, most apparent in their continuing desire for at least nominally autonomous educational institutions, even where they increasingly accepted the mentorship of middle- and upper-class intellectuals. But in the 1830s such patronage by intellectuals was scarcely acceptable: the Chartists and the earlier English radicals from whom they stemmed had no doubt as to the intellectual capacities of their class and, indeed, posed the problem of the intellectuals and of popular "ignorance" in terms of power and class and of class definitions of "useful knowledge." The assumption as to the essentially deluded nature of working-class thought is both a later and an "intellectual" assumption on the part of left as well as liberal theorists. Up till the 1850s, the English working class had its own "organic" intellectuals and, as Richard Johnson has put it, "the relationship between radical leadership and working-class people was extraordinarily close."[47]

Gramsci elaborates the concept of the "organic intellectual" in the *Prison Notebooks*. As a new class develops, economically and associatively, it tends he suggests to create "organically . . . one or more strata of intellectuals which give it homogeneity and an awareness of its own function, not only in the economic but also in the social and political fields."[48] Since Gramsci's category of "the intellectual" is expansive—it would include the scholar, the writer, the man of letters, but also anybody whose social function involves the dissemination of ideas either within civil society or between government and civil society—his category of the "organic intellectual" is expansive too. According to Walter Adamson's gloss on Gramsci's "The Intellectuals," the organic intellectuals of the aristocracy in feudal societies would include not only soldiers and other specialists in "technico-military capacity" but also priests in all their various functions.[49] Under capitalism the organic intellectuals of the bourgeois class are not just specialists in management and industrial organization, but also economists, lawyers, publishers, doctors, publicists—indeed everyone connected with what we now call the "culture industry," and what Gramsci calls "the organization of a new culture."[50] In the instance of the proletariat under capitalism, organic intellectuals comprise all those striving to produce a new proletarian culture as well as productive functionaries in the narrower sense (shop foremen and stewards, machine technicians, trade union economists).

In the instance of subaltern classes like the proletariat, organic intellectuals are defined or characterized prospectively as well as functionally; organic intellectuals seek to inspire the proletariat's self-confidence as an historical actor and provide it with social, cultural and political leadership.[51] Until this process reaches an advanced stage, however, traditional intellectuals are perforce likely to fill the leadership vacuum. These Gramsci characterizes as a relatively "autonomous and independent social group" which experiences through an *esprit de corps* its "uninterrupted historical continuity and [its members'] special qualification."[52] Traditional intellectuals have no single class origin and often imagine themselves to be above or beyond the usual class divisions. Not being organically tied to a class—even to a class in the ascendant—traditional intellectuals tend to be at best aloof from, and at worst antagonistic towards, its interests. Some intellectuals serving the proletariat are likely on Adamson's account to be former organic bourgeois intellectuals who had defected. Others might be survivors of decadent or vanishing estates like the Church or the military aristocracy.

As a class matures into a position where it can begin to assert its power politically, it becomes increasingly important to supplant traditional with organic intellectuals. But this substitution is no simple matter. It is likely to take the form of a complicated and protracted co-ordination "of the form and the quality of the relations between the various intellectually-qualified strata,"[53] one that could well take several generations before proving itself to be irreversible.

Any class developing towards dominance will "struggle to assimilate and to conquer 'ideologically' the traditional intellectuals." Organic intellectuals from within the proletariat must not simply identify themselves in opposition to traditional intellectuals, but must work actively to co-opt them. "[T]he more it succeeds in simultaneously elaborating its own organic intellectuals," the "quicker and more efficacious" this "assimilation and conquest" will be.[54]

Today, on the one hand, "The enormous development of activity and organization of education in the broad sense . . . is an index of the importance assumed by intellectual functions and categories." On the other hand, "Parallel with the attempt to deepen and broaden the 'intellectuality' of each individual, there has also been an attempt to narrow the various specializations." Efforts to promote "the so-called 'high culture,'" are parts of this same attempt: "schools and institutes of high culture can be assimilated to each other" easily enough.[55] On the other hand, while it is axiomatic that proletarian education depends on the active leadership of the organic intellectuals,[56] this in turn cannot be understood apart from the self-education of the masses:

> The process of development [of organic intellectuals] is tied to the dialectic between the intellectuals and the masses. The intellectual stratum develops both quantitatively and qualitatively, but every leap forward towards a new breadth and complexity of the intellectual stratum is tied to an analogous movement on the part of the "simple," who raise themselves to higher levels of culture and at the same time extend their circle of influence towards the stratum of specialized intellectuals, producing groups of greater or lesser importance.[57]

As Gramsci's dialectic unfolds over time, the gap between the intellectual and the masses tends to narrow so that the two elements coalesce into an "intellectual/moral bloc,"[58] which will be the embryo of future socialist society and the basis of a "potential state." "The popular element 'feels' but does not know or understand; the intellectual element 'knows' but does not always understand and in particular does not always feel."[59] It is for this reason that "The philosophy of praxis does not tend to leave the 'simple' in their primitive philosophy of common sense, but rather to lead them to a higher conception of life."[60]

> The active man-in-the-mass has a practical activity, but has no clear theoretical consciousness of his practical activity, which nonetheless involves understanding the world insofar as he transforms it. His theoretical consciousness can indeed be in opposition to his activity. One might almost say that he has two theoretical consciousnesses (or one contradictory consciousness): one which

is implicit in his activity and which in reality unites him with all his fellow workers in the practical transformation of the real world; and one, superficially explicit or verbal, which he has inherited from the past and uncritically absorbed.[61]

Our objection to Gramsci's formulations lies not in the fundamentally "moral," and rather naive question as to whether the intellectual can represent the subaltern. What seems to us problematic is, rather, the tendency, amplified by virtually all Gramsci's commentators, to slip back into the notion that the bourgeois intellectuals are "traditional." Gramsci's initial account in "The Intellectuals" suggests rather that the organic intellectuals of bourgeois society include not only the entrepreneur, the industrial technician and the specialist in political economy, but also "the organisers of a new culture." The fact that these cultural intellectuals include, alongside journalists, advertisers and medical and legal professionals, other groups like academics, "men of letters," artists and teachers, appears to give rise to some confusion both in Gramsci and others. These are of course all functions that have a pre-capitalist existence and can therefore be regarded as "traditional" activities "co-opted" by the bourgeoisie, and therefore furnishing the "traditional intellectuals" who may in turn be co-opted by proletarian movements. But whatever the self-perception of such intellectuals as above or beyond class affiliation, as occupying—in Gramsci's editors' words—"the interstices of society,"[62] we would argue that this understanding of the intellectual's function in bourgeois society is a misrepresentation. What our work will show is that, to the contrary, an irreducible transformation of pre-capitalist intellectual work takes place in time with the Industrial Revolution, producing the "organisers of the new culture" as among the most significant "organic" intellectuals of capitalist society.

What we hope to show in *Culture and the State* is that the *organic* nature of the bourgeois intellectual is structural even before it is explicitly or self-consciously "political" in any sense. This structural positioning of the intellectual ranges from the spatial and temporal location of the teacher in the classroom to the more fully determining position of the intellectual in the spheres of culture and education as these are differentiated from other spheres, principally economic and political, with regard to which intellectuals famously claim "disinterest." The organization of *bourgeois* society (a term which condenses both capitalism and modernity) depends, as many from Weber and Durkheim on have argued, on this differentiation and articulation of spaces. Despite the claim to intellectual disinterest that founds the large domain of culture, intellectuals perform through that sphere in the most fundamental ways work that Gramsci would describe as *dirigente*.

Our discussion throughout this book will suggest that the formation of the intellectual in bourgeois modernity is virtually always determined by this system of "organically linked" social spaces (to use Gramsci's language where we ourselves would prefer "articulated" with all its different semantic resonances). The rapid rearticulation of the intellectuals with the forms of bourgeois society links them to its significant structures regardless of personal ideology, a fact which does much to explain the daily sense of contradiction that now faces radical teachers in virtually every aspect of their practice.

What we argue here, in an interpretation of Gramsci which seeks to extend his insights, is somewhat at odds with Gramsci's argument about the Italy of his times, which is based on the transition of southern intellectuals through the traditional professions of peasant society—priesthood, law, medicine, etc.—to the level of state bureaucracy or academic institutions. What is not evident to Gramsci is that although such intellectuals do in fact lack organic connections to their societies, they enter into an organic relation to the bourgeois state which they serve, precisely because it has transformed the significance of those institutions in relation to the larger system of its apparatuses. They enter, therefore, not into traditional but into organic positions as *dirigente*.[63] But his account of the trajectory of the southern intellectuals is nonetheless suggestive for an account of the possibility of a transformation of the structural position of radical intellectuals that does not entail their directive position as members of an advance party. Gramsci's argument is that the so-called traditional intellectuals are drawn over into the revolutionary party by virtue of the historically superior force of the organic intellectuals' arguments. If, however, we take seriously the implications of his writings on the Southern Question for colonial societies, we can open out a trajectory for the radical intellectual alternative to the narrative of seduction and betrayal given by Gramsci.

Our model for this would be the dynamic of the formation and practice of the anti-colonial intellectual. As many have shown, but most fully Frantz Fanon in *The Wretched of the Earth*, the colonial intellectual is at first formed by the educational and religious apparatuses of the colonial state. Their function is to form the intellectual as a simulacrum of the western intellectual subject in order to constitute an intermediary class capable of administering the colony as "subjects who work by themselves." This formation, however, by its very logic of division and selection, can only produce the colonial intellectual as simulacrum. That intellectual ultimately meets the limits of assimilation in the form of colonial racist structures which deny the full "humanity" promised by the educational and political apparatuses of the empire. The encounter with a structurally ineradicable racism in the relations of empire to colony turns the intellectual towards anti-colonial nationalism. In the first place, this nationalism is articulated by intellectuals as an *equivalent* to the forms of the colonizing power: that is, the imagined nation will replicate both its apparatuses and its universalist and rights-based ideologies in order to constitute a modern state. If this trajectory is followed, Fanon argues, the outcome will be the nation-state's dependence on neo-colonial capital furthered by the statist ideology of bourgeois national intellectuals. If, however, intellectuals are drawn into the popular struggle engaged by subaltern social formations, they will gradually shed the political and cultural assumptions that are the signs of their assimilation to colonial structures, and take on the fluid and essentially non-traditional forms of subaltern resistance, in what Fanon calls "that zone of occult instability where the people dwell." They will cease to be "leaders" and will contribute to the struggle by virtue of what they are learning as much as by what they have learnt.[64]

Our point, of course, is not to idealize such popular struggles, with all their own contradictions and obstacles, but rather to retrieve from the specific conditions of anti-colonial analyses of the role of the intellectual and of popular struggles an alternative scenario to the one posited by a Lenin or a Gramsci in the form of the directive party. We hope to link our genealogy of the position and function of bourgeois intellectuals within the cultural and educational institutions that emerged in the nineteenth century to the alternative lessons that can be learnt from the popular struggles of the same period around political, economic and educational issues. What we shall argue in our Conclusion is that the rather exaggerated discourse on the recent demise of communism and of the decline of prior forms of labor struggle and institution at the present moment betoken less a moment of collapse for the left than a moment of opportunity for the transformation of conceptions of practice. In contemporary capitalism, the increasing fluidity of social spaces, and therefore of the definition of what constitutes the properly political, combined with the corresponding emergence of social movements which redefine both the practice and the objects of cultural, political and social struggle, offers the possibility of new formations of culture and intellectual work and the dissolution of a hegemonic cultural state.

This possibility entails not only practical openings but also methodological ones. What we come to comprehend is that as intellectuals we do not stand before, as examples representing a fuller capacity or as epigones of progress. We come after. We come after a whole repertoire of possibilities, of counter-hegemonic strategies and alternative imaginations, that we cannot claim as our inheritance. In the debris of their passing we find nothing to develop and nothing to mourn as foregone. For in the present, in the gradual collapse of our own inherited spaces and practices, we find alongside the specter of a consolidating and homogenizing capitalism, alternative openings and fluidities that are in no way "exemplary," so specific are they to their given historical moment and to its indeterminacies. Precisely in that different relation to the "ends" of humanity, in the negation of universal claims by contemporary social movements, we discover an unexhausted repertoire of renewed possibilities.

CHAPTER 1

The Culture of the Spectacle

> [T]he more [the spectator] contemplates,
> the less he lives; the more he accepts
> recognizing himself in the dominant
> images of need, the less he understands
> his own existence and his own desires.
> The externality of the spectacle in rela-
> tion to the active man appears in the fact
> that his own gestures are no longer his
> but those of another who represents
> them to him.
> —Guy Debord,
> *The Society of the Spectacle*

It has become a virtual commonplace of postmodernity that we inhab-
it a society of the spectacle. But if, in some analyses, the spectacularity
of the public sphere that engages the modern subject is the sign of a
new and unprecedented alienation of that subject from active participation in political life, it is important not to forget the extent to which
the figure of the spectator has historically been the exemplary, even
heroic, type of political subjectivity. That figure emerges as the moral
or social as well as aesthetic critic of such journals as Addison's *Spectator* in the early eighteenth century.[1] But by the end of that century,
and specifically in relation to the French Revolution, Immanuel Kant
transformed the moral position of the spectator explicitly into a political relation, albeit to an ideal rather than an actual republic. As he
argues in his essay "The Conflict of the Faculty of Philosophy with the
Faculty of Law," it is only the philosophical spectator who can derive
the universally progressive meaning of so violent and potentially

31

disastrous a political event as the recent revolution. That progressive meaning is the emergence of a disposition in humanity towards a republican constitution:

> This moral cause inserting itself [in the course of events] is two-fold: first, that of the *right*, that a nation must not be hindered in providing itself with a civil constitution, which appears good to the people themselves; and second, that of the *end* (which is, at the same time, a duty), that that same national constitution alone be just and morally good in itself, created in such a way as to avoid, by its very nature, principles permitting offensive war. It can be no other than a republican constitution, republican at least in essence; it thus establishes the condition whereby war (the source of all evil and corruption of morals) is deterred; and, at least negatively, progress toward the better is assured humanity in spite of all its infirmity, for it is at least left undisturbed in its advance.[2]

As Hannah Arendt comments, in her *Lectures on Kant's Political Philosophy*,

> The spectator, because he is not involved, can perceive this design of providence or nature, which is hidden from the actor. So we have the spectacle and the spectator on one side, the actors and all the single events and contingent, haphazard happenings on the other. In the context of the French Revolution, it seemed to Kant that the spectator's view carried the ultimate meaning of the event, although this view yielded no maxim for acting.[3]

The gradual transformation of the moral into the political censor in the century preceding Kant has been well plotted by Reinhart Kosel-leck in his *Kritik und Krise*, where he powerfully argues for the virtual inevitability of the process and its foundational nature for the emergence of bourgeois politics.[4] Arendt grasps Kant's oblique engagement with political theory as *critical*, insofar as the disinterested spectator as judge (in the full sense in which the *Third Critique* relates judging and the ascription of *ends*) is split off from the subject as interested agent. The capacity to adjudge ends, and accordingly to grasp individual actions as parts of a totality, is what makes the subject not merely moral or tasteful, as in prior writings on aesthetics and sentiment, but fully ethical. This emergence of the political subject as in the first place ethical also grounds the universal claims of bourgeois politics at the same time as it defines that subject as an entirely formal entity. It is, in the terms of the *Third Critique*, a disposition of the subject rather than an individual and situated consciousness that is in play here.[5]

At this historical juncture, splitting the subject into agent and spectator is absolutely not problematic in the way it comes to be for Guy Debord. On the contrary, it supplies the conditions of possibility for claiming the universality and the disinterest of emergent bourgeois political institutions even as these necessarily sanction the practices of partisan politics. The paradox by which bourgeois states claim a disinterested transcendence of politics while in practice operating through the unceasing articulation of conflicting interests is resolved by this division in the subject. For if at one level what is represented to the state are the competing claims of antagonistic interests, at another, ethically superior level, what the state in its turn represents is the universal, spectating human subject. The state is neither simply a bundle of *ad hoc* institutions nor a purely disinterested idea; it is in effect the productive intersection of both. The contingencies of quotidian practice are regulated by a narrative that precisely moves from the irregularities of contingency to the "regulative idea" (in Kantian terms) of an asymptotically deferred harmony. We can map this narrative through the everyday assumption by which the elected representative who is sent to congress or parliament as the representative of interests and/or localities becomes in that very move from constituency to state a supposedly ethical subject who is expected to submit his or her will to that of the general will.

This brings us to the second point that is implied in Debord's remarks. Again, what Debord finds problematic at this moment seems to us conditional for bourgeois politics at an earlier point. We mean the emergence of a theory of political representation and, more specifically, of the procedures and institutions by which subjects become formed as subjects susceptible of and amenable to representation. The idea of representation is so fundamental to our political and indeed aesthetic culture as to seem virtually inescapably self-evident. So much so, in fact, that it is practically impossible to think outside those terms. Debord regards the inescapability in the postmodern era of "being represented" as an index of disempowering alienation. We will be arguing here and in the chapters that follow that for earlier thinkers, those who contributed to the formation of bourgeois political theory and institutions, to be capable of being represented was not merely to approach one's humanity more fully was but the very condition of political life. Learning to be represented guaranteed, if not empowerment, at least enfranchisement. Neither was it for them by any means a self-evident given of the culture but was rather a condition of political life that had to be produced, and produced by the difficult medium of an unprecedented pedagogical intervention in society. To permit oneself to be represented was by no means the natural and self-evident state of the human individual but the effect of an historically emergent *culture*. For thinkers like Kant, Schiller, Coleridge or Mill, the move from the condition of the subject in a more or less feudal state to that of a human and political subject was equivalent to the larger historical progress of humanity from savagery and barbarism to freedom and civilization. The very history of the usage of the word "subject" implies as much.

Given the difficulty of thinking from our historical perspective into a moment at which representation was not to all intents and purposes the mode of being in the (social) world, we will try to approach the issue theoretically as much as historically by regarding the French Revolution as a watershed between two thinkers whose attitudes to representation are crucially incompatible. We will focus on Jean-Jacques Rousseau's attack on the theater in his *Letter to M. D'Alembert* and Friedrich Schiller's two works, *On the Aesthetic Education of Man* and "On the Stage as Moral Institution." Consideration of these thinkers will allow us to throw into relief the strange and novel discourse on representation that emerges in the moment of the French Revolution; the paradox is that what now seems strange will be Rousseau's antagonism to representation. Accordingly, we will be obliged to regard his writings as a kind of critical fiction rather than a positive blueprint for a "post-representational" society. Later, however, we will suggest the continuities between his understanding of the forms of social relation that ground a non-representational society and subsequent formulations that are similarly at odds with the imposition of state institutions through which representative government is to be grounded. For neither thinker, however, do we claim a direct influence on the specific formation of state institutions or on radical counter-institutions. There may have been in both cases just such an influence, but the object of this chapter is rather to throw into relief the meaning of the discourse on representation that, we believe, was far more contested in radical circles than has hitherto been supposed. In keeping with Gramsci's understanding of the sites in which hegemony and its subjects are constituted, we will reflect on the stage as a paradigmatic institution of the "ethical state."

ROUSSEAU, TRANSPARENCY AND THE FATE OF THE *FÊTE*

> [I]t is necessary to keep subjects apart. That
> is the first maxim of contemporary politics.
> —J.-J. Rousseau,
> "Essay on the Origin of Languages" (1754)

The term "transparency" signifies for Rousseau a mode of perception and communication among human beings that is free from all falsehood and deception. It refers not just to one Rousseauean idea among others; the goal of attaining to an utter transparency in human (i.e., social) relations stands as what we might call Rousseau's recuperative ideal—recuperative in the sense that the state of nature, where people "found their security in the ease of seeing through each other,"[6] serves here as a kind of buried origin. All Rousseau's writings offer different strategies for the recovery of a lost, original, yet always-already prior, transparency; even the *Confessions*, as Starobinski points out, propose to establish a kind of circuit of transparency between Rousseau as author and his readers.[7] There is of course a paradox here, since Rousseau believed that while spontaneous gestures and reactions do not lie, language, which can and does do so, is in principle an obstacle and not a means to natural goodness. Language represents, it re-presents; the difference constitutive of it, between itself and that of which it speaks, makes possible deception, which is in turn linked to vice. Language's ambiguous capacities replace the illusion of communication with the practice of delusion, and this latter is far more difficult to counteract.

But counteract it we must, according to Rousseau, whatever the cost. The drastic measures called for in and by the moral emergency to which he wished to alert his contemporaries means that much more is involved in his *Letter to M. d'Alembert on the Theater* (1759), for instance, than the simple-minded indictment of cosmopolitanism and urban sophistication which that work is often taken to have proffered. In fact, the *Letter* is precisely an argument for the necessity of recovering transparency, an argument that sets up its claims in rigorously binary terms: people in Paris define themselves in, and can only properly see themselves through, the eyes of others; along the axis of their *amour propre* are strung out calculation, emulation, hypocrisy and deceit, all of which reinforce each other in the individuals' relation to their own consciousness as in their relation to others. By contrast, in Neufchâtel, Rousseau's doubtless-idealized village alternative, "each is everything for himself, no one is anything for another."[8] This is not a formula for selfishness, but for its transcendence. To know one's character as a self-contained moral unit is to be able to be accessible, and to gain access, to others. The open, honest, forthright self with nothing to hide is buried—implicit—in all of us, and only on the basis of its unmasking does the establishment of a communicative circuit among such selves become in the truest sense possible. The conditions for this appearance of honesty and transparency are, of course, not simply the moral nature of moral selves. They lie in economic and political arrangements inseparable from transparency: that is, a "republican" constitution in which no one is represented by another and economic relations in which the division of labor and therefore exchange are minimal. The phrase just quoted is at once political and economic in its reference, but stems from a social organization in which that division of spheres is as unthinkable as the division of labor: "Never did carpenter, locksmith, glazier, or turner enter this country; each is everything for himself, no one is anything for another" (p. 61).

It is in Paris, then, political and economic capital of France, and not in Neufchâtel, that people are obliged to dissemble simply in order to attain to sociability. Small wonder that the actor can find there so honored a place. He _belongs_, here, among people who play roles habitually—or, as with Rameau's nephew in Diderot, indiscriminately. The actor typifies society at large by counterfeiting himself in imitating others, or in presenting merely a _version_ of (some aspect of) himself to others. His "disgraceful abasement ... renders him fit for all sorts of roles except the noblest of all, man—which he abandons."[9] It is of the utmost importance that we recall at this point a cognate passage from the "First Discourse": "we have Physicists, Geometricians, Chemists, Astronomers, Poets, Musicians, Painters; we no longer have citizens."[10] In its emphasis on the division of laborer and self, Rousseau's sense of the "abandonment of man" will seem to resemble that which Schiller expresses slightly later. But as we shall see, where Schiller seeks "to restore by means of a higher Art the totality of our nature which the arts themselves have destroyed,"[11] Rousseau seeks the restoration of man _without_ division—in effect, without art, artifice, or artificiality.

The abandonment of humanity and, what amounts for Rousseau to the same thing, of the possibility of citizenship, is of course not complete or utter. But it is severe. It involves a double loss: the loss of the capacity for spontaneous experience and for moral choice. What alone can counteract these tendencies is the kind of immediacy of self to others, and of the self to itself, that is involved in the idea of selfhood as Rousseau understood it. This is the antithesis of an educative ideal, particularly as promulgated by the nineteenth-century tradition of *Bildung* to which Schiller made so marked a contribution. It is a matter, here, not of accretion and growth, but of the removal or stripping away of layers. In the name of his recuperative ideal, Rousseau calls for an absolute unmasking, the elimination of personae, and, through this unmasking, the eradication of deceit, hypocrisy, duplicity, evasiveness, pride and pretense—in a word, of *amour propre*. Only with this eradication would selfhood become generalizable in the required sense, only then would it become the origin or principle of commonality, of what Hegel was to term *Allgemeinheit*. For a truly common ground cannot arise until we are capable of binding ourselves to others directly, self to self, or with as little mediation as possible. Achieving such immediacy may of course be a rather tall order; but what needs stressing here is that, as a personal and political desideratum, it is not something to be striven for through education (unless, that is, we espouse the extremely unorthdox kind of education to which young Emile is subjected). There is a sense, in fact, in which it is not to be *striven* for at all, since a self that neither requires nor performs any mediating functions is always-already there, implicit in all of us, awaiting its uncovering and resuscitation. If it is to emerge, we must learn to heed the lesson of its unlettered (i.e., untaught, natural) language, removing the falsehood layered over it and making, thereby, the latent manifest.

It follows from this that the fewer the layers needing to be removed, the easier the attainment of true selfhood and moral being becomes. Thus the revolutionary dynamite contained between the lines, as it were, of *Emile*: the crude, the unlettered, the coarse and unrefined are in principle more able to attain to the desired state than are the sophisticated, the learned, the cosmopolitan. At this level, there is no great mystery to Rousseau's enormous popularity during the French Revolution among the *menu peuple*: they evidently felt, and were quite right in feeling, that he spoke to and with them. We shall come back to this point presently, but first let us return to the theater and, more nearly, to its topography. For theatrical topography plays a significant part in Rousseau's moralism/moralizing, and his discussion of it carries implications that go beyond his attack on the theater *per se*.

"People think they come together in the theater," says Rousseau, "but it is there that they are in fact isolated. It is there that they go precisely to *forget* their real human relationships: their ties to their friends, their neighbours, their relations."[12] ("L'on croit s'assembler au spectacle, et c'est là que chacun s'isole; c'est là qu'on va oublier ses amis, ses voisins, ses proches"). They go there, that is,

> in order to concern themselves with fables, to cry for the misfortunes of the dead, or to laugh at the expense of the living.... In giving our tears to these fictions we have satisfied all rights of humanity without having to give any more of ourselves; whereas unfortunate people in reality would require from us relief, consolation, and work, which would involve us in their pains, and would require at least the sacrifice of our indolence, from all of which we are quite content to be exempt. It could be said that our heart closes itself for fear of being touched at our expense.[13]

The theater, thus conceived, atomizes us by what it portrays or represents, and this is why it is an arena of moral inactivism in which we forget ourselves and (by the same token) others. But it also divides us by its spatial form. We sit apart from each other, in the dark (this is, as we shall see, crucial), observing through a proscenium arch a "spectacle," a portrayal enacted for us in such a way that the separation and division characterizing our daily lives is augmented and reinforced. It should be clear that for Rousseau the theater is a kind of grotesque parody or inversion of the Assembly in *The Social Contract*, where we cannot bracket, ignore or disregard those around us. The theater petrifies, immobilizes, *divides* its audience; sitting in a somber auditorium, immersed in the "closed" dark character of the theatrical experience, it is as though we all had something to hide from one another—as indeed, in effect, we do. What we have to hide is ourselves—our selves—and hence, on Rousseau's terms, the ground of any possible commonality. The theater at best (re)unites us indirectly, through the intermediacy of the performed play. Scenic, staged action brings everything to us by distancing everything from us.[14] *Fetish* as it necessarily is, the play effectively becomes all that we have in common with each other, and the theater therein reveals itself as a mere counterpart to our unhappy dispersion.

What is most relevant about the *Letter* for our purposes, however, is the way Rousseau counterposes to the theater with which the Genevans were threatened the festival or *fête* which, he reminds them, they already enjoyed *sponte sua*. This *fête*, as Starobinski indicates, is the criterion or norm by which all other spectacles—or, for that matter, all other gatherings—are to be judged.[15] The *fête* is open, transparent, immediate, intransitive, a moment not only of community but of freedom. Starobinski regards it as an epiphany of transparency. It would be wrong even to say that the *fête* gives rise to this openness, that it causes or is the means to man's happiness—Rousseau, we may surmise, was of all people no stranger to the "paradox of hedonism"—for it is rather the case that the festival is the *expression* of people's happiness, or better, the *form* their happiness takes.[16] It admits of no blocked encounters; people are here wholly present to one another. Community, identity, and access are involved in and created by the free act of communication itself. The divisive barriers that ground the moment of theater and constitute the image of a society founded on division have been broken down, in advance as it were, as the *fête* discovers a profound identity between self-recognition and the recognition of others, between the individual and his communal self. This is, of course, a picture of innocence. No one has anything (thoughts, feelings) to hide, and no one hogs the limelight, since there is none to be hogged. No curtain is raised, no mask is donned (Molière's *Tartuffe* was apparently the first play performed at the French court in which the actors deliberately removed their masks). The contrast with the theater is completed and expressed through a number of more or less explicit oppositions: between the open and the closed, the light (daylight: it's important that the *fête* take place *en plein air*) and the dark; between freedom and constraint, movement and stasis, unity and dispersion, authenticity and (dis)simulation—between, in short, transparency and opacity.

The substance of the *fête*, then, is openness and clarity; appraisal of another human being, comparison of myself with another—these are utterly foreign to it and impossible within it. There can thus be nothing traditional, or at least not commemorative about it. Rousseau's depiction of the *fête* (and of other, similar gatherings in *La nouvelle Héloïse* and in his essay on Poland) falls in somewhere between a memory and a glimpse of a public joy that is without object, and which a particular object would destroy by offering itself up as a mediation. The depiction has for us a peculiar interest: the General Will, according to *The Social Contract*, is no less devoid of a particular object. Any specific object would destroy the symmetry between citizen and sovereign and hold community hostage; the General Will must be general in its origin and *remain* general in its application. In this sense, it is unsurprising that Starobinski should refer us, in a rather wonderful phrase, to the "lyrical" side of the General Will as an extension of the affectivity residing in the *fête*.[17] *The Social Contract* stipulates at the level of having what the *fête* realizes at the level of being.

Some fascinating implications for our understanding of Rousseau's thought and of its application thus begin to emerge. Rousseau believes that representative democracy, as opposed to the direct participatory democracy promulgated in *The Social Contract*, is a contradiction in terms. But behind this belief lies a more deep-seated antagonism toward representation *as such*. Representation must have an object; it has to be "of something," and has to be effectively fetishistic, therefore, in that it takes and must take the part for the whole and displace direct human relations. But taking the part for the whole is *prima facie* illegitimate since, by the very logic of fetishism, the part object comes to displace the whole. The will does not admit of representation, says *The Social Contract*, and neither does anything else, if our unity and integrity as many-sided beings is to be respected rather than subverted. The theatrical representation of human character is inherently phony at the most fundamental level precisely because it *is* representation. As Robert Wokler nicely puts it:

> Just as we have ceased to assemble together to determine our civic ideals, so, similarly, through art, science and religion we have been numbed and made passive, displaced from the centre of cultural life and herded into the pits and pews. Transformed from agents of what we do into witnesses of what happens to us, we are, in the modern world, turned into a hushed audience and taught deference and timidity. In the arts, no less than in our political relations, Rousseau observed in his "Essay on the Origin of Languages," "it is necessary to keep subjects apart; that is the first maxim of contemporary politics."[18]

And the implications of this politico-cultural parallelism are, as Wokler goes on to indicate, far-reaching:

> Reverie constitutes the free association of ideas never conceived; democracy [as Rousseau conceived it] comprises a free association of people such as had never been truly envisaged before. The imagery of public participation in all facets of social life was deeply felt and richly drawn by Rousseau, around such aesthetic, religious and cultural symbols of solidarity as he portrays in the military dance of the regiment of Saint-Gervais in his *Lettre à M.*

d'Alembert sur les spectacles, or the uplifting song of the grape pickers in *La nouvelle Héloïse.* Democratic politics as he saw it was infused with the charm, the *joie de vivre* of a cultural festival, a popular banquet, a display of all the people for all the people, held in the open air under the sky. . . .[19]

Doubtless for most contemporary readers such festive scenarios have a smack of the folkloric, at best, of D.H. Lawrence's vision of red-breeched dancing miners or of fascist celebrations of idyllic labor. Koselleck, indeed, argues further that the transparency of Rousseau-ean democracy dissolves all distinction between inner and outer, between individual and general will, and produces a state of permanent revolution which is simultaneously a permanent dictatorship.[20] Whatever the particular elements of Rousseau that give rise to such suspicion as to the tendency of his writings, they stand as salutary reminders of the dangerous ground onto which any critique of representation necessarily steps. But the alternatives to representation are not reducible to fascism, a political form not well known, in any case, for its antipathy to spectacle.

We need, in fact, to reiterate the grounds of Rousseau's antagonism to representational structures. Walter Benjamin's luminous insight as to the nature of fascism is important to invoke here:

> Fascism attempts to organize the newly created proletarian masses without affecting the property structure which the masses strive to eliminate. Fascism sees its salvation in giving these masses not their right, but instead a chance to express themselves. The masses have a right to change property relations; fascism seeks to give them an expression while preserving property. The logical result of fascism is the introduction of aesthetics into political life.[21]

For Rousseau, to the contrary, the festival and its transparency are predicated upon the vision of a society with neither division of labor nor expropriation. That such a vision was already becoming utopian at the moment he articulated it, a moment before any alternative emergent formations could have been described, situates it as a residual critique of the culture of representation rather than as an anticipation of the fascism that will arise from an objective crisis in representative democracy's relation to capitalism. It is in this spirit that we seek to re-read Rousseau.

***

To recur to Benjamin, our own conclusion will of course be that aesthetics did not require fascism to enter political life. The shaping of
the political subject in relation to and by way of aesthetic culture was
already glimpsed by Rousseau and was virtually programmatic by the
time of Schiller. Aesthetic culture becomes the ground or condition of
possibility both for thinking and for forging the political subject.
Indeed, we may be right to suspect that the very instinct to identify
forms of immediacy automatically with the terrors of fascism has an
older genealogy. For if radical Jacobinism comes to be seen as a threat
to the forms of bourgeois civil and political society, that is, to relations
of property, and has accordingly to be contained and expunged, its suppression is legitimated by appeal to the Terror, to the excesses that are
seen to be part and parcel of Jacobinism. The Terror itself is then
derived from the masses' refusal of mediation, their desire for immediate political as well as sensual gratification. As Schiller put it in his
On the Aesthetic Education of Man,

> Among the lower and more numerous classes we are confronted
> with crude, lawless instincts, unleashed with the loosening of the
> bonds of civil order, and hastening with ungovernable fury to their
> animal satisfactions. (*AEM*, p. 25)

And as the very name of the Jacobins implied, the instability of the
masses is seen to be of a piece with Rousseau's own "sentimental"
utopianism. Edmund Burke was only one of the first to make this
identification and not the last to seek to contain the Revolution and
Rousseau by aesthetic means.[22]
Not that this backhanded ideological reading of Rousseau and
Jacobinism is without insight; it is simply that it figures the actual
threat that the revolutionary masses were felt to pose to property and
order in terms that are moral and aesthetic rather than economic
and political. In the revolutionary *fête* were enacted social relations of
a kind profoundly antipathetic to the order that ultimately gained
hegemony. In Mona Ozouf's words,

> The mere fact of coming together seemed at the time to be a prodi-
> gious moral conquest: the festival celebrated the passage from the
> private to the public, extending to all experiences of each indi-
> vidual "as by a kind of electric charge." It allowed "that which
> despotism had never allowed—that is, the mingling of citizens de-

lighting in the spectacle of one another and the perfect accord of hearts." "It should be remembered that under the rule of despotism," Poyet tells us, "men mistrusted one another and, having no common interest, hid themselves from one another. . . . The politics of despotism helped maintain this fatal disunion." The gathering at the Champ-de-Mars [The Festival of the Federation] seemed to everyone to be the reverse of that partitioned world.[23]

Organizers of revolutionary festivals were well aware that the outcomes of their efforts should stimulate and provoke equality by negating or suspending social distinctions and visually contracting the social space between participants. Poyet's question—"does patriotism recognize today those lines of demarcation that pride and pettiness once laid down?"—was rhetorical. But here a note of caution imposes itself. The sheer variety of types and levels of festival during the French Revolution is almost enough to stymie in advance the idea that these amounted to a literal application of Rousseau's prescriptions. True, there was quite enough dancing of the *farandole* around the Maypole to suggest otherwise; but, on the other hand, the Maypole was supplanted with all due dispatch by that much more formalized import, the liberty tree. And who in the end is to say that the former is more Rousseauean than the latter? Rousseau was no Maypole-pulling-down Puritan—misanthropy is not so simple a category—yet many Revolutionary festival organizers, bent upon centralization and hostile to "backward" local custom, were nothing else. It may be that what they pulled down with the *mai* was the very idea of intransitivity specified earlier as the core of Rousseau's defense of merriment. It may yet have been an easy target, much as Hegel, inspired by Montesquieu, would soon insist that we *need* mediating, "representative" institutions.

Rousseau was almost always more despairing than sanguine about the likelihood of transparency's retrieval. And with good reason. The actual history, the fate, of public ceremonials during the French Revolution—serious work on which is only now beginning to be done[24]—suggests that a recast public transparency was never viable to begin with. The point remains, however, that Rousseau's extensive meditations on the motif of transparency serve as a kind of advance critique of the need for reconciliation, or at least the need for "culture" and "the state" as media for reconciliation. A recovered transparency would have short-circuited the need for these agencies by reconciling us at a different and more immediate level than culture or state ever dreamed of doing.

We can begin to get at the difference by looking at what is said to need reconciling in each argument. Rousseau's familiar dichotomies—reason/feeling, calculation/imagination, *amour propre/amour de soi*—refer us to divisions within the variegated but unitary nature of man, within what ought to be a unified multiplicity that never privileges one part over the others. Whether or not man was divided against himself in traditional, premodern society is beside the point here, but what is central is that modernity demands and institutionalizes division, the privileging of certain aspects of the self at the expense of others, to an unprecedented degree. Man *must*, to take but one example, privilege *amour propre* over *amour de soi*, in a world where human relations are mediated by money and universal competition is absolutely of the essence. With this established, we need to ask: if fragmentation and cleavage pervade the modern world, precisely what is it, for Rousseau, that they have obscured? Surely we can no longer give the formulaic answer, "nature." In fact we are forced back quite simply and obviously upon that nebulous but nonetheless substantive concept of unity, of an integral and many-sided plenitude. The authentic self according to Rousseau is not at all what late, nineteenth-century theorists were to claim it was—something culturally or politically defined, something beyond ourselves to which we must aspire. Rousseau's self is (again) a more immediate, more integral unity-in-diversity whose delicate symmetry is equally upset by the aspiration "that a man's reach should exceed his grasp" as it is by any excessive concentration on one of its component parts. And it is only on the basis of acknowledging this unity, which each of us essentially is, that we can build real links with each other. Hence Rousseau's conviction regarding the necessary connection, in conditions of extreme inequality, between social inferiority and moral superiority. This has nothing to do with a romanticization of the poor: it is just that the poor have imbibed far fewer crusty prejudices (about education, the benefits of culture, the beneficence of the state) and have, therefore, a far shorter route to travel toward the sense of coherence that is the basis of moral being.

If, then, "foresight takes us ceaselessly beyond ourselves and often places us where we shall never arrive," Rousseau proposes, alternatively: "Let us measure the radius of our sphere and stay in the center, like the insect in the middle of his web, sufficient unto ourselves."[25] The statement is concerned to deny, indeed, to excoriate, the need for culture defined in pedagogic terms. It stands as clearly against Kantian notions of pedagogy predicated upon disappointed desire as the festival does against the theater.[26] And it does so not because Rousseau fails to see the linkages between pedagogical culture and (what passes for) politics, but because he sees them all too clearly. His thought in this area throws an uncompromising light over the other thinkers and writers with whom this book has yet to deal. For it is not, for him, that we are to be made worthy of "our" politics or of "our" way of expressing ourselves artistically, but rather that these things are to be made worthy of us.

To see this is in effect to draw all kinds of lines together, and to begin to come to grips with the challenge Rousseau threw down to his contemporaries—and, by extension, to his no more receptive successors. It is, for one thing, to recognize that justice in Rousseauean politics does not consist in the balancing out of good and evil impulses and tendencies, as it does in the liberal/constitutional models that were to come into their own after 1789. As Rousseau understood it, justice involves no such via media; it demands instead a clearing away, an eradication of cupidity and competition from human relations, and this is the task of the General Will. By the same token, virtue results from the repression of tendencies toward vice at both the personal and the social levels. But just as it would be wrong to see the Rousseau of the *Letter* as a Maypole-pulling-down Puritan, so it would be a mistake, albeit a common one, to over-emphasize the repressiveness this project would involve. The task, after all, is one of recuperation as well as demolition. If we can manage to put aside passions, prejudices, adventitious events and everything else that can count as the detritus of history, we can cast light on the depths of time and on the meaning of moral being. What would then emerge would be a being whose faculties were virtual and whose liberty remained as yet untried—a being, that is, who could provide more promising *matériel* for social reconstruction than can the cowed miscreant who has shown himself after centuries of "progress." Rousseau's state of nature would thus emerge as a socially lived experience: an age in which history was, in Starobinski's term, "contained," when dislocation had not yet set in; an age when needs had not yet become unhinged from the possibility of their satisfaction; an age, in short—which is also, for the individual, a kind of mental, moral and spiritual stage—when enervation, dissatisfaction and imposture were unnecessary because unthinkable, and unthinkable because unnecessary.

But if Rousseau's call for a return to what is essentially a prehistory points us to the fact that, for him, history *is* on the one hand the development of evil, it does not follow that all history is the repository of nothing else. The world of the Ancients was communal and integral.

People's cognitive faculties and evaluative standards were bound up with communal political experiences. True, the disaggregation of community and the disintegration of individual personality were cognate as well as subsequent processes. But our natural liberty, eroded through this, has not been irretrievably lost. The persistence of *fête* or, for that matter, of the very idea of transparency, suggests that communal antidotes to our atomized and sorry state may yet be available.

CULTURE AS SUPPLEMENT TO THE STATE

We have seen that the notion of transparency, both as it was theorized by Rousseau and as it was expressed practically during the French Revolution, implies equally a notion of *immediacy*: there should be no mediation between people and power, between power and its effects, or between interests and their expression. This means, as well, that no intermediary can "come between" citizen and citizen. Immediacy and transparency demand the full presence of citizens, one to another, in the same space; whether taken as metaphors for social organization or, quite literally, as implying the necessity of a political culture in which total participation is the rule, both notions are necessarily and profoundly antagonistic in the political sphere to any concept of representation. Where all stand in the same space, in radical equivalence, no one can stand *for* any other, nor any voice speak for any other. It is of course perfectly logical that, when taken literally, this model of participatory fullness should seem to lie beyond the capacity of liberal democratic representations, but this by no means "proves" its impossibility of realization outside the framework of, precisely, representation. To insist that the size and complexity of the modern state preclude direct participation and necessitate representative government is to beg the question. For this evocation of a numerically vast population, a *vulgus* that is inevitably also *mobile*, is a political turn on the sublime and, like the sublime in the cultural tradition with which we are here dealing, demands a turn to ethical formation as a means of accommodating the unrepresentable to representation.

We shall be arguing in the following pages that this turn to ethical formation in fact *predates* the legitimating argument for representation that depends on the numerical dimension of the modern state, and that what we have to do with, as we have remarked above, is the kind or quality of citizen who will be enfranchised by that state; Our concern is with the inculcation of a peculiar mode of subjectivity: a mode of the subject that must somehow be produced as a prerequisite to participation in the business of the state, even if participation, here, means no more than accepting "being represented." We will also argue that any transformation in the models of political representation is inseparable from similar transformations of that concept in other spheres. This is particularly the case, and particularly relevant, with regard to aesthetics, both in its original concern with individual psychology and in its later metamorphosis into aesthetic culture. The congruence of these transformations with one another is fundamental to what Althusser will call the "interpellation" of the subject by ideological state apparatuses.[27] More significantly, it is what makes subjective acquiescence in that interpellation seem *probable*—in a sense familiar to poetics—to individuals who otherwise have nothing to gain but their chains by such an association. An argument about representation that is most clearly, and earliest, articulated in aesthetic writings, comes, we believe, so to saturate our culture (in the broadest sense of the term) as to seem to define, in each and every sphere, the inevitable formal contours of human being.

In the wake of the failure of the French Revolution to make good on its promise to emancipate Man by way of politics—and of its devolution into Terror—whatever ideals of transparency informed the revolutionary sensibility were displaced by a number of concepts that we can summarize as designating modes of identification. Identification of the individual subject with the state is to be achieved through the intervention of culture, which acts as supplement to a state perceived to be not yet equal to its ethical idea. Two conditions make possible this identification: first, that culture, in a fashion we will presently elaborate, represent what it claims to be the fundamentally common identity of all humans; and second, that the state be conceived ideally as the disinterested and ethical representative of this common identity. The latter claim is one that Schiller makes unequivocally in the fourth of his letters on aesthetic education:

> Every individual human being, one may say, carries within him, potentially and prescriptively, an ideal man, the archetype of a human being, and it is his life's task to be, through all his changing manifestations, in harmony with the unchanging unity of this ideal. This archetype, which is to be discerned more or less clearly in every individual, is represented by the State, the objective and, as it were, canonical form in which all the diversity of individual subjects strives to unite. (*AEM*, p. 17)

Here, in Schiller's seminal argument, the function of culture is to cultivate the identity between the ideal or ethical Man in every subject and the state which is its representative.

The endowment of culture with such a function demands in the first place, as is well known, that culture should be conceived as a distinct domain—distinct not just from the activities of the state, but also from all other institutions and forms of human labor. The specialized activities and productions of this autonomous sphere are seen, paradoxically, to supply the ground for a conception of the human in general, as well as of the individual subject's relation to this generalized humanity. It is the theoretical articulation of this conception and this relation that we will explore here. Important as the "autonomous" artworks are in their own right—important, too, as would be an investigation into the objective historical conditions that made possible the emergence of artistic and cultural productions/practices conceived of as autonomous—what concerns us for the moment is something else. Our concern is with the cultural theory that, at the very moment of the emergence of an autonomous cultural sphere, effectively delimits the form in which aesthetic works in general, even as they are being reconceived, are to be mediated institutionally. As we will see, this institutional delimitation and mediation of what is now separated out as "aesthetic experience" entails a formalization which is at once strictly indifferent to the artwork as such and crucial to the assimilation of individual subjectivity to the archetypal humanity that the state ideally represents.

For Schiller, influenced in this by his reading of Kant's *Critique of Judgement*, the aesthetic experience is not produced by any determinate quality of the object itself; it is, rather, a peculiar modulation of subjective activity such that harmony is achieved between the passive reception of a sensuous impression and the active process of form-giving. Indeed, it is crucial to Schiller's argument that the aesthetic object be "indifferent" as to its specific qualities, material or formal, in order that, conceived as mere matter, it may undergo the process of form-giving which is the proper activity of the subject in its autonomy. Only in this way can the aesthetic moment establish the harmonious balance of those two, eternally distinct, aspects of the individual subject which Schiller defines in Letter 11 as "person" and "condition": that which is the eternal and unchanging substance of the subject on the one hand, and, on the other, the subject *passively* subjected to the world of sense impressions. Since, moreover, each of these aspects of the subject is associated with one element of a series of

dualities—form/matter, sense/reason, reality/thought—which structures *On the Aesthetic Education of Man*, it is the aesthetic moment
which establishes, however momentarily, the unity of man in all his
aspects. We are a long way from the unmediated and inherent unity of
being that Rousseau considered the foundation of community, the cor-
nerstone of moral being. Here, division of the self appears instead as an
ontological given.

For man's harmonious unity is achieved, for Schiller, through the
mediation of what he terms, in Letter 14, the "play-drive." To return
to the opposition: "person" expresses itself through the form-drive, a
striving toward pure form that endangers all relations between the
subject and its material conditions in the world of sense; "condition,"
which takes the form of a sense-drive, subjects the subject to the flux
of sensations and threatens, thereby, to abolish the freedom proper to
it *as* subject—which means, also, to annihilate its personhood. While
we can thus say that the identity of the subject is conserved in the person, it is nonetheless only by way of condition and the sense-drive that
the subject can in any way realize the human potentialities implicit in
this person:

> From this there proceed two contrary challenges to man, the two
> fundamental laws of his sensuous-rational nature. The first insists
> upon absolute reality: he is to turn everything which is mere form
> into world, and make all his potentialities fully manifest. The sec-
> ond insists upon absolute formality: he is to destroy everything
> within himself which is mere world, and bring harmony into all
> his changes. (*AEM*, p. 77)

Between these two "contrary challenges" intervenes the play-drive,
whose end is "reconciling becoming with absolute being and change
with identity," and whose object is beauty ("the most perfect possible
union of reality and form" [*AEM*, pp. 97, 111]).

At a later point in this chapter we will return to a discussion of the
play-drive's "recreationary" aspect: its abstraction (*Absonderung*) from
those conditions of the division of labor which Schiller considers
responsible for each individual's failure to realize his full potentialities
yet crucial for the development of the species. For now, however, it
is important to emphasize how his analysis of the play-drive, and of
the aesthetic disposition which it produces, introduces into what is at
first a synchronic, transhistorical schema of ineradicable duality a
developmental narrative from which the aesthetic derives its fullest

ideological force. For it is through this developmental narrative that Schiller finds a way to overcome what would otherwise remain an *aporia* for bourgeois political thought: to theorize concretely the relationship between the individual subject and humanity in general. It is also in the formation of this narrative that aesthetic culture assumes its crucial function in relation to the state.

In its first elaboration in Letter 14, the play-drive appears to mediate between two opposed yet equally necessary drives—the formal and the sensuous—the balance between which is the aesthetic experience. Reconciliation is achieved, here, by "annulling constraint" and setting man free, both "morally and physically" (*AEM*, p. 97). The harmony thus established within the subject's dual nature represents, equally, a momentary wholeness since, as we have seen, the potentiality of the person is at this point no longer at odds with the subject's determination by condition. Already, though, what is produced in such a moment is conceived by Schiller as a mere intuition of an as yet unfulfilled destiny:

> Should there, however, be cases in which [the individual] were to have this twofold experience simultaneously, in which he were to be at once conscious of his freedom and sensible of his existence, were, at one and the same time, to feel himself as matter and come to know himself as mind, then he would in such cases, and in such cases only, have a complete intuition of his human nature, and the object which afforded him this vision would become for him a symbol of his accomplished destiny, and, in consequence (since that is only to be attained in the totality of time), serve him as a manifestation of the Infinite. (*AEM*, p. 95)

The aesthetic moment, constituted in the subject's relation through the play-drive to the beautiful object, is thus no more than a prefiguration of that human nature which is posed throughout as the end of aesthetic education—which is to say that it is, in a word, *inadequate*.

The partial, prefigurative aspect of the aesthetic experience is not conceived here, as it often is by later, more critical thinkers, to be the unreconciled expression of a negative utopianism, but rather as partaking of a fuller structure of representation. Within this structure, the partial aesthetic experience does more than simply prefigure the "accomplished destiny"; it contributes productively to that destiny's accomplishment. Implicit throughout has been an understanding of representation that goes beyond the purely binary and spatial terms of the presentation of an object to a subject, and posits instead an ethical narrative to which the representational function of aesthetic experience is crucial. Letter 20 makes this understanding explicit. Here, what had been conceived as the mutual interdependence of the sensuous and formal drives becomes reconceived as a temporal structure within which the sensuous is prior to the formal which must overcome it: "We know that he begins by being nothing but life, in order to end by becoming form; that he is an Individual before he is a Person, and that he proceeds from limitation to infinity" (*AEM*, p. 139). Within this narrative, which is, as we shall see, at once that of the individual and that of the species, aesthetic experience plays an indispensable, transitional role. For if, in the first place, the individual is determined passively by sensuous experience, remaining prehuman insofar as his will is still subordinated to external necessity, this determination must be overcome before the passage can take place into the self-determining autonomy of moral necessity (*AEM*, pp. 139-41). The function of the aesthetic is to annul this first determination by producing a state which Schiller describes as one of "pure determinability," which reproduces "in a certain sense ... that negative state of complete absence of determination in which he found himself before anything at all had made an impression upon his senses." The crucial difference is that the sensuous content of this state is now determined by form. In the aesthetic condition, once again, the simultaneous activity of the sensuous and formal drives leads to their "cancel[ling] each other out as determining forces"; but whereas previously the resultant "determinability" had merely produced an equilibrium between opposed forces, here it becomes the condition for a transition from the dominance of one to the dominance of the other.

It is true that the narrative structure of representation within which the aesthetic functions is often occluded by Schiller's continual insistence upon the ineradicable duality of human nature as a transhistorical phenomenon. Nevertheless, an attentive reading of his argument shows more than this; it shows not only that this duality implies a hierarchy in which reason, morality, or form are valorized over sensuous matter and in which human destiny is realized in the gradual predominance of the former over the latter, but, further, that the very manner in which the aesthetic condition produces a prefigurative intuition of human nature by mediating between these dualities is in fact the means to its *producing* that human nature. This is, of course, once again a question of the representational function of the aesthetic; but here, the mediation of the form–sense duality actually displaces the intuition of a harmonized human being with a formalization which is more than a mere term in the aesthetic condition. For what Schiller is inevitably unable to articulate is that the aesthetic condition itself involves a formalization of human subjectivity without which the assertion of its duality would make no sense. The "pure determinability" of the aesthetic state demands not only the indifference of the object but also that of the subject, since without this second indifference the material specificity of any individual subject would reintroduce interest into the experience of the aesthetic. What may appear at first as an inward turn towards the most private and specific, the most *unique*, of subjective experiences, turns out to be an extreme assertion of the formal identity of all subjects.

This formalization guarantees the productivity of the aesthetic. Where, in the first place, any given aesthetic experience provides an intuition of complete and harmonious human being, it is the formality of the experience that assures that the individual not only intuits that state, but, however momentarily, partakes of it. For as Letter 21 explains, the aesthetic restores to the subject its still purely determinable human potentiality:

> For as soon as we recall that it was precisely of this freedom ["the freedom to be what he ought to be"] that he was deprived by the one-sided constraint of nature in the field of sensation and by the exclusive authority of reason in the realm of thought, then we are bound to consider the power which is restored to him in the aesthetic mode as the highest of all bounties, as the gift of humanity itself. True, he possesses this humanity *in potentia* before any determinate condition into which he can conceivably enter. But he loses it in practice with every determinate condition into which he does enter. And if he is to pass into a condition of an opposite nature, this humanity must be restored to him each time anew through the life of the aesthetic. (*AEM*, p. 147)

"Each time anew": this is the foundation of any aesthetic pedagogy, assuring the productivity of the aesthetic through the repeated identification of each subject with the species in general. It is at once the condition for every subject of becoming-universal and the ground for the ethical (and, as we shall see, political) demand that every subject *be* universal, i.e., that we all be formally the same.

For what the restoration of "humanity *in potentia*" finally means is that, in the aesthetic mode, we do not judge as individuals but as the species. In potential, as pure determinability, any subject is every subject. This is the logic of the tendency of aesthetic theory to valorize the formal over the sensuous: just as the subject as Person is indeterminate potentiality, so it is where "the formal drive holds sway" that "we are no longer individuals, we are species" (*AEM*, p. 83). More than this, however, it is precisely and only through this formalization of the subject that representation itself and the narrative of representation become conceivable.

ON THE STAGE AS MORAL INSTITUTION

The extreme formalization of the aesthetic subject in *On the Aesthetic Education of Man* might leave Schiller, as if in some prefiguration of the Absolute Spirit of a Hegel whom he certainly foreshadowed, without a moment in which that subject can be formed or instantiated. More explicitly, but no less inexorably than Kant's *Third Critique*, Schiller's writings on the aesthetic formation of the subject drive towards a pedagogical moment in which, simultaneously and contradictorily, that subject is formed as if it were individual and autonomous but by way of institutions in which it comes into identity with others. Divided by class, occupation and status, "man" must be harmonized and unified in himself and with others through an aesthetic *education*. We will recall that, by contrast, Rousseau's understanding of transparency was predicated not on identity among subjects but by the play of differences through an undivided space. It is correspondingly instructive that where, for Rousseau, the theater, the "spectacle," is among the many sites of division which "keep subjects apart," for Schiller, in the absence of the fully developed educational institutions of the following century, it is the stage which offers a paradigm for the formation of an ethical citizenry. This argument he elaborates in a brief but significant essay, "On the Stage as Moral Institution" (1784).[28]

That Schiller turns to the stage is instructive for a number of reasons which we will elaborate in turn. The stage is self-consciously a public institution. There existed in Germany, as elsewhere in Europe, a long tradition of "self-cultivation" by way of the private act of reading, practices formed in relation to the scriptural tradition of biblical devotions but secularized of late for middle-class audiences in the various forms of the periodical, poetry and the novel. But Schiller's insistence on the theater as a site of moral formation rather than corruption or mere distraction is relatively new. While Kant, in the *Third*

Critique, still valorizes the private act of reading over quasi-public activities (including the hymn-singing that he detested), Schiller makes a definitive connection between the public form of the theatrical performance and its formation of subjects explicitly for the state. The reasons may lie in the very phenomenology of theatrical presentations that Rousseau treated with such suspicion. For where Rousseau, as we saw, sees the stage merely as a site in which subjects think they come together but are really divided, Schiller implies a dialectical relation in "On the Stage as Moral Institution" between the semi-private form of the theater's mode of consumption and its constitution of a public. It synthesizes, that is, the privacy of the contemplative aesthetic subject and the gathering of a number of such subjects around a common object. The very material conditions of the theatrical performance instantiate Schiller's claim in *Aesthetic Education* that it is the unique characteristic of the aesthetic work to be a "*common* property." At the same time, the theater overcomes the potential for the "idiotization" of the aesthetic subject, the withdrawal of the subject into a contemplation divorced from any relation to public activity. Offering neither the transparency of the Rousseauean or revolutionary festival nor the open-ended and therefore potentially divisive dialogics of interested public debate, the stage offers an aesthetic object whose dialogues achieve closure and accordingly present through the medium of time a singular object around which divided subjects can come together. It is a most evident instance, along with the classroom or lecture room whose geography and narrative assumptions it shares, of the dialectic by which fundamentally identical beings meet in their divided individuality in order to come together in a unity produced in relation to a common object of attention.

Hence, the importance of Schiller's choice of a *recreationary* space for the prototypical "moral institution." As we began to indicate above, implicit in the theory of culture is a notion that it is at once recreationary and re-creationary and that this pun embodies the deep relation between the *space* of culture and its processes. As we have already seen, the efficacy of the aesthetic derives from its pure "determinability," from its not being conditioned by one or other of the given states or occupations by which humans are divided while at the same time presenting the pure formality of the as-yet-to-be-determined subject with an actual object for its play. In social terms, such a manifestation is only possible in what we have since come to term, for reasons embedded deeply in the very logic of culture's relation to political and to economic society, the space of "recreation." That is, only in a space which is set apart from either material or political interests can an object become the undetermined matter for the contemplation of a disinterested subject "at play." In a paradox instantly contained by what we have described as the narrative dimension of the discourse on the aesthetic, the division of spheres, and the divisions of interests and subjects it implies, is overcome by a final division that distantiates the sphere of culture from the spheres of interest. In that sphere of recreation, of the "play-drive," the divided subject is re-created into wholeness. Accordingly, it is the very recreationary space of the theater that is able to guarantee the process of re-creation that it repeatedly performs. For this reason, in the service of the state, the theater effects the transition from a merely private need for harmonization in the individual to the formation of the people as citizens:

> Man, neither altogether satisfied with the senses, nor forever capable of thought, wanted a middle state, a bridge between the two states, bringing them into a harmony. Beauty and aesthetics supplied that for him. But a good lawgiver is not satisfied with discovering the bent of his people—he turns it into account as an instrument for higher use; and hence he chose the stage, as giving nourishment to the whole soul, without straining it, and uniting the noblest education of the head and heart. (*SMI*, p. 333)

The stage, furthermore, not only secures a harmonious relation between the sensual and the intellectual bents of humans, between "person" and "condition." It also stands institutionally between laws, which "only prevent disturbances of social life," and religion, which "prescribes positive orders sustaining social order." Religion, moreover, "acts mostly on the senses" and therefore loses power once its precepts lose the support of imagery and symbols (*SMI*, p. 333). As an institution, and this is the crucial element which will make of the stage a paradigmatic scene of fundamental *political* pedagogy, the theater forms the *disposition* of subjects as citizens, mediating between the prohibitive or coercive force of the law and the prescriptive but abstract principles of religion. "Where the influence of civil laws ends, that of the stage begins" (*SMI*, p. 334).

Since it is a question of forming the *disposition* of the spectator, it is the social form of the theater rather than its actual content that is of importance. Though Schiller provides us throughout the essay with a great number of actual instances of plays which might, each in their own way, bear a particular moral message, in the end, the actual object

which is viewed by the spectator is of little matter or, to put it another
way, a matter of indifference. This is entirely in keeping with the
indifference of the object in his more formal aesthetic theory. What
the spectator carries away from the performance is not the particularity of a moral judgment but the unifying—and edifying—vision of a
humanity identical to itself. For, in the theater:

> Effeminate natures are steeled, savages made man, and, as the
> supreme triumph of nature, men of all ranks, zones, and condi-
> tions, emancipated from the chains of conventionality and fash-
> ion, fraternize here in a universal sympathy, forget the world, and
> come nearer to their heavenly destination. The individual shares
> in the general ecstasy, and his breast has now only space for one
> emotion: he is a *man*. (*SMI*, p. 339)

This passage, the conclusion of the essay, nicely exemplifies how the
discourse of culture draws together the narrative line of development,
from savage to man, from effeminacy to masculinity, with a spatial
synthesis that overcomes the contingencies of region and class, to produce an identification of the individual with the figure of universality,
"man." It is easy to see, once again, how the temporal axis in which
"man" emerges supervenes upon the spatial one, making of universal
"fraternization" a future project rather than an immediate and revolutionary demand. Such a deferred project is, of course, the antithesis of
the Rousseauean festival and the very form of the institutions by
which the emergent bourgeois states will come to regulate and limit
the revolutionary demand for Liberty, Fraternity and—especially—
Equality.

At the heart of Schiller's difference from Rousseau—and this would
be our third remark—is his insistence that the individual becomes
man by way of representation. Once again, Schiller's understanding of
the theater (which we might set against Rousseau's undivided spaces
and immediacy of social relation) is simultaneously topographical and
temporal. Numerous individuals come literally together—assemble—
in the space the theater furnishes in order to confront one and the
same representation. It is as if the lines of sight that connect them to a
common object also unite them in a common identification. But the
condition of possibility for that identification is the fact that, as they
unite, they unite in the same form, as *spectators*. In order to come to
the theater, they have left behind them the contingencies of gender,
class or "condition" to become the recreationary aesthetic subject that

is the archetype of "Man." The formal relation of spectators to the stage is accordingly itself exemplary of the institutional "assemblies" that emerge with the gradual emergence of representative democracies: the classroom, the parliament, the political rally, the recreationary "event."[29] At the same time, the narratives that the theater stages are, at least according to the canon that Schiller selects, equally exemplary of the passage from contingency to "justice," that is, to universal validity. The "representations" that the theater presents to the public replicate as normative narratives the very conditions that their assembly there enacts: to overcome contingency it is necessary to identify with the representative figure of man. The understated obverse of this demand lies precisely in the exemplary quality of the theater: precisely because it is a recreationary space, its representations can never be more than prefigurative instances of an equality that is always yet to come. Deferral is inscribed in both the narrative and the spatial assumptions of the stage as moral institution.

Presented by Schiller as an exemplary state apparatus, the theater, perhaps inadvertently, betrays equally the secret of the fetishism of representation. The discourse on aesthetics that founds the possibility of a culture of representation is one which emerges in reaction to the French Revolution as a means to deferring its more radical possibilities, possibilities for which in many ways Rousseau and the "Jacobinism" his name evokes came to stand. But such is the force, the success of that discourse, such the degree to which its terms have come to saturate modernity, that it is very difficult for us, located in our moment and our institutions, to imagine again the strangeness of that discourse and to reenvisage a moment in which it seemed "improbable" rather than self-evident. It is no less difficult to recover the articulate resistance or the inarticulate recalcitrance which emergent institutions of representative democracy encountered at all levels of society. Certainly, the resistance of feudal remnants, of the *ancien régime*, of aristocracy, of Toryism, to the gradual inroads of liberalism is the stuff of European political historiography. Resistance to representation and to the political reforms it entails is cast within the grand narratives of the nineteenth century as the prerogative of reaction. But there is also another narrative, embedded in the liberal writings of that period, which is that of successive attempts to school working-class subjects in the discipline of representation, to convert the mob into citizens, to transform "savage" into "man." What it is all too easy to lose sight of, given the cultural power of the image of the anarchic crowd, of the formless mass, is the significance of the recurrence of the discourse on representation and pedagogy. Its very repetitiveness speaks to the diffi-culty of the task: clearly, it was not so easy to gain acceptance for the notion that representation, being represented, was the normative mode of one's relation to political life. Stressed continually is the recalcitrance of working-class subjects to being represented. That re-calcitrance is seen time and again as a preference for unruly and immoral assembly, or as an inability to submit to "deferred gratifica-tion" in place of a headlong and unrestrained demand for immediate satisfaction. This assumption disguises the possibility that "recalci-trance" is not predicated on a lack of consciousness or forethought but on different assumptions embedded in social forms that are incom-mensurable with the divisions of civil society that subtend the bour-geois state. E. P. Thompson has grasped such incommensurable formations for an earlier period in elaborating the "moral economy" of the poor.[30] We would want to stress, in keeping with the kind of argu-ment made by Stallybrass and White when they explore the gradual containment of popular spaces in the nineteenth century, that the emergence of representative institutions does entail the active destruction of other social formations which become recalcitrant, even where the resistance appears not to be fully articulate, by virtue of the state's systemic antagonism to their political and cultural impli-cations and to their survival. But the recalcitrance is not always sim-ply that; at significant moments, whose number may only appear limited as an effect of what at this juncture it seems possible to retrieve, the British radical tradition produced a sustained and articu-late resistance to the imposition of representative government and its educational institutions. In the following chapters, we will attempt to elaborate the nature of that resistance and the reasons for its gradual occlusion. We have chosen to do so in relation to the great moments of liberal historiography, the Reform Bills of 1832 and 1867, in order to highlight the tensions between the culture of representation and the gradually diminishing opposition to it. We have chosen to do so also in order to bring out the degree to which reform itself was consciously predicated by liberal thinkers upon a considerable work of disciplining and pedagogy, such that the emergence of the citizen may seem insep-arable from the efficacy of another kind of reform and another mode of pedagogy, that of the reformatory.

CHAPTER 2

Cultures of Representation

AN ENGLISH JACOBIN

The Jacobin forces of the French Revolution, who took both name and inspiration from their readings of Rousseau, had their counterparts among the English radicals of the 1790s. In the wide spectrum of English radical positions, ranging from the rights-oriented positions of John Thelwall, Richard Price or Mary Wollstonecraft to the political anarchism of William Godwin, a handful of thinkers and writers advocated the abolition of private property as the only real foundation for political and economic equity.[1] Among these, the teacher, bookseller and journalist Thomas Spence is in retrospect the most prominent and forceful in his attacks not only on monarchical government but on the doctrines of political rights made famous by Thomas Paine. Spence's work indicates the possibilities of a popular revolutionary discourse in Britain far more radical than the ideology of representation that was emerging coevally among middle-class thinkers as the rights-based ideas of Paine began slowly to enter into "compromise formations" with more conservative positions. That such a compromise became possible, and could eventually flourish in the work of Samuel Taylor Coleridge and others, is in large part due to the derivation of the doctrine of rights and of its account of the origins of civil society from the rights of property that Spence radically opposed. Accordingly, before we turn to the shaping of that ideology in the work of by now canonical figures, it is salutary to be reminded of a quite widely disseminated radical discourse which, however occluded by government suppression and the greater resources of middle-class writers, continues to have a place in the vital political debates of the 1830s.[2]

Spence's positions were laid out in works like *Pigs' Meat, or Lessons for the Swinish Multitude*, a penny weekly paper, which included both his own writings and quotations from his own voluminous reading that retrieved passages from writers as various as Milton, Swift, Rousseau or Goldsmith for radical arguments; and the pamphlet *The Meridian Sun of Liberty; or the Whole Rights of Man Displayed and most Accurately Defined*, a speech on the end of private property and the decentralization of rule into parish-republics. In a briefer pamphlet, *The End of Oppression*, clearly intended for popular consumption, and probably for reading aloud, Spence expresses in simple terms an argument against private property, a plan for revolutionary action and an outline for post-revolutionary society based on parochial government. In the first place, through a dialogue between an Old and a Young Man, Spence's radicalization of Paine is proclaimed:

> *Young Man.* I hear there is another Rights of Man by *Spence*, that
>   goes far beyond *Paine's.*
> *Old M.* Yet it goes no further than it ought.
> *Y.M.* I understand it suffers *no* private Property in Land, but gives
>   it all to the Parishes.
> *O.M.* In so doing it does right, the earth was not made for Individuals.[3]

Whereas, in Paine's *The Rights of Man*, it is presumed that the emergence of distinct rights of private judgment and opinion depends on the pooling of social force in government in order that private property might be protected, Spence castigates this political vision as tending only to "a barren Revolution of mere unproductive Rights, such as many contend for" (p. 9). Instead he offers a plan for a revolution whose first act would be the repossession of private lands in the name of the population of each parish:

> If [the revolutionary committee] published a Manifesto or Proclamation, directing the People in every Parish to take, on receipt thereof, immediate possession of the whole Landed Property within their district, appointing a Committee to take charge of the same, in the name and for the use of the Inhabitants ... the grand resource of the Aristocracy, the Rents, would be cut off, which would soon reduce them to Reason, and they would become as harmless as other men.   (pp. 8–9)

Spence's irony concerning the difference here between an abstract and a "practical" reason is part of the subversiveness and counterhegemonic force of his writing. Equally important, especially for our subsequent argument, is his unswerving reliance on the capacity of the people to manage their affairs: to the Young Man's apprehensions as to the potential for "mismanagement" by the people, the Old Man replies that "it does not become Democrats to doubt concerning it. For if Men cannot manage the Revenues and affairs of a Parish, what must they do with a State?" (p. 7). This question as to the capacity of the people, of the working classes, to participate in, let alone govern, the state is the fundamental legacy of the fear and suppression of revolutionary tendencies in Britain during the French Revolutionary wars. As we shall see, the question reverberates throughout the century and shapes the arguments for and institutional forms of culture and education in both middle-class and working-class writing on the subject. What originate through the same political events as quite separate lines of discourse will maintain their distinctness and effective incommensurability until their gradual convergence in the 1860s. In what follows, we seek to establish the genealogy of these separate discourses and the history of their convergence, not least because they speak to the constitution of hegemony and the occluded survival of marginalized concepts.

THE EXEMPLARY PARSON

In this section we begin to examine the emergence of a discourse on culture, politics and education among nineteenth-century bourgeois thinkers which was to become forcefully hegemonic within less than a generation. We will focus on both its institutional forms and on the more intimate "structures of feeling" which it presumes and prescribes. Given their still current canonical status, we will examine the issue of representation, in the multiple senses outlined in the previous chapter, through the work of the founding Romantic writers, Coleridge and Wordsworth.

Samuel Taylor Coleridge's seminal role in the diffusion in Britain of a discourse on culture that had largely German antecedents will scarcely be contested. Though other British thinkers of a younger generation, notably Thomas De Quincey, Thomas Carlyle and John Stuart Mill, also turned to the German tradition independently of Coleridge and often for different purposes, he remained a crucial influence on the reception and dissemination of the concepts of *Kultur* and *Bildung*. Raymond Williams, in *Culture and Society*, puts it as follows:

> It is from Coleridge, and later from Ruskin, that the construction of "Culture" in terms of the arts may be seen to originate. Yet this is only a partial conclusion, for the arts, essentially, are only a symbol for the kind of "substantial knowledge" which Coleridge sought to describe. The same criterion is at least as necessary in other aspects of our whole activity.[4]

The phrasing, so characteristic of Williams, betrays Coleridge's influence on him as on others: it is impossible to tell whether the invocation of "our whole activity" is a paraphrase of Coleridge or Williams's own judgment. The claim made for Coleridge, again in ways typical of *Culture and Society*, at once draws attention to the large significance of his formulations yet obscures their full import. For Williams, as so often, grasps the function of cultivation for Coleridge in the dimension wherein it is opposed to the alienation and specialization characteristic of industrial society but thoroughly effaces its equally powerful conjunction with the work of the state. But what is critical in Coleridge's thinking is precisely the deep linkage he everywhere asserts between the aesthetic formation of the subject, or cultivation, and the education of citizens for the state.

We will highlight those significant moments of suppression in Williams below. But first we should clarify that it is not our intent to demonstrate Coleridge's pervasive and effective influence on the specific institutions of education that emerged in Britain in the course of the nineteenth century, any more than we would want to reiterate the history of his indisputable influence on the emergent discipline of literary criticism. Although we will be indicating subsequently that at a later moment Coleridgean formulations with regard to cultivation were fully diffused even in working-class periodical literature, they remain "regulative" rather than "constitutive" concepts. To this extent, we would agree with Ian Hunter's *Culture and Government* in dismissing any idea that there was a programmatic application of ideas emanating from the discourse on culture in the forging of pedagogical institutions. As we have suggested in the Introduction, however, we would contend that the discourse on culture, precisely insofar as it intersects with a simultaneously emergent theory of the state, does establish the discursive parameters within which, to borrow from Benedict Anderson's important formulation, the citizen can be imagined.

Accordingly, we would like to establish more closely the kind of intersection of an aesthetic with a political discourse out of which the terms emerge that regulate what kind of subject citizenship came to presume. This will involve us exploring further, and in the specific context of the formation of British Romanticism, the concept of representation as it is articulated at every level: aesthetic or poetic, social, and political. We will do so both through Coleridge's *On the Constitution of the Church and State* and through Wordsworth's poetic theory and practice, where a more intimate phenomenology of what it means to be representatively "man" is elaborated. In relation to the revisions that one of Wordsworth's *Lyrical Ballads* undergoes between its initial publication in 1798, when the poet was still considered a "radical," and 1815, by which time Wordsworth had famously undergone his transformation into a Tory, we will instantiate a crucial shift in the meaning and purview of the concept of representation. In relation to our sense of the ways in which a modern understanding of representation emerges at this moment, we will finally explore the instability of the concept in radical circles at the time of the first Reform Bill: their debates can only be grasped in their still radically critical dimension if we comprehend their distance from assumptions which, formed within discourses on aesthetics and politics, have come to appear normative parameters for subsequent thought.

The chapter of *Culture and Society* immediately preceding Williams's discussion of Mill on Bentham and Coleridge is entitled "The Romantic Artist." A chapter that might well have devoted some consideration to Coleridge's important investigations of the processes and *techné* of poetic creativity, not to mention Coleridge's late and systematic deployment of poetic concepts in his political writings, is remarkably sparse in extended reference to that writer. But the formulations that Williams does make here on the nature of Romantic conceptions of the artist in relation to society are instructive, not least because of their affinity with a long tradition of understanding poetry as aesthetic social critique, when we seek to understand precisely what Williams silences in Coleridge's writings. "The Romantic Artist" opens with what stands as an important correction of the misperception of the Romantic artist as removed from social and political concerns:

> Than the poets from Blake and Wordsworth to Shelley and Keats
> there have been few generations of creative writers more deeply
> interested and more involved in study and criticism of the society

of their day. Yet a fact so evident, and so easily capable of confirmation, accords uneasily in our own time with that popular and general conception of the "romantic artist" which, paradoxically, has been primarily derived from study of these same poets. . . . What were seen at the end of the nineteenth century as disparate interests, between which a man must choose and in the act of choice declare himself poet or sociologist, were, normally, at the beginning of the century, seen as interlocking interests: a conclusion about personal feeling became a conclusion about society, and an observation of natural beauty carried a necessary moral reference to the whole and unified life of man.[5]

The assertion Williams makes here seems now as incontestable as he claims. Equally important, if now commonplace, was the emphasis he places on the paradox which poses the universal and totalizing claims that Romantic poetry makes about humanity against both the emergent autonomy (or specialization) of the artistic sphere and the commodification of art—developments which are, after all, recto and verso of the same processes. What interests us here is how Williams's elaboration of these issues ultimately obscures the manner in which the political and the aesthetic are imbricated by focusing on the "culture/society" opposition.

Later in the chapter, bridging Wordsworth's and Shelley's critical writings on the nature of poetry and the poet, Williams remarks that:

The emphasis on a general common humanity was evidently necessary in a period in which a new kind of society was coming to think of man as merely a specialized instrument of production. The emphasis on love and relationship was necessary not only within the immediate suffering but against the aggressive individualism and the primarily economic relationships which the new society embodied. Emphasis on the creative imagination, similarly, may be seen as an alternative construction of human motive and energy, in contrast with the assumptions of the prevailing political economy.[6]

Our question will be: what makes the necessity of such compensatory formations *(self)-evident*? The question arises not simply from a general theoretical scruple about the ideological force of the evident (though that is no unimportant scruple), but also from our perception of the irrelevance of such formulations in radical writings as late as the 1820s and 1830s which we will shortly be examining. But

Williams continues in a manner which raises a further and connected set of questions. Noting Shelley's tendency to specialize the critical energy that opposes industrialism "to the act of poetry, or of art in general," he continues:

> The positive consequence of the idea of art as a superior reality was that it offered an immediate basis for an important criticism of industrialism. The negative consequence was that it tended, as both the situation and the opposition hardened, to isolate art, to specialize the imaginative faculty to this one kind of activity, and thus to weaken the dynamic function which Shelley proposed for it.[7]

With all due respect to and sympathy for the preference on which this criticism is based, that is, Williams's emphasis on "the idea of culture as a whole way of life" as opposed to "the idea of culture as art,"[8] we are drawn to question the adequacy of the model whereby culture offers "an alternative construction" to industrial society and political economy. Adequate at one level, the oppositional structure Williams outlines nonetheless reduces the significance of the profound imbrication of politics and culture for Romantic poets, precisely by obscuring the *differential* emergence of the relation between culture and society. Culture, as a distinct domain, works and is defined by its differentiation from other spheres, in a relation, that is, which is always dynamic and not statically in opposition. Its significance, as the domain in which freedom and harmonious wholeness are to be realized, derives from its relation to those spheres in which "man" is divided. Its transcendence of specialization and division in order to provide a space of reconciliation nonetheless depends itself on a differentiating specialization of function. This differential relation, which expresses a specialization that is to overcome the effects of specialization, establishes culture's analogical and finally instrumental relation to the state insofar as each emerge from division as sites in which division is supposed to be transcended. As we have suggested earlier, without such a recognition it is impossible to resolve the apparent contradiction by which cultural artifacts as "oppositional" as Shelley's poetry, or even Wordsworth's, come to integrate so unproblematically into the canons of state pedagogy. Once, however, we grasp that the figure of man within which that overcoming of division is represented is indissociable from the figure of the citizen of the state, the possibility of integrating an oppositional culture with a state project will no longer seem so paradoxical. At the same time, it is important to recall once more that the terms of representation that now seem normative to us were highly contested throughout the "Romantic" period, both culturally and politically. Culture and the modern state are coeval and, against considerable resistance, bring each other's terms into being: we might say that Shelley's opposition to certain aspects of his society helps to bring into being the state by which he can be received.[9] Romantic "humanity" was by no means self-evident but struggled to displace a prior conception of Man which was considerably less troubled by division, for division itself only becomes problematic where equality or equivalence are asserted as political values.

Of all the British Romantic writers, it is Coleridge who most systematically elaborates a new relation between the work of culture and the equally new pedagogical labors of the state. What is everywhere implicit in the figure of man or of humanity that grounds the universality of Romantic claims is in Coleridge made explicit: the domain in which the full humanity of the modern individual can be realized is that of citizenship, but only insofar as citizenship is shaped by way of cultivation. In this respect, the emerging conceptions of man and of cultivation differ markedly from those which dominated the previous century. There, where appeal is made to a general notion of "man," his position relative to the cosmos, that "isthmus of a middle state" between the animal and the divine, underwrites analogically a polity which is predicated on the naturalness of division itself.[10] The radical force of Romantic claims, as is well known, is to universalize the claims of humanity from moral to political ones. The stabilizing and often conservative recourse of Romanticism is to contain those terms within the political register, offering what Marx termed *political* rather than human emancipation. Coleridge, who is typical of this tendency in the sense of bringing its many elements into the clearest conjunction, effectively succeeds in the unthinkable task of synthesizing Rousseau's radical identification of "Man" and "Citizen" with Burke's insistence on the necessity of "men of light and leading" to maintain the stability of society. He does so by bringing to bear a "Germanic" notion of culture that predicates both citizenship and humanity on the diffusion of "light" through pedagogical institutions which it is the state's duty to organize and maintain. In *On the Constitution of Church and State*, he entitles these institutions "the National Church." This National Church stands precisely between the forces of Permanence, that is, the landed interests of society, and the forces of Progression, by which he understands the mercantile and manufacturing interests whose tendency is constantly to destabilize society by their volatility. As such, the National Church is an institution of civil society which functions as what Gramsci would have seen as an instrument of the *ethical* state. Our point is, accordingly, that culture designates not a discursive formation in opposition to society but rather a set of institutions within society at the point of its intersection with the state. The oppositional relation between culture and society can only be maintained ideally; in practice, the very formulation of the space of culture demands, as we have already seen, its actualization in pedagogical institutions whose function is to transform the individual of civil society into the subject of the state. That naturalization of the often violent production of citizens overlaps with the universal historical narrative of the evolution of humanity from animal or savage to civilized being.

Williams's desire to maintain the opposition of culture and society requires that he omit from his lengthy citations from Coleridge the final sentence of the following passage:

> But civilization is itself but a mixed good, if not far more a corrupting influence, the hectic of disease, not the bloom of health, and a nation so distinguished more fitly to be called a varnished than a polished people; where this civilization is not grounded in *cultivation*, in the harmonious development of those qualities and faculties that characterize our *humanity*. We must be men in order to be citizens.[11]

The burden of Coleridge's argument here is not simply to pose cultivation or the cultivated individual as domains of "harmonious development" against the depredations of society, but rather to provide for a complementary principle through which culture will develop in individuals the capacity to be citizens for the state. The problem for us is to comprehend how that formation of the subject as citizen is to take place, a problem that must be posed at two levels: first, at that of its institutional actualization, that is, how is the cultivation of individuals into citizens to be practically achieved; second, what is the precise form of this new subject, who nowhere exists but is everywhere projected, and how is this new subject supposed to embody the principles that will make it work for the state?

Coleridge elaborates the first question through the institution of the National Church which, it bears reiterating, is modeled on but is not identical with the established Church itself. The model, which really gives the form of the institutions which will supplement and then displace the functions of the Church proper, is the hierarchy of the

Anglican Church from the Archbishop down through the humblest curates. This hierarchy is designed to ensure pastoral care even in the smallest and most dispersed communities of the realm; it becomes the model for the dissemination of learning generally through the institution of a specialized class (or estate) of the "clerisy":

> A certain smaller number were to remain at the fountain heads of the humanities, in cultivating and enlarging the knowledge already possessed, and in watching over the interests of physical and moral science; being, likewise, the instructors of such as constituted, or were to constitute, the remaining more numerous classes of the order. This latter and far more numerous body were to be distributed throughout the country so as not to leave even the smallest integral part or division without a resident guide, guardian or instructor; the objects and final intention of the whole order being these—to preserve the stores, to guard the treasures of past civilization, and thus to bind the past with the present; to perfect and add to the same, and thus connect the present with the future; but especially to diffuse through the whole community, and to every native entitled to its laws and rights, that quantity and quality of knowledge which was indispensable both for the understanding of those rights, and for the performance of the duties correspondent. (*CCS*, pp. 43–4)

The structures of the Church provide the model for the institution of national education, and, indeed, the elementary foundations of what will, in its *ad hoc* way, become a system of national education. But they can only do so at the very moment when it becomes possible, even necessary, to envisage the displacement of the feudal Church, with its function of forming and disciplining *subjects* for the monarch, by the institutions of culture, whose very terms are derived from, but in fact extend those of the Church to the formation of *citizens*. For where the function of the Church had been to rationalize the division of society into markedly unequal estates, that of culture is to universalize political identity in the form of citizenship and, as we have argued, produce a formal equality that seeks to overcome the actual material inequalities of civil society. Even as Coleridge acknowledges the "precedency" of theology, he writes out the terms of its displacement by an education whose forms are really given by aesthetic culture:

> It [theology] had precedency, because, under the name theology, were comprised all the main aids, instruments, and materials of

NATIONAL EDUCATION, the *nisus formativus* of the body politic, the shaping and informing spirit, which *educing, i.e.,* eliciting, the latent *man* in all the natives of the soil, trains them up to citizens of the country, free subjects of the realm. (*CCS*, pp. 47-8; emphases in the original)

The extended series of struggles and accords between a secularizing state and the private educational establishments of various religious sects that characterize the history of nineteenth-century education are at least in part explicable in terms of what we might call this parasitic displacement of theology by culture.[12] And it is not that Coleridge programmatically influences these struggles—his work, as Williams points out, could be appropriated equally by liberals or conservatives—but that he grasps and articulates the very process through which the new citizen-subjects must come into being, be "educed," and the corresponding institutional forms that their education requires. And we would emphasize again that it is not the specific materials of pedagogy that are at stake here, not, for example, the actually rather late replacement of biblical scripture with literary texts, but the way in which the citizen-subject is imagined in terms most fully defined within the discourse of aesthetic culture.

Coleridge does not elaborate the intimate formation of the subject in a way which would account for its suturing with the state. In order to pursue that issue further, we will turn in the next section to the writings of William Wordsworth, from whom Coleridge in any case derived his closest understanding of aesthetic processes. What Coleridge does provide, however, is a figure that condenses the institutional apparatus of an incipient state education with the mode of its interpellative practices. This figure is that of the parson, a term which Coleridge glosses as

Persona κατ'ἐξοχήν; persona *exemplaris;* the representative and exemplar of the *personal* character of the community or parish; of their duties and rights, of their hopes, privileges and requisite qualifications, as moral *persons,* and not merely living things. (*CCS*, p. 53n; emphases in the original)

Coleridge is at pains to emphasize here the quality of the *person* that the parson represents or exemplifies for the people. He has already defined the *person* in Chapter 1 as one who, unlike a mere thing or instrument, "must always be included in the end" (*CCS*, p. 15). The definition asserts the quality of autonomy as that which differentiates

the man and the citizen from the mere "native of the soil." It also suggests, since the parson exemplifies personhood, that it is a quality that
he possesses and which is, in Coleridge's phrase, merely "latent" in
other individuals, awaiting its eliciting by the exemplary force of the
parson and, by extension, the schoolmaster whose model he is. The
parson is the exemplary representative man by virtue of his cultivation
and stands for a more proximate actualization of harmonious humanity than others have attained. It is, therefore, in relation to and by way
of his exemplary standing, rather than through any particular matter
that he teaches, that the parson/teacher interpellates individuals into
"citizens of the country, free subjects of the realm."[13]

What Coleridge effects here is a shift from a conception of representation as based on communities of interests to one founded in an ethical narrative. Without this shift, the apparatuses of the ethical state
could never emerge. In this sense it is of primary importance that the
exemplary person comes *to* rather than *from* the community for which
he is to be representative. We could formulate this as a minimal but
absolutely critical semantic revision of an early and famous formulation of Wordsworth's: if the poet of 1802 is "a man speaking to men,"
Coleridge's parson is "Man speaking to men." As we shall see, however, by 1815 at least, Wordsworth's own poetry had enacted just such
a shift and in doing so provided a canonical instance of the emergence
of a discourse on representation which inescapably founds our understanding of both subjectivity and subjectification. And it is doubtless
no accident that for Wordsworth the poet as representative man is virtually indistinguishable from the poet as exemplary pedagogue.

FREEDOM OF ASSOCIATION

In his "Preface" to the *Lyrical Ballads* (1800), William Wordsworth
provides us with a description of the creative process. The passage is as
justly celebrated as it has been influential on subsequent understanding of the phenomenology of creativity, but it is usually too selectively
recalled for its full import to be grasped:

> From such verses [contemporary, trivial poetry] the Poems in these
> volumes will be found distinguished at least by one mark of differ-
> ence, that each of them has a worthy *purpose*. Not that I mean to
> say, that I always began to write with a distinct purpose formally
> conceived; but I believe that my habits of meditation have so
> formed my feelings, as that my descriptions of such objects as

strongly excite those feelings, will be found to carry along with them a *purpose*. If in this opinion I am mistaken I can have little right to the name of a Poet. For all good poetry is the spontaneous overflow of powerful feelings; but though this be true, Poems to which any value can be attached, were never produced on any variety of subjects but by a man who being possessed of more than usual organic sensibility had also thought long and deeply. For our continued influxes of feeling are modified and directed by our thoughts, which are indeed the representatives of all our past feelings; and as by contemplating the relation of these general representatives to each other, we discover what is really important to men, so by the repetition and continuance of this act feelings connected with important subjects will be nourished, till at length, if we be originally possessed of much organic sensibility, such habits of mind will be produced that by obeying blindly and mechanically the impulses of those habits we shall describe objects and utter sentiments of such a nature and in such a connection with each other, that the understanding of the being to whom we address ourselves, if he be in a healthful state of association, must necessarily be in some degree enlightened, his taste exalted, and his affections ameliorated.[14]

The passage is at once an expansion into greater psychological detail and a contraction into the intimate sphere of the individual subject's interiority of that narrative of representation which informs both Schiller's letters On the *Aesthetic Education of Man* and Coleridge's *Church and State*. For poetic creation is described as the processing of a primary material, supplied by the feelings, which only by dint of repeated "re-presentation" attains to the general status of a representative moment of truth. Reflection occurs in the course of this meditative process on the *form* of any given experience insofar as each past experience becomes a "general representative" in thought. The formalization involved here is the guarantee that the poems so produced will have a "worthy purpose," precisely because the repetition demanded by formalization permits the discovery of "what is really important to men." Poetry is devoted to the essential forms which men have in common rather than to the accidents which divide them. It is, moreover, *intrinsically* ethical, since the particularity of any private experience is elevated within it to general representative status.

The intrinsically ethical nature of poetry is further replicated in its ethical function with regard to the reader. For poetry is not only the product of a being ethically formed by dint of meditative repetition, but is also operative in the formation or development of an ethically cultivated disposition in its reader, who is to be "in some degree enlightened, his taste exalted, and his affections ameliorated." Wordsworth's description of the phenomenology of creation is deliberately general enough not only to embrace creative processes *per se*, but to constitute an account of human ethical development as intimately bound to acts of generalizing rememoration. Accordingly, if poetic creation is a refinement of a process common to human reflection in general, so in turn reading is "a repetition in [the reader's] mind" of the act of poetic creation itself.[15] The poem supplants structurally other modes of primary feeling, becoming for the reader the object of reflection and—as the "Preface" frequently insists—of comparative judgment which will release its moral purpose only through a series of readings as repetitive as those habits of reflection which, for the poet, precede composition. Only the higher degree of formal organization of the poem endows that reflection with a direction, governing the *process* of enlightenment rather than its product, and, at the most basic somatic levels, establishes a dialectic between the pleasures of repetition and the labor to produce shocks of "mild surprise" which repetition represents.[16]

Numerous critics have noted the necessity of repeated readings to be an intrinsic demand of the *Lyrical Ballads*. This is not to say that as "classics" they reward study and frequent savoring, but, rather, to make a claim for a process of repetition being fundamental to their structure and to the ironic pedagogy which is their "purpose." The vast majority of the ballads are narratives of misrecognition which operate on two levels, that of the poet-narrator who is caught time and again in errors of judgment or of expectation and that of the reader for whom ironic signals are carefully implanted as potential guides to the process of misrecognition which we share with the poet. Just as the course of the narrative demands a moment of reflection upon the genesis of prejudice, elevating momentarily the particular anecdote into a "general representative" of judgment, so in turn the reader is brought to reflect on the narrative and its purpose in such a way as to oblige a rethinking and a re-reading for error. At this second level, it is actually impossible to "understand" the poem without—at the least—a second reading.[17]

Constantly, Wordsworth's reflections on creativity—which are virtually consubstantial with his poetry as a whole—recur to acts of repetition which reconstitute and "ameliorate" perception. Such reflection has, of course, become so standard for literary pedagogy in the intervening period as to seem virtually self-evident. What we wish to do here, however, is to explore the *political* implications of what we describe as the ironic pedagogy which Wordsworth's poetry inaugurates. One of the well-known *Lyrical Ballads*, "Animal Tranquillity and Decay," will serve to exemplify both the processes involved in an ironic pedagogy through poetry and the by no means self-evident process of revision through which it became "habitual" to Wordsworth. With peculiar appositeness to the discussion of re-vision, the poem is generally better known in the revised version published in 1815. A comparison of this with that of 1798 is a vivid indication of the intervening transformation in both the "place" and the mode of articulation of the politics of poetry.

ANIMAL TRANQUILLITY AND DECAY
    The little hedgerow birds,
That peck along the road, regard him not.
He travels on, and in his face, his step,
His gait, is one expression: every limb,
His look and bending figure, all bespeak
A man who does not move with pain, but moves
With thought—He is insensibly subdued
To settled quiet: he is one by whom
Long patience now doth seem a thing of which
He hath no need, He is by nature led
To peace so perfect that the young behold
With envy, what the Old Man hardly feels.   (1815)

OLD MAN TRAVELLING;
ANIMAL TRANQUILLITY AND DECAY,
A SKETCH
    The little hedge-row birds,
That peck along the road, regard him not.
He travels on, and in his face, his step,
His gait, is one expression; every limb,
His look and bending figure, all bespeak
A man who does not move with pain, but moves
With thought—He is insensibly subdued
To settled quiet: he is one by whom
All effort seems forgotten, one to whom
Long patience has such mild composure given,
That patience now doth seem a thing, of which

He hath no need. He is by nature led
To peace so perfect, that the young behold
With envy, what the old man hardly feels.
—I asked him whither he was bound, and what
The object of his journey; he replied
"Sir! I am going many miles to take
"A last leave of my son, a mariner,
"Who from a sea-fight has been brought to Falmouth,
"And there is dying in an hospital."   (1798)[18]

Examination of the revised version shows minimal revision if we dis-count the most glaring, that is, the omission of the concluding six lines of the 1798 version. The revisions which do occur clearly tend in the direction of generalization: the capitalization of certain substantives which allegorize the purely *social* relations of 1798, and most signifi-cantly, the cuts in the title. The version of 1815's title introduces the poem as a moral meditation upon the peacefulness of old age whereas that of 1798 deliberately poises that meditative topos against the pur-posiveness of an old man's traveling, a word which mobilizes, in this version, notions of ends and, etymologically, of labor or "travail." The poem is also self-confessedly a *sketch*, at once provisional and immedi-ate, open and unfinished, experiential and experimental. If it has been declared a sketch that fails to produce a masterpiece and which is revised to conform to another poetic than that to which, momentarily, it opened up, examination of the grounds for what seems, now, so self-evident an aesthetic judgment will illustrate how bound up with polit-ical representation our aesthetic norms of verisimilitude are.

What the reader objects to in "Old Man Travelling" is of course the interruption by the old man, which also clearly offended the aesthetic, or political, sensibility of Wordsworth around 1815. A rude shock frac-tures the moral judgments of "the young" at this point, as an object for meditation of a clearly compensatory kind transforms into a subject who has both his own objects and determination and the capacity to represent himself. The Old Man suddenly ceases to be a personifica-tion and becomes a *person*. It is, in our earlier terms, a narrative of the spatiality of *self*-representation: as the old man enters within range of immediate interpellation, his speech *in his own voice* makes ludicrous any act of representation of the old man by another. Representation in this mode is displaced, not by any reflection on errors of judgment in general, but by the particular resistance of another human subject to assimilation within a meliorative narrative. The travail of the old man is the end of his travel and what both entail is not any consolation of nature for decay, but, rather, a radical disordering of what might have been the "natural" end of an old man by social forces which sacrifice the young for what are, to all intents and purposes, the ends of a rather different bunch of old men. At an "aesthetic" level, what is offensive is the rendering of the dialogue in a manner so crude that the regular meter of the foregoing lines completely disintegrates. The Preface's discussion of the soothing effects of the repetitions makes quite clear that this has to produce an experience of displeasure since in the absence of regular meter one is defenseless against the irruption of shock. One might want to add that the disintegration of the meter is simultaneous with the disintegration of the singularity of poetic voice: one is faced here with a really quite radical heterogeneity which refuses reintegration even at the general level of style.[19]

By contrast, the discrepancy between the thematic title of "Animal Tranquillity and Decay" and its object is only mildly and ironically insinuated in the later version. Only by gradual sedimentation of understanding over time does one grasp the incoherencies: the word "regard"—as an activity in which birds might, but don't, engage—signals either a gross anthropomorphism or, in its complex semantics, more deftly draws attention, in the midst of such anthropomorphisms, to the fundamental incommensurability of a nature indifferent to pain and a human nature whose language is unable to separate the perceptive act of looking from the complex emotions of compassion and respect; the intrusion of the word "seems" sheds a frisson of doubt over the young man's conclusions, as does the designation of "patience" as "a thing"; a seeming contradiction appears between the states of "insensibility" and "thought." Embracing all this is the larger reflection, which is central to Wordsworth's meditations on the function of poetry throughout his career, on the incompatibility of a rememorative act like writing with any simply consolatory philosophy of nature: to reader and writer alike, the transcendence of particularity intrinsic to their activities must oppose any mode of natural consolation since it has effectively nothing to say to a humanity that such activities, in a quite strong sense, define.

What makes for the strength of that definition is the extension of poetic notions of verisimilitude into the domain of human subjectivity in general. Alternatively, one might equally well say that what governs poetic verisimilitude is the extension into the cultural domain, or the sublimation in that domain, of fundamentally political claims to the representation of man in general. According to the supplementary function of culture which we have been exploring, both arguments would be correct. There is probably quite a literal sense in which poetry for Wordsworth, as indeed for many other Romantics, including Coleridge, actually supplanted politics in the years of "disillusion" with the Terror and with the war against France. Certainly the *Lyrical Ballads* were written under the pressure of coming to terms with these events. But not only do we not have space to explore these questions fully here, we wish in any case to make the stronger claim that, aside from any accidents of biographical experience, it is the theoretical claims of both culture and politics to represent the figure of Universal Man which determines a priori the mode of verisimilitude within or through which subjects must be interpellated in order to be citizens.

Wordsworth is clear and explicit about the relationship between political and poetic discourse, a relationship at once analogical and historical.[20] What underlies both the analogy and the historical contiguities is a two-fold claim expressed, for poetry, already in the brief "Advertisement" to the 1798 edition of the ballads. Poetry is the representation of humanity in general and as such is simultaneously antagonistic to inherited prejudice, "that most dreadful enemy to our pleasures, our own pre-established codes of decision" (*LB*, p. 3). Not unlike political revolutions, it is the function of poetry to shatter prejudicial "habits of association" in order to produce that "healthful state of association" in which, as we have seen, poetry can have its ameliorating effects. Where the analogical relation breaks down at one level is of course in the fact, as Williams notes, that poetry is to achieve its ends in dissociation from the social world against which it is increasingly defined. Wordsworth's withdrawal to a more "natural" environment is famous, but it is wrongly interpreted as simply a reactionary Romantic resistance to the encroachments of urban and industrial civilization. It is, rather, a species of detour through which to return to civilization with cultivating effect, and the withdrawal cannot be understood without reference to the urban civilization against which it is differentially defined. As we shall see, withdrawal has a quite strictly understood recreationary function for the subject, whether mediated through actual geographical movement or through the movements of poetry.

It is, in fact, only the temporality inscribed in poetry as understood through Wordsworth that gives geographical withdrawal its ethical recreationary effect. For if at first the rationale for Wordsworth's choice of rural life for his settings seems founded in a rather naive assertion of an homology between simple and permanent forms of nature and simple and permanent modes of language, it is rapidly made clear that poetry subjects the primitive or "elementary" to a process of refinement, "purified indeed ... from all lasting rational causes of dislike or disgust" (*PW*, p. 735).

Poetry is not the compensatory reproduction of a natural social life, but in a quite strict sense the repetition of a (natural) language "arising out of repeated experience and regular feelings." Rural life is by no means glorified in itself or as it is, solely on account of the effects of its re-presentation in poetry. For what poetry inculcates by its very processes is an ethical habit of generalization of particular experiences within subjects who are, by virtue of their "freedom of association," presumed capable of autonomous judgment in contradistinction to those whose "sameness and narrow circle of ... intercourse" is represented. Two equally important assumptions are at work here: firstly, that the subject to be interpellated by the poetry be, at least potentially, autonomous; and secondly, that it is in the first place within such a subject, and not upon society as a whole, that poetry is to have its effects.

If the subject of poetry is thus distinguished from the "elementary" humanity which, in the fullest sense, it comes to represent, it is at one and the same time to be distinguished from another humanity which, in a degenerate rather than natural or originary fashion, is equally "primitive." This humanity is that of the cities and is distinguished from the regularity of the rural by a paradoxical simultaneity of multiplicity and homogeneity: multiplicity by virtue of the "encreasing accumulation of men in cities," homogeneity by virtue of "the uniformity of their occupations" (*PW*, p. 735). What Wordsworth, in an as yet incompletely developed form, is grasping here is the fundamental contradiction of individualism: unleashed from the narrow circle of traditional social bonds, the individual emerges only to enter into the uniformity of interchangeable units of abstract labor. The autonomy gained in the process is purely formal, since only within the most limited of parameters can that freedom be expressed in the form of realized difference. This social effect of industrial capital upon individuals reduces them, in Wordsworth's terms, to the condition of a "savage torpor": the homogeneity of the individuals corresponds, within a schema which is once again that of the ideal temporality of development, to the indifference of the not-yet-individuated savage. To this correspond, in turn, modes of representation disseminated by the press which satisfy "a craving for extraordinary incident." Sensational journalism produces representations of events which are purely interchangeable, their effect measured in terms of quantity of immediate effect. Immediacy of effect (what Benjamin will analyze as *shock*) is intricately related for Wordsworth to an incapacity to develop.

Against immediacy of representation is posed the narrative of representation which informs poetry. If the urban condition of "this degrading thirst after outrageous stimulation" is liable to produce a sentiment of "*op*pression" at the heteronomy of modern life, the "*im*pression of certain inherent and indestructible qualities of the human mind, and likewise of certain powers in the great and permanent objects that act upon it" opposes that oppression. Poetry produces within the subject a transformation of external stimulus into autonomously regulated impression, repeated mediation converting the shock of immediate perception into the internal form of that which is "inherent and indestructible in the human mind." The narrative of representation—the progressive formalization of particular experiences into "general representatives"—establishes within the individual subject a law of ethical verisimilitude by which its cultivated interiority represents, both to and in itself, the essential universality of human nature. The narrative by which poetry transforms the disintegrative effect of the multiplying shocks of modern experience into a principled phenomenology of perception in turn replicates the universal history of man's progression from "savage torpor" to true culture. The reversibility of the analogy between the history of the subject and the history of the race will come to have invaluable legitimating force in arguments for restricting franchise: the uncultivated are never yet ready for the responsibility of ethical judgment taken on by the representative citizen.

Poetry thus enacts the transformation of political into ethical categories, retaining in the process a submerged set of political analogies. The poet, "man speaking to men," is representative man, different only in degree of sensibility, not in essence. Ideally, he enacts the transformation of particular and private experience into general representative reflection, thereby recreating the original identity of human nature through a narrative which repeatedly presents as essential its own movement of formalizing generalization. The process is analogous to that of political representation, wherein the representative, standing in the first instance for the private and particular interests of civil society, ideally transcends those interests in the ethical sphere of the state. By way of this analogy, poetry acquires a double function as an agency of cultivation. First, and this involves gradually its institutional mediation in forms as yet unknown to Wordsworth, it provides a kind of training in ethical development through cultural pedagogy.

Poetry here represents a cultural form whose function is to *produce* internally a mode of subjectivity proper to citizenship. Second, and ideologically more significantly, poetry, and by extension culture in general, comes to supplement the state as the state fails to emerge as a sphere in which human equality is genuinely achieved. Within the sphere of culture, free and uncoerced relations of judgment theoretically exist which *represent*, in the sense of prefiguring, those which are elsewhere absent. But the disinterest of poetry is attained only by virtue of denying *formally* (since the actual content of the work is secondary to its formal disposition within an ethical structure) its relation to the actual social interests or utopian longings which it *supposedly* protects. Confined to the sphere of recreation, by virtue of which confinement it gains its *re*-creationary force for the divided economic subject, it consoles for the absence of that equality whose promise, according to some readers, it keeps alive. But more importantly, and on account of the institutional mediation it will finally attain, this poetry reproduces social hierarchy in the form of the poet as master-teacher whose ironic disposition always reestablishes him as a being of superior ethical development. The lines of progress, as Malthus once noted of Godwin, are directed at a point which can only be reached at infinity.[21] In the meantime, to the earnest appeal of Mathetes, the pupil, as to "What is to be done?" once the poetry has been read and assimilated, the master poet can only reply, since the pupils are not poets, that what poetry teaches is the ethical duty to submit voluntarily to society's labor:

> neither will that portion of his own time, which he must surrender to labours by which his livelihood is to be earned or his social duties performed, be unprofitable to him indirectly, while it is directly useful to others: for that time has been primarily surrendered through an act of obedience to a moral law established by himself, and therefore he moves then also along the orbit of perfect liberty.[22]

Poetry, for Wordsworth, not merely occupies but regulates the space of recreation. It returns the subject re-created to labor and in doing so naturalizes the division of spaces, aesthetic and economic, through which the subject ethically accommodates to the division of labor. That movement of "self-subordination," on the part of those whom Althusser will come to term "subjects who work by themselves," constitutes "the orbit of perfect liberty." Aesthetic culture here is in no simple sense antagonistic to or compensatory for the fatigue and narrowing of workaday existence; it forms the subject who must accommodate to labor. For precisely this reason, it is not so much that the subject must pass by way of poetry (or any other given aesthetic form), but that the qualities Wordsworth understands to reach their highest expression in poetry regulate the value of what occupies the recreationary sphere. Insofar as recreation approaches the condition of poetry, it conduces to the "amelioration" of the human and helps to produce a "healthful state of association."

As we shall see in the following chapter, the regulation of recreation in the wake of Acts controlling hours of labor will become crucial to the discourse on education and franchise. In this, the conjunction emerges between the accommodation of the subject to labor through recreation and the formation of that subject as simultaneously but distinctly—in another sphere—a citizen. To revert to the concept of "alien politics," the subject is at liberty in political and cultural spheres that leave economic disenfranchisement untouched. But in order for that to occur, as we have been arguing, what must come to seem self-evident, a matter of "common sense," is the separation between spheres that permits the separation within the subject of distinct modalities that correspond to distinct spaces for social agency. A worker in one place, a citizen or political subject in another, an aesthetic being in another, the putative wholeness of the individual is always to be realized in an alien place and at another time: "his" labor is fulfilled in the totality of a political economy; "his" partial and interested citizenship is realized in the form of the state to which "he" is subjected; "his" humanity is represented in cultural forms whose very formal principle, repetition, ensures the perpetual deferral of self-possession.

This is why the ironic form of the "mature" Wordsworth's poetry is so instructive. What is enacted in the revision of "Old Man Travelling" into "Animal Tranquillity and Decay" is the displacement of the conflictual *spaces* of radical dialogism, where none allow themselves to be "represented," by the *time* of ethical formation, a never-ending and strictly interminable correction and supplementation of always partial perceptions. The voice of the Old Man, a voice that was the mainstay not only of a Rousseauean version of popular wisdom but of an English radical tradition that was at its height in the 1790s, gives way to an apparently subversive but finally normative notion of unceasing "growth" or "maturation" of "the Young."[23] This overcoming of the conflictual spaces of radicalism by the narrative of representation, precisely because it shapes the pedagogical project of the state, eventually transcends the party political lines of conservative and liberal, Tory or Whig. But it was by no means either a rapid or easily completed achievement. What we will show in the next section is that at the very moment that Romantic artists like Wordsworth and Coleridge were formulating the terms of representation out of aesthetic considerations, an entirely different and distinctly critical set of debates persisted in radical circles virtually until the middle of the nineteenth century. The persistence of these debates marks the difficulty of the process by which certain singular and linked concepts of representation could come to delimit democratic possibilities.

AGAINST REPRESENTATION

Our own researches with regard to the persistence of radical culture in England have been profoundly instructive at a personal as well as an archival or interpretive level. Attempting to locate a counterhegemonic discourse on culture critical of the bourgeois tradition that we have been outlining, we turned to radical and working-class publications of the late 1820s and early 1830s, the historical moment, that is, of the first Reform Bill and of Coleridge's *Church and State*. Expecting to find some critical acknowledgment of and engagement with the concept of culture and education developed in this and other contemporary bourgeois writings, we were at first considerably disappointed to find scarcely a mention of such concepts. Reading further into the material, mostly in penny papers and other ephemeral publications, it rapidly became apparent that this ignoring of what has seemed since *Culture and Society* the dominant tradition was by no means simple ignorance but a systematic refusal on the part of working-class and some petty-bourgeois radical writers to accept the division of education, politics and economics into separate if interinfluential spheres. What is critical here is that the terms by which, from Coleridge to Arnold or Mill, the notion emerges that education must precede franchise and that such education should be disinterested, or ethical/cultural, simply do not have the self-evidence in radical writings that they do in the dominant discourse.

Furthermore, the very concept of representation, which in the dominant discourse is narrativized into a developmental schema running from savages and the working class, who are said to be too self-interested and narrow to represent themselves, to the intellectuals, ethical apices of civilization and representative humans, is remarkably fluid and shifting. There is, for example, none of the self-evidence by which, for Coleridge, representation at the local level of classroom or parish, or for Wordsworth in the minimal example of the "representative" moment of poetic apprehension, folds over into representation at the level of state and parliament. To the contrary, concepts of representation that would seem quite contradictory according to that narrative are held at one and the same time within the same periodicals and about different institutions. Writers able to accept representation at the state level reject it vehemently within working-class institutions like trade unions while other writers who argue against political representation by others may be found supporting a representative structure within those same unions. What is being discussed, immediately before and after the first Bill which promised but did not deliver a massive extension of the franchise, is the very nature and value of representative structures themselves. Within these debates, despite the occasionally "avant gardiste" positions on enlightening the laborers taken by some petty-bourgeois radicals, there is little call for a discourse on culture in which "whole men" become representative archetypes of fulfilled humanity. There is, to the contrary, remarkably little interest in the supposedly destructive effects of the division of labor, but plenty of attention to the fact that lack of political power or even representation was closely bound up with the inability of laborers to put an end to their exploitation. For this reason in turn, education is to be directed not toward cultivation and harmonization of the inner man but toward political knowledge. As John Henry Baden Lorymer put it in *The Republican* of April 1832, echoing Spence's *Pig's Meat*:

> If a Nation be almost unanimous in its demand for REPRESENTA-
> TION, what should prevent those citizens who are desirous of
> being represented, from actually having representatives?
>
> Nothing can prevent them but a most beastly ignorance of their
> RIGHTS, and a most pig-like apathy with regard to the mode of
> acquiring them.

Or, as one "C. H." put it somewhat later in "Plain Reason—Useful Knowledge," in Richard Carlile's *The Gauntlet*, December 15, 1833:

> In a country where every thing relating to the science of Govern-
> ment has grown radically corrupt—where both precept and prac-
> tice are inimical to, or destructive of, true liberty, and where the
> oppression of the administration, is the most grievous burden
> borne by the state, *political knowledge* is necessarily the most
> "useful knowledge."

There is here no claim that what is to be "cultivated" by this education is disinterest: it is an explicitly political education but by no means an education directed at politics for its own sake. Education is rather directed at producing political understanding that will ultimately enable the transformations in the material conditions of the working classes which will free them from exploitation.

It is possible to trace among the more centrist of the radical papers, such as James Morrison's *Pioneer* or George Pilgrim's *Cosmopolite*, the outline of the notions that education must precede the attainment of the franchise or that education is a good in itself in calming the passions of the people, notions that later become the staple of liberal discourse on education and franchise. But the more radical writers argue uncompromisingly against the hegemonic use of education to defer the franchise, whether by the State or by individual reformers. "Senex"—once again an "Old Man"—in one of a series of remarkably uncompromising articles "On Associated Labour" for the *Pioneer*, makes the following comments "On the Pretended Ignorance of the Labouring Classes":

> Under this pretence [lower class ignorance], they rob us, and almost work us to death; and yet there are persons who really mean well to us, crying out, Ah, this is but too true! the majority of the people are not sufficiently instructed to be entrusted with power: we must illuminate their minds before we can venture to advocate their elevation in the scale of society!
>
> Brethren, there is an immensity of benefit in what is called education; but do not suffer yourselves to be tricked and bamboozled out of your rights under the notion that you must have education before you are fit to have justice. Education is a very good thing; but men and children must live as well as learn; besides there is such a thing as education without knowledge, and there is also such a thing as knowledge without education, and of these two things the last is much better than the first.... All useful knowledge consists in the acquirement of ideas concerning our condition in life; and there are few men of common observation who do not get into their minds, whether they can read and write or not, the ideas that are most serviceable to them. The position of a man in society, with its obligations and interests, forces ideas upon him which all the theory of education would not have impressed upon him as long as he was not called upon practically to make use of them.

At stake in this and other such writings, which strikingly prefigure later theorists like Gramsci, is in effect the mediating function of educational institutions, in at least two senses. The first thing criticized here is the assumption that knowledge is valid only when mediated through institutions defined by their distance from the conditions of labor. Such distantiation permits the "representative" claims of educational institutions by asserting their emancipation from interests or class positions while at the same time disenfranchising knowledge that derives from what become the merely "local" conditions of oppression. Senex, to the contrary, radically affirms the value of such knowledge, not because of any essential class basis for it, but because of its relation to specific "obligations and interests" and the practical uses that constitute and further them. Connected to this is the second mediating function of education, which is Senex's most explicit target, its invocation as the necessary but, of course, infinitely extensible, condition for the exercise of the political franchise. The two kinds of mediation are closely related within the general concept of representation, for the differentiated space of the educational institution is a spatial correlative of the temporal deferral demanded as the precondition for participation in representative democracy.

Though much of the discussion of representation in the radical papers of the moment circulates around the Reform Bill and strictly political concepts of representation, there is a constant awareness that what is at issue in both the radical appeals for reform and conservative opposition is the relation of the state to production. Putting an end to exploitation is the rationale for political reform and the processes are not distinct precisely because the formal equality offered by bourgeois notions of representation is never accepted. But the debate on representation and the need for a working-class legislature constantly opens on to the question of representation within other organizations and institutions. Two instances of debate will serve to indicate the range of the discussions and the variety of positions taken in the realm of education and trade unionism as well as in politics.

Henry Hetherington, "the Poor Man's Guardian," was editor of one of the most radical of working-class periodicals, the *Penny Papers for the People,* from 1830 to 1831. A printer and proprietor of his own press, he militated weekly against the Reform Bill's splitting of the middle classes from the working classes through the £10 franchise, against the property qualification and against deferral of the franchise on grounds of laboring-class ignorance. At the same time, as his *nom de plume* suggests, he espoused a kind of intellectual avant-gardisme, believing—unlike Senex but to the same end—that the poor do not know what they want:

> the working classes are, by the blessing of our blessed constitution, generally speaking, too ignorant to form a correct opinion for themselves; they only call for a change, because their animal feelings tell them that a change is necessary, without knowing or imagining *what* change it is that they require: they want an adviser—they want a Guardian; we, for want of a better, have elected ourselves into that situation; and we, in their name, assert our unqualified disapprobation of the proposed measure. . . .[24]

At the same time as he claims the right to represent the poor given their ignorance, Hetherington does not proceed to extend this judgment to deferral of franchise. To the contrary, here he agrees with Senex:

> [A]narchy and confusion of any sort, though it might for a short time exist, would very soon give place to *"order,"* which would every day improve, while *ignorance* would every day diminish; and why? because the ignorant and disorderly would have their interests represented by persons capable of sympathizing with them—by persons, in fact, who would themselves be interested in removing the disabilities and misfortunes under which they labour, instead of by persons interested in keeping them as they are, in order that their ignorance and their wretchedness may be excuses for not rendering them their rights.[25]

Representation can take place on grounds of sympathy but is always a prelude to the removal of disabilities which hinder self-government. In the sphere of trade unionism, however, Hetherington's probably complex rather than simply contradictory position runs him into trouble. The *Penny Papers* for April 23, 1831 carries a report of a meeting concerning an "Important Union of the Working Classes" held to discuss the constitution of that Union. Among the resolutions proposed for it is the following:

> That as this Union is intended to raise the working classes from their present degraded condition, it is necessary that it should be done by *themselves*, therefore no person shall be eligible to act on

the Committee unless he be a wealth producer; that is, one who gets his living by his labour.[26]

The report recounts that Hetherington, among others including Benjamin Warden, a saddler, opposed this resolution on the grounds of its exclusive spirit; its restriction of choice of officials; and its infringement on the liberty of the Union's members. The resolution was accordingly amended to permit all members to participate on committees. This organizational dispute was immediately grasped by more radical unionists to be an instance of appropriation of working-class institutions and to have far-reaching implications. A letter from "A Friend to the Poor" appears in the following week's issue which connects a general statement of principles on representation to the events that had just transpired at the Union. The letter is worth quoting at length since it articulates very clearly a position radically opposed to representative democracy in any sphere, and belongs in a long-standing tradition of British radical thinking running back at least into Thomas Spence's writings in the 1790s:

> People who live by plunder will always tell you to be submissive to thieves. To talk of *representation*, in any shape, being of any use to the people is sheer nonsense; unless the people have a house of working people, and represent themselves.... Representation, therefore, by a different body of people to those who are represented, or who live by an opposite source, is a mockery, and those who persuade the people to the contrary, are either idiots, or cheats.... The people should drop all contention, therefore, about electing a legislature in its present shape, and contend night and day, every moment of their lives for a legislature of their own, or one made up of themselves.... This resolution spoke a volume, by showing the people's desire to take the lead in favour of themselves. This resolution you and Mr. Warden destroyed (not from bad, though from mistaken motives) by insinuating, like the present lawmakers, that the people were not *intelligent* nor *honest enough to conduct their own concerns*. I shall only observe on this matter that if the wealth-producers be *intelligent* and *honest* enough to raise every thing in the world, from a pin to a first-rate ship of war, they are certainly *intelligent enough* and *honest enough* to regulate the affairs of an union among themselves. You and Mr. Warden, then, will do well in withdrawing yourselves from their committee, and every one else who is not absolutely a man

who works for a master, or working man. Attend their meetings, hear what they have to say, report their proceedings, and encourage them to go on; but at the same time give them the lead, learn them to go alone, and encourage them to be no longer slaves but men. There must be a house of the people.... *The people, therefore, to be well represented* must represent themselves. This is the way in which representation began, and this is the way it must end.

Passages like these from Senex and "A Friend to the Poor" do more than recall Marx's characterization in *The Eighteenth Brumaire of Louis Bonaparte* of the French peasantry of a later year: they "cannot represent themselves, they must be represented." Senex and "A Friend to the Poor" indicate the degree of critical consciousness in English working-class circles as to the stakes involved in the discussion of representation and of the close relationship between being represented, being educated and being appropriated. Neither seeks to constitute a culture, by any means, if we mean by culture a distinct recreationary domain of disinterested reflection, but rather criticize the very terms which require and maintain that separate domain. Culture is not invoked here precisely because what is being envisaged allows for no separation between economic, political and educational self-management. What is perhaps most striking is that this refusal of aesthetic culture, unlike Rousseau's, is not predicated on an already nostalgic desire for other forms, but is forged in a vivid apprehension of the political, economic and social relations that are emerging in urban, industrial England. It is not a preservative appeal to the virtues of a traditional "moral economy" but a very contemporaneous understanding of the transformation of social relations, as the industrial bourgeoisie begins to seize political and legal hegemony alongside, and in conjunction with, economic domination.

This brief exchange within English radicalism has a counterpart in an encounter between a radical position on education and liberal/utilitarian patronage some six or seven years before. This second episode is part of a longer story involving the emergence of what is now Birkbeck College out of the London Mechanics' Institute. The *Mechanic's Magazine,* founded in 1823 and edited by Thomas Hodgkin and James Robertson, was a polytechnic encyclopedia designed to promote self-instruction among working-class mechanics. Its principal aim was to make better mechanics of its readers, yet, though a very different kind of periodical from the penny magazines or unstamped press of the next decade, it contains frequent editorials connecting the process of self-education to the political process and to the self-management of working-class institutions. A long article by the editor on October 11, 1823, "Institutions for the Instruction of Mechanics," brings these issues together in calling for the foundation of a London Mechanics' Institute on the model of those already established in Edinburgh and Glasgow. Robertson is quite explicit on the necessity for self-education:

> The education of a free people, like their property, will always be directed most beneficially for them when it is in their own hands. When government interferes, it directs its efforts more to make people obedient and docile, than wise and happy. It desires to control the thoughts, and fashion even the minds of its subjects; and to give into its hands the power of educating the people, is the worst possible extension of that most pernicious practice which has so long desolated society, of allowing one or a few men to direct the actions and control the conduct of millions.... The people only want to have the means of educating themselves left in their pockets untouched by the tax-gatherer, and there is no doubt but they will employ those means more for their own advantage than they can possibly be employed by men who, for the very reason they belong to the *upper* classes, can know little or nothing of what the *lower* classes need, nor what is fitting for them. They know, indeed too well what is proper to them as *subjects*, as *tax-paying machines*, as *slaves*, but not what is suitable to them as labourers and as men.[27]

Robertson's proposal was successful, and a Mechanics' Institute was founded which included among its institutional laws, that two-thirds of the thirty-member committee "*must* be taken *from the working classes.*" William Cobbett concurred with Robertson, apparently, remarking at the Public Meeting for the Institute's establishment that "the thing should be managed by the mechanics themselves.... If they allowed other management to interfere, men would soon be found who would put the mechanics on one side, and make use of them only as tools."[28]

Robertson's and Cobbett's fears were rapidly realized, as Henry Brougham, Whig M.P. and promoter of "Useful Knowledge," and George Birkbeck, a philanthropist who had been closely involved in the founding of the Edinburgh and Glasgow Institutes, indeed began to set aside the mechanics. Birkbeck's interventions, not unlike

Hetherington's, were "from mistaken motives" rather than bad ones; they radically undermined the autonomy of the Mechanics' Institute all the same.[29] He donated money for a lecture theater and for courses of lectures which, as Robertson put it in a lengthy and frustrated editorial in July 1825, should have been erected *"with their own savings, and with their own hands."* The upshot, he argues, is that

> Instead of the men being encouraged to depend entirely on their own contributions, they have been taught to place their chief hope on the benevolent assistance of the great and wealthy, and to applaud, to the very echo, every announcement of a new subscription from Lord this and Sir that.[30]

Robertson's protestations, and those of a number of other correspondents who discuss especially the principle of paying for lectures as a crucial element in self-governed education, were evidently of little avail. They indicate, nonetheless, the widespread and articulate nature of English working-class awareness of the stakes involved in the intricate connections between self-representation, education and economic self-management. Rather than accepting passage through the intermediary institutions of a disinterested education, they insist on self-determination in that as in other spheres. The *Mechanic's Magazine*, like the penny magazines, has little to say to the question of culture, precisely because its definition of knowledge is devoted to making mechanics better mechanics rather than to assimilating them to bourgeois notions of wholeness and harmony. In both kinds of publication, what is emerging is a highly articulate conception of what is meant, in the later phrase of Gramsci, by the "organic intellectual." Even though the concentration on political and practical/mechanical information may scandalize those who see the remedy to the damage inflicted on working-class culture as lying in more *cultural* freedom and development, a shrewd if ultimately unsuccessful political intelligence clearly determined these options. The future history of the Mechanics' Institutes indicates that middle-class educators and philanthropists were not less aware of the political implications of working-class resistance to "being represented" and their demands to represent themselves or by-pass representative structures altogether. On the one hand, the new directors of the Institute censured Thomas Hodgkin's lectures on Political Economy, published in 1827 under the title *Popular Political Economy*,[31] and countered them by the dissemination instead of work by economists like Charles Knight, whose work was, like so much widely distributed and popularized political economy of the time, designed to show the inevitability and even the benefits of class differences, "security of property" and control of wages. As early as 1825, Brougham wrote in his *Practical Observations upon the Education of the People* that much good could come from expounding "the true principles and mutual relations of population and wages." Indeed, he argued, the most effective way to ensure liberty and "good order," of securing "the peace of the country and the stability of the government" was "the universal diffusion of this kind of knowledge."[32] But in order to do so, and to control the kinds of "useful knowledge" that might be disseminated, it was crucial to control popular education through its institutions. Accordingly, as the system of Mechanics' Institutes spread across the country, the workers themselves were originally allowed no representation whatsoever on their governing boards, while political or religious discussions, even newspapers, were banned from them. Their purpose became rather "the rapid promotion of general science," "an extensive diffusion of rational information among the general mass of society" and "the creation of intellectual pleasures and refined amusements, tending to the general elevation of character."[33]

What we will carry over to the next chapter, and to the latter part of the century, is the question as to how what was perceived by Robertson and others as a kind of *coup d'état* in the Institute could come to be the expression not, in Gramsci's terms, of domination but of hegemony. We seek to explore the possibility of a convergence between working-class self-representation in a cultural sense and the desires of middle-class reformers to produce a "general elevation of character" precisely by regulating the spaces of recreation. Without such a convergence, whose logic lies in the emergence of a new state formation and the need to address it, the hegemony of a singular understanding of representative democracy might never have been achieved. But if what follows is the increasing hegemony of the view that "universal education must precede universal franchise" (to cite Mill's *Considerations on Representative Government*) we should not foreclose the many-aspected debates current among English radicals of the 1820s and 1830s. Nor should we assume that their recalcitrance to the "culture and society" tradition has nothing to teach us at this juncture about the value of a political and material critique that emerges from self-consciously positioned knowledge.

CHAPTER 3

Capitalism vs. the Democracy

FROM MORAL ECONOMY TO SOCIALISM

At first glance, E. P. Thompson's characterization of working-class constitutionalism as "the illusion of the epoch"—he means the epoch that culminated in 1832—appears to be complemented by Gareth Stedman Jones's insistence that Chartism too suffered from a cognate "illusion." Chartism, a response to the setbacks the workers' movement suffered in 1832 and 1834, was in Stedman Jones's view stymied by what was "first and foremost a vocabulary of political exclusion"[1] —exclusion, that is, from the franchise. The Chartists on this view were misled by their commitment to a shopworn legacy of natural rights and of traditional forms of protest. They signally failed to see that by the 1830s these resources were no longer appropriate, having been overtaken by that convenient alibi of the historian (and of the political economist), the "logic of events."

Stedman Jones's criticism points forward as well as back, to the way in which (in Dorothy Thompson's words) "the political impulse of Chartism [was to become] constricted into the narrow confines of popular liberalism in the second half of the [nineteenth] century."[2] Even later than this, Stedman Jones reminds us, working-class aspirations in Britain were to find political expression only through a Parliamentary Labour Party that was self-consciously constituted as the "political" (read "parliamentary") arm, or tail, of an otherwise relentlessly and defensively economistic trade union movement. The argument is that working-class politicians were to bite the fruit of parliamentarianism because this fruit had so long been forbidden them; and that they were to do so even though parliamentarianism deflected the socialist impulse and made possible a series of betrayals of socialism[3] at the hands of successive political stalwarts, not all of whom even called themselves socialist.

That such betrayals were to take place is not at issue. What is at issue is Stedman Jones's casting of the Chartists as having been fixated on the franchise in a way that made those betrayals possible. His argument, like so many prospective arguments, is armed with hindsight— hindsight about later developments about which the Chartists could have known nothing. Stedman Jones's thesis is in any case not immune from what E. P. Thompson memorably termed "the enormous condescension of posterity";[4] it judges and condemns Chartism in the light of the very distinction between "the political" and "the social" that during the Chartist decades had yet to take shape. To the contrary, the theoretical and practical grasp of what Ellen Meiksins Wood, in her critique of Stedman Jones, terms "the *unity* between political and appropriative powers"[5] was made possible by the 1832 Reform Act and made manifest in the New Poor Law of 1834. It was to the Chartists themselves neither a concept, nor a threat, nor yet a distant prospect. It was lived reality.

It was in response to this looming reality that the working-class movement rethought constitutional reform, after 1832 as before it.[6] But in 1832 the working-class reform movement still needed middle-class representatives like Francis Place, who used the threat of working-class insurrection, and the reality of revolution in France, alongside that of the Swing Riots, melodramatically ringing London with flames,[7] to negotiate a line of retreat acceptable to all but the most diehard defenders of "Old Corruption."

A second scholarly and political dispute, this time between Thompson and Perry Anderson, makes clear what's at stake in how we read the history or evolution of Chartism. Thompson paraphrases Anderson's position in the following terms: Chartism having been "wrecked by its pitifully weak leadership and strategy," the working class retreated in a state of "extreme exhaustion"; its "élan and combativity" proceeded to evaporate. "A profound caesura in English working-class history supervened"; henceforth, the working class "evolved, separate but subordinate, within the apparently unshakeable structure of British capitalism." As a description (Thompson admits) this is partly true. Nonetheless, according to Thompson, the demise of Chartism marks a significant turning point in the direction of working-class agitation, a turning point that can be identified (usually later, and not always in so decisive a form) in the history of other nineteenth-century capitalism elsewhere. "What was going on," in Thompson's words, "is a far-reaching shift within the working class itself . . . the pulling apart of different occupational groups, newer and older, skilled and unskilled, organized and unorganized, metropolitan and provincial, which had been momentarily united in the great agitations leading up to the Chartist climax in 1839," a unity which was never to re-form—a unity which *could* never have re-formed—in the same way again.[8]

For some 15 years, Chartism succeeded in fusing tendencies that after its demise proved centrifugal. These tendencies can be registered in various ways—for instance by the introduction of "no politics" rules into certain trade unions (e.g. the Miners' Association in 1842), or by the "new model" consumers' cooperation movement of the Rochdale Pioneers in 1844. What can be observed throughout these and other developments (there is no shortage of examples) is, in Thompson's words, "that the workers had come to fear, above all, not the machine but the *loss* of the machine—the loss of employment."[9] In consequence, the workplace gradually became the main site of class conflict, and only in the 1860s did working-class activism converge once more with political struggle around reform agitation. Thompson then argues that the working class,

> having failed to overthrow capitalist society, proceeded to warren it from end to end. It was part of the logic of this new direction that each advance within the framework of capitalism simultaneously involved the working class far more deeply within the status quo. As they improved their position within the workshop, so they became more reluctant to engage in quixotic outbreaks, which might jeopardize gains accumulated at such cost. Each assertion of working-class influence within the bourgeois-democratic state machinery simultaneously involved them as partners (even if antagonistic partners) in the running of the machine.[10]

But this appears to us to overlook the evanescent nature of the status quo, a point already famously made by Marx's description of the dynamic of capitalism in the *Communist Manifesto*. We will go on to argue rather that an emergent proletariat continues to shape its own interpretation of social relations, existing and desirable. What to some appears as conformism or assimilation, appeared to working-class intellectuals as, in their own terms, "self-reliance."

For a working-class "alternative" had in fact enjoyed a real existence, one which overlapped both with Chartism and with Owenism, and which found its characteristic means of expression in the unstamped press. It would be unwarranted to characterize this alternative either in terms of the working-class economism and constitutionalism that succeeded it, *or* in terms of the eighteenth-century radicalism from which it emerged. In particular, there was and could have been no apolitical trade unionism at this time; the repression of the 1790s alone, by penalizing conspiracies among workmen and movements for parliamentary reform simultaneously and by means of the same statutes, had effectively coupled together economic and political radicalism: "The aristocracy were interested in repressing Jacobin 'conspiracies' of the people, the manufacturers were interested in defeating 'conspiracies' to increase wages: the Combination Acts of 1799 served both purposes."[11] The "working-class 'alternative'" in any case denoted a shift within this coupling, a shift in Gregory Claeys's words "from moral economy to socialism," which helps give the Chartist decades their specificity.

Radicalism at the end of the eighteenth century, prior to the systematic repression of British Jacobinism, primarily entailed a drive to reform a visibly corrupt Parliament and extend the franchise. It envisaged no specific economic program.[12] The point of no return to this political universe was reached when early "socialism discarded the notion that there should be any connection between the right of the franchise and the ownership of property"; rejecting such a connection became practically obligatory among those who were so painstakingly denied the franchise in 1832. Ownership of property was now "perceived as itself a fateful source of social and political corruption, blinding the possessors to the suffering of the dispossessed, and with the increasing inequality of wealth gradually threatening the entire society with cataclysm."[13]

1832 marked the emergence of a new and glaring contrast, between "the political" (the narrow caste in power, which had proved itself capable of controlling access to its ranks) and "the social" (the rising demands of the unenfranchised majority, and the notion of popular participation in general). "The political" came to coincide with individualism and competition, "the social" to connote the problem of poverty, working-class movements of all kinds, and the condition of labor in general. The working class came to see itself, and to be seen by some others, as the most "social" or even "sociable" (in the sense of moral) of classes, as well as, at the same time, "the democracy," the largest class or the numerical majority of the population.

These distinctions help us comprehend Chartism, "the democracy's" most characteristic mass movement. "What they wanted was a voice in making the laws they were called upon to obey; they believed that taxation without representation was tyranny, and ought to be resisted; they took a leading part in agitating in favor of the Ten Hours question, the repeal of the taxes on knowledge, education, cooperation, civil and religious liberty and the land question, for they were the true pioneers in all the great movements of the time."[14] Chartism, we should remember, *was* a social movement, not just a political doctrine; as such, like the Owenism with which it frequently intersected at the local level, it "provided cultural facilities, ways of life, and modes of identity linked to what was largely understood as a common ideal, a world in which all were accorded dignity, a decent standard of living and a full range of civil, religious and political liberties, privileges which far too many were denied under the existing system."[15] Chartists, far from being fixated on the franchise as a nostrum or a panacea (as, for instance, Stedman Jones would have it), constantly stressed that economic and social reforms were expected to follow from the inception of popular government. "What else has the [People's] Charter ever been regarded as but as the means to social ends?" asked the O'Connorite Chartist Thomas Clark in the 1850s. In the words of Joan Wallach Scott, "Stedman Jones does not entertain the possibility that economic grievances are about power and politics, that Chartists might have sought economic change by political means, that their visions of power intertwined economics and politics."[16] Eileen Yeo has put the point equally well:

> The six points of the Charter, however revolutionary for their time, were not all that the Chartists meant by self-government.... The very way in which the Chartists tried to govern their movement disclosed a blueprint for collective control which involved much more than periodic voting for parliament.... It is interesting to speculate on how parliamentary democracy might have been different if won by the Chartists and erected on a foundation of vigorous local self-activity.[17]

As "a Christian Socialist" (probably F. D. Maurice) put it in 1850:

> The Democratic Politician looks now upon political reform, but as a means to an end—that end being socialism. The watchwords of Chartism in 1839 were "a full day's wages for a full day's work." That cry long since gave way to the more defined idea of the "organization of labour." This latter opinion is, we are quite aware, far too little comprehended by many of those who are loudest in their

demands for the Franchise, but it should also be borne in mind
that the leaders of the Popular Party in this country are not so ill-
informed thereon.[18]

Our "Christian Socialist" is by no means alone either in pointing up
debates, contested terrain, among the Chartists or in noting the shift
that was taking place among them "from moral economy to socialism." We might notice in passing that Christian Socialism is not here
reforming Chartism, but learning from it. Older slogans were commonly seen among the Chartists themselves as invoking the habits
and assumptions of a bygone, but by no means necessarily pre-market
age when master and man were more intimately acquainted and
where competition had not yet erupted into universal viciousness,
before the great extremes of wealth and poverty had made the two
nations so sure of their mutual antagonism. This was not mere nostalgia, but the means to imagine alternative social relations with a future
inflection. In Asa Briggs's words, "During the last years of the agitation there was an unmistakeable shift in emphasis from the demand
for political reform within the framework of a parliamentary ideal, a
demand which grew naturally out of eighteenth-century radicalism, to
the search for social democracy, a search that led some Chartists—
notably [Ernest] Jones and [George Julian] Harney—into socialism."[19]

Dorothy Thompson misprises the openness of this agenda by insisting, against the evidence, that Chartism contained "no proposal for the
complete replacement of existing property relations," and by asserting
that, in the eyes of the Chartists, labor as the property of the laborer
was "*as much* in need of protection by the law as any other form of
property."[20] This is a misleading way of making the valid point that
Chartists were not, by and large, opposed to property *per se*, since it
overlooks the central fact that there was one form of property to which
they were unalterably opposed: the property called capital whose
untrammeled movement the laws of political economy were bent
upon establishing, defending and extending. While this position may
fall short of a wholesale theorizing of expropriation, the point remains that there is no warrant for unduly liberalizing it, as, in effect,
Dorothy Thompson does. As far as the Chartists were concerned, political liberalism and economic liberalization were assailable by virtue of
their intrinsic connection one with the other. Conversely, democracy,
understood expansively, and socialism were cognate concepts which
involved each other for the good and simple reason that each aimed to
promote people's control over the conditions of their own existence.

Democracy and capitalism were by contrast antithetical principles; liberalism and capitalism stood and fell together. This perception helps explain Chartism and by so doing points beyond it. It helps us confront the question of whether political and economic liberalization have ever been more than contingently related—a question that is (as we write) being raised all over again in the very different context of Central and Eastern European societies in the 1990s. Had there been democracy of the kind the Chartists espoused in early-nineteenth-century Britain, would there, could there, have been capitalism too? The question strikes us as an open one, since genuine democratization would have enabled the populace to resist capitalism, and there is much evidence that they would have seized the chance of doing so.

POLITICAL EDUCATION

This line of argument, of course, had no claim to monopoly and in fact jostled rather uncomfortably with others. Chartism was in the first instance a multifarious movement within which desire for the franchise—for "universal suffering and animal parliaments," as one contemporary wag put the matter—was primarily a least common denominator that helped keep the movement together. It is important to keep this multiplicity of beliefs in mind, in view of the danger of selecting some of them arbitrarily, wresting them out of their context and then deciding that the chosen few are the important ones because later developments appear to echo them. Chartist actors and beliefs that seem to prefigure liberalism are cases in point. It has often been pointed out that Ernest Jones made the fateful transition to liberalism in his old age; and Bronterre O'Brien, for his part, is on record as having favored, in 1848, a middle-class alliance—even if this proposal did provoke the withering and scornful opposition of Feargus O'Connor. There again, William Lovett can readily enough be seen (as he is seen by Dorothy Thompson, for instance) as having prefigured later working-class liberalism. Lovett, indeed, is particularly important for our present purposes not only because he was the foremost Chartist theoretician of education, but also because in this capacity he shifted from the quintessential radical early Chartist view—that political participation was the form of education that alone could make possible other forms of education—to the quintessentially Victorian-liberal view—that prior education was needed in order to prepare the lower orders for the exercise of political rights (understood now as the suffrage).

It has often been argued that only when Lovett convinced himself
and others of the temporal and logical priority of education over the
suffrage did he gain significant support from the middle class. And we
should take note of the fact that this support was rejected by many
Chartists, especially those who disputed Lovett's conclusions—as did,
to give the most prominent example, Feargus O'Connor, whose *Conservative Chartism, Christian Chartism and Temperance Chartism*
(1841) was a broadside directed at Lovett. For, of course, middle-class
support as it was extended to Lovett may eventually be regarded as one
of a series of attempts to define a "respectable" element in Chartism
and to sever it from the disreputable remainder. But much more is at
stake here: it is equally the case that Chartist debates around education and politics provided the very means for middle-class intellectuals and administrators to draw together a rather incoherent Radical
project to disseminate "useful knowledge" with one which had begun
to emphasize the effort to form "moral" citizens through a govern-
mentally subsidized system of education. That this process took place
in response to a very articulate working-class debate on alternatives in
politics and education is as important historically as the resistance to
middle-class, sectarian and state education among other Chartists. For
even where "assimilation" appears to take place, we would stress
rather the *convergence* of state-based education projects with an
autonomous working-class set of precepts which pre-existed and influenced middle-class "reforms."

But vigorous resistance there also was, and it matters not only that
we acknowledge this resistance, but that we also see the implications
of the measures that were resisted, since this issue went beyond Lovett
himself. Educating the poor was not just a Victorian philanthropic obsession. It merits reading as an ideology, since it served at once as a
means (and often as *the* means) to shelving dangerous political
reforms, and at the same time operated as an important mechanism of
social control. Time and again, crudely deterrent legal and penal mechanisms of control were supplemented by officially sanctioned attempts
at educational rehabilitation, which were themselves an expression
of the same imperative. Chadwick's New Poor Law (1834) was duly
supplemented by Dr. Kay's workhouse and district schools; factory
inspectors' reports were similarly supplemented by riders in their concluding paragraphs about the pressing need for tightly-regulated and
closely-supervised education. As Richard Johnson tersely puts it, "the
condition of the poor came almost to *mean* the condition of their education."[21] Dr. J. P. Kay, who later became Sir James Kay-Shuttleworth

and who gave his name to the influential "Kay's *Minutes*,"[22] represented education as being, for the employer of labor, analogous to the use of profit to ensure against capital loss.

The "legitimate educator" was, in the idiom of Kay's *Minutes*, there (or supposed to be there) in order to preempt the "socialist." His task was to be aided by the fact that the "appalling concatenation of evils that would reduce the working population to utter debasement, destroying the very structure of society by the explosive violence of volcanic elements" had a "remote or accidental origin" and was in no way inherent in capitalist society as such. By "judicious management" this concatenation might be "entirely removed." After all, continued Kay, with no discernible irony, "a system which promotes the advance of civilization and diffuses it over the world cannot be inconsistent with the happiness of the great mass of the people." Utopian as it was, Kay's optimism was tempered by two conditions, "environmental" and "moral." The first involved public health, sanitation, adequate policing and—needless to add—the repeal of the Corn Laws; the second entailed "teaching the poor man his political position in society, and the moral and religious duties attendant upon it." In insisting that "environmental" reform could not do its work unaided by "moral" reform, Kay was, in Richard Johnson's words, "attempting to express the connection between environment, consciousness and culture in the language of moral censure [and] of providential causation." This language should not obscure the fact that Kay's moralistic and paternalistic admonitions were superimposed upon arguments that were, at root, economic. He was attempting to denounce working-class decadence—his emphasis on "disorganizing doctrines" was designed to link irreligion, sedition and moral iniquity—moralistically and "scientifically" at the same time. His words of 1838 are not disarming: "The attention the [Poor Law] Commissioners have given this subject [education] is likely to prove a means for vindicating their opinions and designs from the imputation of being under the influence of cold-blooded economic speculations, without the infusion of a more generous sympathy for the happiness of the poorer classes."

Since working-class parents were by definition disqualified, incapacitated from fulfilling their "natural" role as educators, "a little artificial world of virtuous exertion"—Kay means the school, not the workhouse, though his language (here as elsewhere) betrays him—is to be substituted for parents' baleful influence on their young. By substitution is meant not addition but replacement. "We cannot let farmers or labourers, miners or mechanics be judges of our educational work.

It is part of that work to educate them all into a sense of what true education is." Salvation in other words must come from outside if the vicious circle of iniquity is to be broken. The teacher, a social "emissary" and exemplar is himself to be tightly controlled lest he "go native" among his charges. Small wonder, then, that Richard Johnson characterizes Kay's *Minutes* as "an enormously ambitious attempt to determine, through the capture of educational means, the patterns of thought, sentiment and behaviour of the working class" and concludes that as "a system of control ... the *Minutes* rival any Parliamentary statute dealing with a social matter in the first half of the nineteenth century."[23]

Contrary to Ian Hunter's assertion of the ad-hoc and non-ideological character of early reform,[24] arguments about what these "educational means" should now teach were commonplace even in the 1820s. Brougham's *Practical Observations upon the Education of the People* (1825), for instance, duly observed that much good could come from expounding "the true principles and mutual relations of population and wages." Indeed, as Brian Simon puts it in his discussion of Brougham, "[t]he most effective way of ensuring liberty and 'good order', of securing 'the peace of the country and the stability of the government', was 'the universal diffusion of this kind of knowledge'."[25] Such knowledge, unsurprisingly enough, tended most readily to be "diffused" (an interesting choice of word in its own right) at times of crisis. The Society for the Diffusion of Useful Knowledge (SDUK), which was launched by Brougham with the help of Matthew Davenport Hill in 1826, and with Charles Knight as the main publisher of its pamphlets, tended at first "to provide intellectual fare of a kind to solace those whose lives were given to manual labour"—"miscellaneous scientific and cultural information, ranging from Lepidoptera to 'Autumnal Customs in Kardofan',"[26] rather than disseminate the precepts of political economy. But this anodyne phase was not to last. With the economic crisis of 1830, combined as this was with serious outbreaks of rick-burning and agricultural machine-breaking throughout the Home Counties,[27] the SDUK set out directly to tackle economic issues. By this time Robert Owen's socialist ideas as well as Hodgkin's economic theories—and we should bear in mind that the latter did not so much displace the former, as Place appears to have believed they did, as augment them in the minds of many readers[28]— had gained some purchase among the working class. Place and others were party to a deep-seated fear of a "convulsion" in which the middle classes "will be swept away—no matter which party conquers" unless they "at once go amongst the people" and "instruct" them.[29] In April 1831 a sharp attack was launched by the house organ of the Radicals, *The Westminster Review*, appealing for a fundamental change in policy. What did the SDUK do, thundered the *Review*, once it was faced with riotous assemblies, forcible raising of wages, open attacks on private property, machine-breaking and the firing of ricks and barns—at a time when London appeared to the alarmed to be ringed with fire? Why, it produced a spate of irrelevant and obscure treatises in science, and promised "[t]o a people ignorant of everything most intimately connected with their welfare ... two treatises ... [one] on the Polarisation of Light, and another on the Rigidity of Cordage!"[30] Brougham himself was singled out in the same article as "quailing with fear" before the "vile and interested clamour" of clergy and aristocracy and hence avoiding the publication of those whom Place had called "the greatest enlighteners of the people," i.e., the Political Economists. Brougham in truth managed to combine staunch support for the New Poor Law and the principles of political economy with an apparent belief that despite the impact of these the working class could somehow elevate itself. "To the working classes I would say, that this is the time when by a great effort they may secure the inestimable blessing of knowledge."[31]

The editors of the *Review* were presumably unaware that the shift they sought had already taken place, with *An Address to the Laborers on the Subject of Destroying Machinery* (1830) and the *Results of Machinery, Namely, Cheap Production and Increased Employment Exhibited: Being an Address to the Working-men of the United Kingdom*, both written by Charles Knight. Brougham said of the latter that it was "eminently conducive to allaying the reckless spirit which ... was leading multitudes to destroy property and break up machines."[32] Knight followed these with *Capital and Labour*, addressed to those who might otherwise fall victim to teachers like Thomas Hodgkin. Hodgkin and other "ministers of desolation," if they had their way, "would be able to sing their triumphal songs of 'Labor defended against the claims of Capital' amid the shriek of the jackal and the howl of the wolf."[33] In 1831 there came the *Short Address to Workmen on Combinations to Raise Wages*, characterized by Simon as so overdrawn and patronizing that Place himself disowned it: "Every such essay as this makes it more and more difficult to drum sound doctrine into the people."[34]

It may be, as Simon thinks, that here the utilitarian perspective of molding minds "like wet clay in a plastic hand" (as Brougham put it in a speech to the House of Lords in May 1835[35]) "is "less directly ex-pressed";[36] but "drumming doctrine into people" is scarcely subtle. The idea of doing so ran up against a predictable internal obstacle in any case, predictable because familiar. In the first year of the reformed Parliament, Arthur Roebuck made a new appeal for "the universal and national education of the whole people." Even though he had the sup-port of Joseph Hume, James Bowring, Francis Place and others—the usual suspects rounded up from the radicals—he found few other tak-ers for his scheme to establish infant schools, technical schools and normal schools (for the training of teachers), controlled by a minister of Cabinet rank and administered by local committees. Effectively, Roebuck's wild-eyed scheme was fully forty years too soon. Even so, it had an air of *déjà vu* about it as early as 1832. Brougham's 1820 Bill "For the better education of the poor in England and Wales," which had also advocated a system of universal compulsory elementary edu-cation provided by the state, on grounds drawn straightforwardly and almost literally from Adam Smith's *Wealth of Nations*,[37] went down to resounding defeat: it ran up against the reality principle of the times, the need for child labor in the mines, factories and mills, as Robert Owen had pointed out at the time. By 1833, once again, "few industri-alists took [Roebuck's] proposal seriously: so far as they were con-cerned, children were first and foremost an indispensable adjunct to the labour force."[38] It may well be that, in Simon's words, "once the middle class felt itself to be in the saddle, the task of teaching the working class to recognize its claims ["to drum sound doctrine into the people"] seemed much less urgent"—particularly if to do so would run the risk, however indirectly, of encouraging the working class to for-mulate and recognize claims of its own.[39] Brougham by 1833 had already announced with no small flourish that he no longer supported the principle of compulsory education, but was in favor of leaving edu-cation to voluntary bodies—which meant in practice primarily the very religious bodies that were to have made themselves impregnable by the time the 1870 Education Act eventually rolled around.[40] James Kay, in *The Moral and Physical Condition of the Working Classes Employed in the Cotton Manufacture in Manchester in 1832*, adds to the Radical belief in universal education—not that there was much left of this to add to—the admonition that religion must be closely linked to education: "With pure religion and undefiled, flourish frugality, forethought, and industry."[41] The various kaleidoscopic nonconform-ist denominations, whose complexity is much more bewildering than that of the various early-nineteenth-century socialisms that were also peppering British society, were with such arguments being given a new lease of life, and all the encouragement they might have needed to rule many a local roost.

What needs to be stressed at this point is not just the internal incoherence of middle-class Radical ideas about education, but also the fact that this was perceived and acted upon by their working-class adversaries. This needs to be stressed alongside our more basic points: that there was what Tholfson calls a "robust autodidactic culture" among the working class in the 1820s;[42] and that there is widespread evidence of working-class radicals coming into conflict with middle-class efforts to use education, particularly adult education, as a vehicle for propaganda.[43] Simon cites chapter-and-verse on this latter. Thomas Hodgkin: "Men had better be without education than be educated by their rulers; for then education is but the mere breaking of the steer to the yoke; the mere disciplining of a hunting dog which, by dint of severity, is made to forego the strongest impulse of his nature and, instead of devouring his prey, to hasten with it to the feet of his master."[44] John Doherty of the Lancashire Cotton Operatives (in Simon's words "the most influential Trade Unionist of his time"[45]): "Let the huckstering owners of the misnamed Mechanics' Institution, and the would-be rulers of mechanics' minds, see that the day is gone by when the million will be satisfied with the puny morsels of mental food which aristocratic pride and pampered cunning have been wont to deal out to them. Let them see, in reality, that 'the schoolmaster is abroad'."[46] The *Pioneer* (Birmingham), 2 November 1833: "the Mechanics' Institutes already established in this country are anything but such."[47] "This Brougham was always a great stickler for popular education. Indeed the whole bunch of Malthusian conspirators signalised, and still signal themselves, by an affected regard for the 'mental culture' of the people." Small wonder that Cobbett had

> held in the utmost abhorrence the wretches who, mouthing "education," tried to make [the workers] slaves. In our day, the Educationists are still what they were in Cobbett's time—the pretended friends, but the real enemies of the people.... Ah gentlemen, we see through your craft.... You would educate us, not, as you sometimes pretend, to fit us for the exercise of political rights, but to make us indifferent to these rights. And you call yourselves "Philosophical Radicals!"[48]

Already before 1825, men such as Doherty, who were directly involved in the struggle with employers and the establishment of trade unions, grasped this point and consciously set out to promote independent educational institutes. Hetherington's *Poor Man's Guardian* warned its readers in 1831 that, notwithstanding the wooing of the workers in the political field, the intention was to exclude them from the franchise, that the Reform Bill was a "Humbug Bill" to be exposed and opposed as such.[49] The reform government of which Brougham was Lord Chancellor persecuted the working-class press even more viciously than had the Tory administration of 1819,[50] while paying lip service to the need to expand the franchise and promote education. Radicals connived the while at policies in the industrial field which made increased education for the workers and their children impossible. While opposing the limitation of adult hours of work, they gave outright support to the New Poor Law.[51] We know about the working-class response to this, the most reviled and hated piece of legislation ever foisted upon the British working class. In Oldham, Lancashire, working-class radicals who did not have the vote nevertheless succeeded in preventing implementation of the Poor Law Amendment Act for thirteen years after 1834.[52]

The workers' movement's fervent opposition to this draconian measure suggests that working people understood full well what later historians proved able to ignore: that the 1832 Reform Act could be considered an advance in democracy (as opposed to liberalism) only in the light of subsequent developments that 1832 was designed not to encourage or promote but expressly to forestall.[53] The newly augmented ruling-class coalition, however divided on issues of principle (most dramatically, the Corn Laws) it may have been, could at a pinch always close ranks against the (rarely insurrectionary) threat of universal suffrage from below. This is why there was no solid phalanx of aristocratic opposition to the rise of industry and of political economy, its intellectual counterpart. The landed classes duly survived the repeal of the Corn Laws in 1846. The landed gentry continued to populate the Cabinet, to monopolize the representation of rural areas in Parliament and often to represent urban areas too. It never needed to fight a rearguard action against capitalism. The manufacturers, for their part, gained virtually unlimited freedom of maneuver from the 1832 settlement. George Loveless described the Whig governments of the 1830s as a "tyrant faction," and there is no reason to regard this view of them as exaggerated. We need only look to the measures they enacted. Repeal of the Corn Laws in 1846, and the Tithe Commutation Act of 1836 were hits at the aristocracy, to be sure, but the hits at the workers were much more serious, concerted and bitterly contested. There was the Irish Coercion Act (1833); the Poor Law Amendment Act (1834); the Tolpuddle Martyrs episode of the same year, the Municipal Reform Act (1835); the Newspaper Act (1836); and, to cap this legislative barrage, the proposal to set up constabulary forces in rural districts in the late 1830s—forces which, it was feared, would busy themselves both with regulating the leisure and educational activities of the working class in the unincorporated towns that were to be important centers of Chartist support, and with enforcing the New Poor Law and employers' interests during trade disputes.[54]

At one level, as is well enough known, the struggle for economic demands (such as the Ten Hours Bill), for repeal of the New Poor Law, for freedom of speech, for the extension of the franchise, and for independent institutions, all fused in the Chartist movement. Indeed, it is possible to trace out a marked pattern of indigenous working-class protest against the work of the Mechanics' Institutes and of the SDUK, one that is far more coherent, far more thoroughgoing than anything proceeding from the ranks of the middle-class Radicals. Francis Place was surely right when he wrote that the workers "will read nothing which the Diffusion Society meddles with. They call the members of it Whigs, and the word Whig with them, means a treacherous rascal, a bitter, implacable enemy."[55] The Co-operator James Watson writes of the SDUK:

> Has it any tendency to improve [the working class's] condition, by giving them more of the fruits of their labour? Would it lead them any better to understand their rights, or to comprehend or act upon the principle of cooperation? No. They had been amusing the people with the fruit of their antiquarian researches about Charing Cross and the fruit of their researches at the Zoological Gardens. That was all very well and very useful in its place; but while he and others—tens of thousands of others—felt degraded in the land of their birth, having no participation in their political and social rights, and carrying about the brand of the slave on their foreheads, they were not in a condition to sit down coolly and philosophically to such investigations."[56]

A very different idea of useful knowledge—useful because open and contentious—is suggested by a mordantly-worded advertisement in the *Poor Man's Guardian* for "Lovett's Coffee and Conversation Rooms," which had a library of several hundred volumes. "Do you wish to read of the Contentions of the Whigs and Tories for Places and

Emoluments? Do you wish to hear the opinions and speculations of the proppers, patchers, and repairers of Church and State? And do you wish to know what the Radicals, Destructives, and Republicans think of all those parties? Consult the following list." There follows a list of twenty-eight journals including the *Mechanic's Magazine*, Cobbett's *Register*, the *New Moral World* and the *Westminster Review*. The advertisement continues; "The Malthusians, Political Economists, Co-operators, and Anti-Co-operators, Believers and Unbelievers, are especially invited; as they all profess to have knowledge to impart, and to be the advocates of the Truth."[57]

In 1836, in the wake of the failure of Owen's Grand National Consolidated Trades Union, and in the wake of the Tolpuddle Martyrs episode (both of 1834), Lovett, Hetherington, Cleave, Watson and others founded the London Working Men's Association, which in short order, in 1837, issued its "Address on Education": "Could corruption sit in the judgment seat—empty-headed importance in the senate-house—money-getting hypocrisy in the pulpit—and debauchery, fanaticism, poverty, and crime stalk triumphantly through the land—if the millions were educated in a knowledge of their rights? No, no, friends; and hence the efforts of the exclusive few to keep the people ignorant and divided. Be ours the task, then, to unite and instruct them; for be assured the good that is to be must be begun by ourselves."[58]

The Owenite *New Moral World* sounded a similar note in the 1840s. "Educate! Educate!! Educate!!! ... Let every institution forthwith have its Sunday and Day school, distribute tracts and works explanatory of the Social System with unsparing liberality ... let the lecture rooms be made as attractive as possible, private classes, lyceums, reading rooms and other means of instruction and innocent recreation. Let us not be outstripped in this endeavour."[59] Mechanics' Institutes according to the *New Moral World* were by contrast willing to educate working people only insofar as the instruction given squared with "the interests of the clergy and the wealthy classes." They were no more than "halfway houses to the attainment of social knowledge."[60]

As Lovett, for his part, saw the situation, "While a large portion of the hawks and owls of our society were seeking to perpetuate that state of mental darkness most favorable to the securing of their prey, another portion, with more cunning, were for admitting a sufficient amount of mental glimmer to cause the multitude to walk quietly and contentedly in the paths they in their wisdom had prescribed for them."[61] (Lovett here had more than a "glimmer" of the future, as we are about to see). What is noteworthy in the meantime is the confidence and scorn with which the Chartists and others dismissed middle-class ideas about their "ignorance" and therefore their unfitness for the franchise. "[T]hey tell us ... we are ignorant, at the very time when a tool-cutter and a cabinet-maker are engaged, even in the dungeon to which ... tyrants had unjustly consigned them, in writing a system of education, before which their modish plans, and 'abstract theories', and 'histories of birds and fishes' sink into insignificance."[62]

The (mistitled) *Chartist's Friend*, one of the earliest journals to try to appropriate Chartist ideas for middle-class purposes, argued that the working classes, being "too ignorant to discuss complex issues," should rather follow the Bible and "submit to the powers that be ... [which are] ordained by God."[63] William Linton scornfully replied that the working class could scarcely be worse at exercising the franchise than were the "current fools and felons" who already did so. He added that with or without an educational franchise to exclude the illiterate, there could be no better judge of the interests of the working class than its members themselves.[64] The *Chartist Circular* responded to the arguments of the *Chartist Friend* with similar indignation:

We are perpetually met, in our struggle for universal suffrage, by the answer—You are too ignorant, too drunken and improvident; you could not be trusted with the Franchise. This smells strongly of the old-school slang of "swinish multitude", "vulgar herd", "unwashed mob".... Yet it is evident, that an appearance of argument is assumed; they admit the principle, but do not wish us to get it "as yet"; wait a little, fifteen, twenty, maybe fifty years' training will make you all right, you'll get it.... As far as ignorance is concerned, we could affirm that the working classes have turned the circumstances that surround them to far better account, in the acquisition and use of important knowledge, than either the middle classes or the upper classes. Their scientific associations, their mechanics' institutions, their well-stocked libraries, are convincing proofs that the working man, jaded though he always is by excessive toil, yet seeks for, and appreciates useful information.... [L]ook to the circumstances with which the working millions are surrounded, and it is indeed astonishing that the onward march of improvement is so rapid amid all their difficulties ... knowledge is spreading fast, a mind, a spirit, a soul, has descended into the depths of society, and a reanimation is taking place; like a glorious river, knowledge has overflowed its ancient channels which priests and legislators cut for it.... Tremble, tyrants, for the voice of discontent is abroad. Knowledge is conferring on us its power. It is opening our eyes to see that our interests are opposed to yours."[65]

Democracy was associated in the *Chartist Circular* "not with a social system where people were scarcely to blame for the wretched condition they found themselves in, but with a progress of popular political knowledge as the people became cognizant of their rights—a knowledge of which the Charter itself was an embodiment."[66]

The larger solution was to be a policy of national education—a policy the Chartists contrasted with the recommendation of political exclusion on the basis of ignorance.[67] Participation in politics was held to be an educational experience in its own right, and was to be encouraged on educational grounds, among others.

Educational grounds were not to be used, *per contra*, as a justification for the denial of political participation.[68] Popular participation in politics would enrich the political process and become essential to the practice of democracy. In, by and through their agitation to make the People's Charter the basis of the Constitution, "the people would gain a political education on the great questions of national and social rights ... truth, liberty and justice."[69] These priorities, this ordering, were not universally adhered to. The *Northern Star* of 11 July 1846, for instance, reverses them: a truly human education, we read, "can only be attained when the people are all politically equal." Hence, "the political enfranchisement of the whole male adult population is an indispensable preliminary to every kind of educational, social and physical improvement." On 12 September 1846 we read: "Education will follow the suffrage as sure as day follows night."[70] These are differences of emphasis rather than outright inconsistencies, however, differences which correspond to the differences between Lovett's "knowledge Chartists" and the rest, and not too much should be made of them. In general, Simon seems to us to be entirely justified : "Small wonder that the Chartists indignantly rebutted the taunt of 'ignorance', flung at the workers as reason for refusing them the vote. There is no doubt that the general cultural standard maintained by their press was extremely high."[71] And this in any case was but the tip of the iceberg. We have only to consider what the Chartist press busied itself with reporting. Dorothy Thompson, with whose assessments we have at times disagreed, is surely quite right to indicate how widespread the reporting in Chartist newspapers was, extending as it did even beyond the panorama of Chartism, Owenism, Cooperation, Christian Socialism, trade unionism and more.[72]

The radical working class that absorbed such arguments could scarcely have been any less indifferent to the implications of a barrage of newly-enacted industrial legislation signaling a shift to a new form of state control: the Master and Servant Act of 1823, the passing of which in some respects overshadowed the more paradoxical, more dogmatic repeal of the Combination Acts the following year; the Truck Act of 1831; the Mines Regulation Act of 1841; the "Gagging Bill" of 1848 which for the first time made seditious speech a felony and significantly increased its penalties. Masters-as-magistrates looked likely to sit in judgment over court cases where they (or their cohorts) were interested parties. These cases often involved industrial practices that were being redefined as crimes. Traditional perks such as the garnering of waste material, wood and coal, as well as "fents" of cloth, were being refigured as theft, and their perpetrators prosecuted accordingly.

Even though five labor laws were passed between 1802 and 1833, adult hours of work remained entirely unregulated, while the Cotton Factories Act of 1819 was disregarded. "Under these conditions, to talk of the diffusion of knowledge, of universal education was little more than self-deception if a little less than hypocrisy."[73] Hence it came to pass that "[t]he real struggle for the very possibility of education for the working class had to be fought out by the workers themselves on another issue altogether, that of the working day; and fought out against the determined opposition of the Radicals."[74] The mass movement for the reduction of hours of labor, which was developed in the 1830s around the Ten Hours Bill, eventuated in a Factory Act in 1844 which did not include the Ten Hours clause, but instead limited the working day for children under thirteen in the textile industry to eight hours, laying down also that they must have two hours' education a day.[75] These clauses were in line with the Benthamite theory that although the state should not "interfere" in the case of adults, children were by definition not yet in a moral position to make "free" contracts, and so should be protected and, of course, educated. On the one hand, provision was made for inspection; on the other, no funds at all were allocated and no administrative machinery was set up to ensure compliance with the Act's provisions, "an absence," in Marx's words, "that again makes the compulsion illusory."[76] Yet the barrier had been breached: the principle of compulsory education had for the first time been conceded. Even in the 1840s, "In general, the political struggle for education was inseparably linked with continuing action to secure a shortening of the working day."[77] According to the *Northern Star*, "[t]he educational reform that Lord John Russell will undoubtedly propound, according to his political creed, will be more advanced by a Ten Hours Bill than by the mere establishment of schools, which, under the present system, the working man's child has not much leisure to attend—even though an educational grant should equal that to Her Majesty's stables."[78]

Simon's analysis is in important respects borne out by Anthony Howe's more detailed, more localized study of "Cultural provision for the Working Classes" in *The Cotton Masters, 1830-1860*. In the period Howe discusses, factory masters in Lancashire patronized an increasingly "vast array" of educational and recreational activities. These were designed to cater to workers whose formal education, if any, ended at the age of thirteen, and whose leisure time had been increased with the progressive impact of factory legislation, especially after the act of 1867 that further limited the working hours of women and children of 1847.[79] Facilities ranging from public libraries to working men's clubs were often initiated and supported financially and organizationally by the masters, although they remained throughout part of the pattern of "self-help" culture. Such financial help remained important as the Mechanics' Institutes belied the hope that they would become self-supporting.[80]

It is the patterning *within* this general framework that is important to us. "The Mechanics' Institutes began with high-minded aims. Education was to prepare the working classes for social and political emancipation, while a knowledge of science would fructify in new inventions enabling Britain to overcome foreign competition. These aims were rapidly diluted. Instruction in science was largely irrelevant to the labour of all but a few factory operatives, being required neither by the nature of the product nor by cotton technology. . . . Instruction moved from physical towards moral sciences; scientific experiment gave way to libraries, concerts, excursions and soirées. . . . If the cultural apparatus supported by the masters had been devised to instill the tenets of political economy, then it . . . notably failed" to do so.[81]

The masters' institutions more nearly offered "some instruction and much entertainment"—"Workers' Playtime"—"as an alternative to drunkenness and ignorance. In this way the manufacturer no doubt believed the working class to have become more 'orderly' and 'respectable', while at the same time he fulfilled his social duty to bridge the gulf between master and man which had threatened to become unbridgeable in the 1830s."[82] Unsurprisingly, "pubs and singing rooms retained greater appeal to the proletariat, though not to the white collar groups who often became the mainstay of such institutions in their search for self-respect and independence." Public libraries, "the cheapest form of police" to Joseph Brotherton,[83] were also supported by Charles Dickens: "books ... will cheer [the working man] through many of the struggles and toils of his life, will raise him in his self-respect, will teach him that capital and labour are not opposed, but are mutually dependent and mutually supporting [hear, hear—applause]—will enable him to tread down blinding prejudice, corrupt misrepresentation, and everything but the truth, into the dust."[84] In general, "operatives were considered far more lacking in politico-economic" than in technical education. "Had there been a demand for technical education, many industrialists would ... have looked to private and voluntary provision rather than to an increased role for the state. Technical education never became a major philanthropic venture of the masters, whose patronage was to be confined to educational movements of social rather than industrial application."[85]

Much cultural philanthropy so understood was aimed not at the working class *per se* but at a middle class that needed the assurance of seeing the upper strata of the working class as becoming "respectable" and "independent"—"independence" being a good example here of the inversion of words' meanings at which the Victorian era was so adept. As we have already suggested, the "respectability" of the working class was seen by themselves in relation to their own longstanding moral self-reliance not as an aping of middle-class values. Their "superiors," however, continued to affirm the virtues of a "cultivation" that most often took the working class as its object. Art in particular "was to lead to intellectual cultivation: a craving for the beautiful would lead to order, contentment and prosperity. Art would therefore replace nature in the discipline of the industrial town, as a leisure pursuit more desirable than the 'perusal of frothy and pernicious publications' and 'indulgence in sensual propensities.'"[86]

[P]atronage of the arts was part of the stewardship of wealth, and not mere gratification. To that extent, the textile masters escape the weaker sense of the charge of "philistinism", the use of wealth for wealth's sake. However, they fall down in the stronger sense—for art was regarded, not as part of the culture of liberal education and self-development, but as part of a broader spectrum of philanthropic activities with social utility firmly in view, however ineffectual in practice.... [T]he mind of the middle class had been opened, and its culture broadened. The cotton masters had helped achieve one of Arnold's ambitions, to reinforce the middle class "force of ideas" against the "less spiritual force of established power, antiquity, prestige, social refinement."[87]

In Ruskin's terms, "illth" was being transformed into "wealth." Men of the latter fulfilled a "glorious office" and were, "in reality, the pilots of the power and effort of the state . . . the arbiters of the will and work of England."[88]

In view of this now canonized series of developments, it is unsurprising that for many historians of the British working class in the nineteenth century the mid-Victorian era—stretching roughly from 1850 to the late 1870s—represents an age of compromise, disappointment, even betrayal. In the heroic age of the Chartist '30s or the "hungry '40s," class antagonisms and agitation seemed as though they might foreshadow the agenda proffered by a broadly Marxist account of the relation between the development of British industry and that of the British working class considered as a revolutionary agency. Both Engels in Manchester during the early 1840s and Marx in London after 1848 were only too aware of Moses Hess's "European Triarchy" conception of the development of European revolutions in the nineteenth century—according to which schematization the "social" revolution was to begin in England, among the class most aware of the growth of and tendencies of modern industry, while "political" and "philosophical" revolutions unfolded the while in France and Germany respectively. From this teleological perspective the British proletariat, which was politically quiescent until the reform agitation of the late 1860s, had failed to play its prescribed part. It appeared to be misled by leaders from the more "aristocratic" trades, by slogans drawn from an individualistic ethos of "self-help" and Victorian respectability, and by the combined appeals of cultural conformity and (comparative) material security. In John Walton's words, which again admit of a broader application than that of Lancashire, "a composite picture could be assembled to suggest that the working class was bought off by rising real wages, assimilated by political concessions, propaganda, and the lure of 'respectability', and internally divided both horizontally, between the 'labour aristocracy' and the rest, and vertically, between the liberal improvers and the Tory hedonists and bigots."[89]

On the other hand—and here we are beginning to move into what is the main area of our concern—it does seem fair to indicate that there is an ideological quality to words like "respectability" and "improvement," and therefore to the various (and they were various) cultural and educational means to the attainment of these objectives. Working-class self-improvement as an ideal was in other words not *just* a prelude to or presentiment of the Gladstonian liberal complacency which read it as a mark of the acceptance of hegemonic ideas of "respectability."From Cobbett to O'Connor and Lovett, the attempt to by-pass the precepts of Whiggish political economy and middle-class liberalism in the tradition of Spencean, Owenite or Jacobin social radicalism was a matter of principle. Nor indeed, as Claeys points out,[90] was it an unpopular one. The ideal of mutual independence, and not of the dominance of any one class, which became an important source of working-class reformism was an important source of working-class revolutionism too. More broadly, mid-century reformism was not just a product of an upswing in the trade cycle and the moderation of an upper stratum of workers. It must have had precedents, some of which were detailed by E. P. Thompson in *Whigs and Hunters*.[91] More specifically, within the compass of the nineteenth century, the ethos of self-help and independence which seems to contribute so much to the bonding of the working class to the "status quo" after 1850 was in fact an aspect of mainstream radical Chartism, as well as of the London Working Men's Association, well before the mid-century compromise kicked in.

Chartism was essentially a fusion of economic and political insights—a fusion of a particular kind that took place in a particular historical context whose elements were never to reconfigure themselves in quite the same way again.[92] This characterization of Chartism entails the important corollary that engagement of the working class with the prevailing system of rewards and expectations required a shift of emphasis from political to economic grievances.

It was largely for these reasons that the tendency of class conflict turned in the mid-Victorian era not in the direction of the cooperative movement, the temperance movement or Christian Socialism (all of which were to prove much more accomodationist) but towards trade unionism. For where else—in the process of elimination that presented itself—was there to turn? This deflection of energies has to be assessed very carefully. On the one hand, social realities such as class conflict and antagonism that had been blurred (or wished away) by formal consensus universalism here came stridently and vividly into the open: workers who were genuinely interested in behaving rationally, responsibly and courteously in the workplace found out in short order that the only trait that really mattered to their masters was sheer subservience.[93] Above all else, again in Walton's words, "where questions of power and status predominated, the liberal writ did not run,"[94] this being precisely the internal contradiction from which liberalism has suffered all along. On the other hand, the very division between an area where the liberal writ "did not run" and others where it ran very powerfully had to be resolved by the incorporation of aspects of the tradition of working-class "self-reliance," an incorporation which changed and domesticated the very meaning of the term. Ironically, the very critique of "useful knowledge" modes of education undertaken in the radical tradition and in Chartism came to converge with a middle-class recognition, based on quite different premises, of the limits of utilitarianism. As we shall see in the next chapter, thinkers like Mill and Arnold develop that criticism by way of an aesthetic idea of culture, but their impetus comes not just from Schiller or Coleridge. On the contrary, the trenchancy of working class antagonism to piecemeal education obliged advance liberals to rethink the modes whereby the education of the working class can be incorporated with the work of the state. This involved a shift, in Gramsci's terms, from domination to hegemony. Brougham and others had unabashedly sought to subordinate working-class institutions to their own utilitarian purposes, often under the shelter of class-interested and coercive state legislation. The new liberal paradigm, which blended a Coleridgean "Christian Socialism" with the work of Mill, Arnold and others, succeeded in incorporating working-class critiques into the process of parliamentary reform and into arguments for a national education system whose work would precede universal franchise. This time, as we shall see, the condition for middle-class hegemony lay rather in the forms of civil society that had been consolidated with the strengthening of the state in the decades after Chartism than in coercive measures.

CHAPTER 4

Facing the Ethical State

EDUCING THE CITIZEN

The decade from 1860 to 1870, the decade of the second parliamentary Reform Bill, enacted in 1867, and the Education Act of 1870, sees the crystallization of the Victorian state and its transition from a predominantly coercive to a hegemonic form. We mean by this that through that decade a convergence takes place between the ideological formulations of liberal thinkers on culture, education and representation and the state institutions that emerged in order to contain the demands of a highly mobilized and articulate working class. This convergence entails the consolidation of what Gramsci termed the "ethical state," a state represented not merely in its legal and police apparatuses, but in the extension of its paradigms into the organs of civil society itself: schools, trade unions, even religious bodies. What characterizes the ethical state is, beyond the antagonisms of particular classes, groups or sects to the actual practice of a given government, the saturation of discourse on society with an "idea of the state" or, more evidently, with the subordinate conception of the proper relation of the subject as citizen to the state. "Dominant ideology" ceases simply to legitimate the coercive imposition of regulation through the force of law and becomes a deeply embedded paradigm for social organization at every level. Beyond the *ad hoc* measures of "governmentality," the idea of the state and its concomitant notion of the ethical subject as citizen take on a self-evidence that regulates the very form of social institutions from the family to parliament itself. Such is the force of self-evidence over discourse that any utterance that questions its terms is likely to be relegated in the first instance to

115

the terrain of non-sense, violence, deviance or perversity: to virtual irrepresentability.

The emergence of a given form of self-evidence or "common sense" is of course a slow and complex historical process, both theoretically and practically.[1] Here we have chosen to focus on two of the principal figures in the debates on education and the state during the period, figures whose careers and writings embodied the nexus between theoretical formulations and practical engagements, and whose works continue to this date to exert an influence on our conceptions of modern culture and liberal society. Matthew Arnold is now most famous for his work *Culture and Anarchy*, composed in response to working-class agitation for reform, but in the course of his work as a government School Inspector prior to 1867, he produced several lengthy reports on education which already emphasized the necessary conjunction between the state and education. John Stuart Mill, whose *On Liberty* and *Considerations on Representative Government* were in his time definitive statements of what was then called "advanced" liberalism, was no less an active public and parliamentary advocate of reform in the crucial debates leading to the passage of the 1867 Act. Not that in any respect Mill and Arnold occupied at the time identical or even complementary political positions on particular issues. Rather, they occupy antipodal positions in the spectrum of liberal thought, not least around reform agitation. Arnold, indeed, regarded Mill as a latter-day Jacobin for his qualified support of the Hyde Park marchers, whom he himself famously regarded as "a mob marching where it likes, meeting where it likes, bawling what it likes, breaking what it likes."[2]

Arnold's response to the riots which followed the government's refusal to permit a demonstration in favor of the extension of franchise appeared in what is probably his most famous and influential work, *Culture and Anarchy* (1867-1869). Arnold diagnoses the "condition of England" in terms of a spirit of liberty that finds its expression "in doing what one likes," in an excessive faith in mere machinery (from technology to governmental measures), and in the struggle among the three classes that had emerged, the aristocracy, the middle classes and the working classes (the barbarians, the philistines and the populace, as he put it). He accordingly suggests a reconciling remedy to the potential for anarchy that lies in the tendencies of the interested "ordinary self" that "does as it likes," that remedy being found in the "best self" that is forged by culture:

> Well, then, what if we tried to rise above the idea of class to the idea of the whole community, *the State,* and to find our centre of

light and authority there? Every one of us has the idea of country as a sentiment; hardly any one of us has the idea of *the State*, as a working power. And why? Because we habitually live in our ordinary selves, which do not carry us beyond the ideas and wishes of the class to which we happen to belong. . . .

But by our *best self* we are united, impersonal, at harmony. We are in no peril from giving authority to this, because it is the truest friend we all of us can have; and when anarchy is a danger to us, to this authority we may turn with sure trust. Well, and this is the very self which culture, or the study of perfection, seeks to develop in us; . . . So that our poor culture, which is so often flouted as so unpractical, leads us to the very ideas capable of meeting the great want of our present embarrassed times. We want an authority, and we find but jealous classes, checks, and a dead-lock; culture suggests the idea of *the State*. We find no basis for a firm State-power in our ordinary selves; culture suggests one to us in our *best self*.[3]

This extended citation adequately encapsulates the core of Arnold's argument. Arnold draws at once from a political tradition which, deriving principally from Hobbes, views civil society as the site of the war of each against all and finds its counterpoise in the authority of the monarch or the state, and equally from the tradition we have already discussed, of Schiller and Coleridge. Arnold synthesizes the regulatory and the formative functions of the state, recognizing that the state cannot operate once the franchise has begun to be extended unless it assumes an *ethical* function. That is, its coercive powers meet all too much resistance if it cannot forge a citizenry that willingly submits not only to the criteria of "disinterest" but to a dominant paradigm of the well-formed subject. The principal characteristics of that subject are, again, that it should develop over time and through cultivation; that it should seek wholeness or harmony of its faculties against the narrowing effects of specialization and class perspectives; that its highest expression lies in judgment or critical spectatorship rather than in the unbalancing absorption of political activism; and that it should find in the state its natural representative.

What is perhaps most striking about this model is its enduring effectivity: even in the present moment it informs a spectrum of political and social assumptions across a broad spectrum of conservative to liberal and even socialist thinking. We would ascribe that effectivity to the model's capacity to integrate the formation of the subject with the emergence of the state as a form so that the identification of the ethical subject with the state is enabled by their identical logic: both are historical forms that develop, that provide sites of reconciliation and disinterest, and that are mutually representative. The state's priority lies in its greater development and consequently in its right to assume the function of "educing the citizen" in every individual. Arnold is entirely cognizant of this complementarity of the cultivation of the "best self" and the authority of the state: he is, after all, recasting Schiller's dictum that the state represents the "archetype or canonical form" of the individual. Culture is not a mere supplement to the state but the formative principle of its efficacy. It is, in other terms, a principal instrument of hegemony. And it is so, precisely because it is not merely a contingent or *ad hoc* intervention of a bureaucratic agency, but is constitutive of an "idea," of the state and of the subject, that founds and disseminates the "common sense" of an emerging representative democracy.

Ian Hunter is doubtless substantially correct to point out that the institution of literary teaching, or "English," as a major "discipline" in education and as the principal site of cultural formation is a late emergence, long post-dating Arnold's interventions. It is no less certain that Arnold, as the first Professor of Poetry at Oxford to lecture in English and as a lifetime poet and literary critic, was extremely influential in that development. But that is still to mistake the instrument for the concept. Culture, for Arnold, is by no means restricted to the reading and judgment of literature and *belles-lettres*, however important that may have been to him. Culture is primarily for him and for other Victorian thinkers a question of the harmonious development of the faculties and of the ethical judgment, a fact which does much to explain how such thinkers could be appropriated by Raymond Williams and others as offering a critique of capitalism.[4] Our position is, however, that Arnoldian and cognate arguments do constitute a partial criticism of capitalist social relations, of their effects, but, unlike the working-class writings of the 1830s, or of Marx and others in the 1860s, they nowhere touch on the critique of capital itself. Furthermore, Arnold's work is embedded in practice and in theory with the work of the state and is instrumental as well as influential in the forging of a new mode of hegemony.

Indeed, Arnold's reports on education, composed in his capacity as a government School Inspector in the ten-year span preceding the publication of *Culture and Anarchy*, in no way contradict that work's guiding assumptions. This is not surprising of *Schools and Universities on the Continent* (1868), which was composed exactly contemporaneously. What is more noteworthy is the extent to which *The Popular Education of France* (1861), a report for the Royal Commission on Education based on Arnold's tour of French, Dutch and Belgian schools in 1859, already formulates the principal concepts of his better known *Culture and Anarchy*. In his introduction to the report, which he republished as a separate essay entitled "Democracy" in 1879, he states in germ his later and more extensive conception of the state as representative of the nation's "best self" and as responsible for the education of the people:

> The State is properly just what Burke called it—*the nation in its collective and corporate character.* The State is the representative acting-power of the nation; the action of the State is the representative action of the nation....
>
> .... Only, the State-power which it employs should be a power which really represents its best self, and whose action its intelligence and justice can heartily avow and adopt; not a power which reflects its inferior self, and of whose action, as of its own second-rate action, it has perpetually to be ashamed. To offer a worthy initiative, and to set a standard of rational and equitable action—this is what the nation should expect of the State; and the more the State fulfils this expectation, the more will it be accepted in practice for what in idea it must always be.[5]

"Democracy" is thus striking not only for its early anticipation of Arnold's subsequent terms, or for its insistence on the responsibilities of and need for the exercise of "State-power," particularly in relation to the extension of education, but also in its grasp of the *exemplary* function of the state as representative of the people. The state ideally represents the nation's "best self," and represents that self to the individuals who compose the nation even as it represents them. In this representative exemplary function, the state becomes ever more adequate to its "idea" and in itself already educates the people in the realization of their individual selves. The state is already the paradigmatic exemplary teacher, functioning in relation to the populace in a way that repeats the ethical architecture of the classroom whose emergence Ian Hunter documents in *Culture and Government*. In this, Arnold's work, from *The Popular Education of France* through *Culture and Anarchy*, grapples with the principal question of middle-class reformers through the century, that is, how in a time of political reform to educate the people to be willing to be represented.

Arnold's formulations are, then, in effect only one culmination of an "idea" that had been driving middle-class reformists and bureaucrats for some time, an idea that is crucial to the form and vision of education as it is actualized and gradually made uniform. We have suggested before that such an idea of the *exemplary* function of the teacher underlies the very geography of the classroom that earlier reformers like Kay-Shuttleworth espoused. That form spatializes not only the operation of disciplinary surveillance, but facilitates the eliciting of response—that is, the interpellation of students—as it were by their own consent. As so many other institutions will come to do, the topography of the classroom simultaneously symbolizes and naturalizes the temporal and ethical advance of the teacher over the students, thus making self-evident the necessity for a narrative of development by which the child becomes human through the unfolding at once of moral and intellectual powers. That narrative, without which the emergence of educational institutions of a hegemonic rather than coercive kind could hardly be envisaged, was already in place in bourgeois thinkers like Schiller, Coleridge, and Wordsworth; it achieves a canonical recapitulation in Arnold's thinking. As we shall now see, it informs equally the contemporaneous work of John Stuart Mill and, with no less significance, the advocates of working-class self-education through whom hegemonic and working-class goals came to converge.

Mill might, in many respects and from other perspectives, be regarded as Arnold's virtual antagonist. A utilitarian by formation, a reformist deeply interested in the machinery of government and the economy, and a thinker far more "advanced" as a liberal than Arnold would ever be, Mill nonetheless may better be regarded as a thinker whose work converges with Arnold's within the limits of the emerging dominant paradigm that practically determines the formation of the liberal state in Britain. From the moment of his famous encounter with Wordsworth's poetry that pulled him out of severe depression, Mill's utilitarianism became deeply informed by conceptions of cultural improvement drawn principally from the same direct sources as Arnold's—Samuel Taylor Coleridge and Wilhelm von Humboldt, younger friend and admirer of Schiller and later Prussian Minister for Education. Mill's 1840 essay on Coleridge not only contains the germs of his later *Considerations on Representative Government* (1861) and its critique of Coleridge's division of the forces of Permanence (landed property) and Progression (mercantile capital), it offers a far-reaching endorsement of Coleridge's arguments for national education and for its role in the stabilization of the state.[6] Mill's debt to the German tradition of aesthetic self-cultivation, and in particular to von Humboldt, is no less evident in his enormously influential *On Liberty* (1859). As with *Culture and Anarchy*, *On Liberty*'s epigraph is drawn from von Humboldt but it is in the chapter "Of Individuality" that the German philosopher's work emerges most explicitly as fundamental to Mill's thinking about the relation of individual to society.

Our point here is that the ideal of the individual for Mill, no less than for Arnold, is that which culture, in the large sense of ethical and aesthetic development, alone can produce. Mill thus paraphrases von Humboldt's principles early in the chapter:

> that "the end of man, or that which is prescribed by the eternal or immutable dictates of reason, and not suggested by vague and transient desires, is the highest and most harmonious development of his powers to a complete and consistent whole"; that, therefore, the object "towards which every human being must ceaselessly direct his efforts, and on which especially those who design to influence their fellow-men must ever keep their eyes, is the individuality of power and development"; that for this there are two requisites, "freedom and variety of situations"; and that from the union of these arise "individual vigour and manifold diversity", which combine themselves in "originality."[7]

Full individuality is equally the unattainable goal of personal and human history, devolving as so often on the occasional manifestation of genius that lies beyond what culture can systematically produce.

The precepts on individuality that Mill extends from von Humboldt —above all, that "Individuality is the same thing with development"[8] (*Considerations on Representative Government*)—are not without implications for his thinking on world history (and therefore on British imperialism) and for his understanding of the necessity and limits of extended franchise. Both lines of thinking are taken up and largely interwoven in his subsequent *Considerations on Representative Government.*[9] For *Representative Government* is in part a world-historical overview of the conditions of possibility for the emergence of different modes of government, culminating in representative government as the form most conducive to both liberty and progress. It is no less a study of the conditions of possibility within the modern state for extended rights to political representation, conditions which fundamentally repeat the paradigms of Mill's world-historical overview. That is to say, that the development of politically capable or autonomous individuals within the nation-state repeats the development of nations and peoples capable of self-government in world history.

Mill's categories are familiar. The lowest stage of humanity, the savage, is incapable of government of any kind, let alone "civilization," and requires the force of an extraneous authority to prepare it for higher forms of government:

> Thus ... a people in a state of savage independence, in which every one lives for himself, exempt, unless by fits, from any external control, is practically incapable of making any sort of progress in civilization unless it has learnt to obey. The indispensable virtue, therefore, in a government which establishes itself over a people of this sort is, that it make itself obeyed. (RG, p. 394)

This is not only a condition relating to political capacity, but one which equally addresses the capacity for disciplined and continuous labor:

> Again, uncivilized races, and the bravest and most energetic still more than the rest, are averse to continuous labour of an unexciting kind. Yet all real civilization is at this price; without such labour, neither can the mind be disciplined into the habits required by civilized society, nor the material world prepared to receive it. (RG, p. 394)

Mill does not shirk the implications of these assertions, which lead to an acceptance of slave societies and despotism as necessary stages in the development of the first requisite of civilization, discipline. A little further on, this will become also a justification for British imperial policies of the kind emerging in India, since despotism itself rarely provides the terms by which a people may transcend the state of slavish obedience:

> A despotism, which may tame the savage, will, insofar as it is a despotism, only confirm the slaves in their incapacities. Yet a government under their own control would be entirely unmanageable by them. Their improvement cannot come from themselves, but must be superinduced from without. The step which they have to take, and their only path to improvement, is to be raised from a government of will to one of law. They have to be taught self-government, and this, in its initial stage, means the capacity to act on general instructions. What they require is not a government of force, but one of guidance. (*RG*, p. 395)[10]

The capacity for self-government emerges accordingly as the result successively of the rule of force and the rule of law, supplemented in the latter stage by the enlightened guidance ("the government of leading strings" [*RG*, p. 396]) of ethical superiors.

This model holds no less for the relation between individual development and the capacity to be represented in Britain itself, both historically and, as we will be mostly concerned to show, contemporaneously. There are significant parallels, to begin with, between Mill's characterization of the English working class and his characterization of the savage:

> It is not sufficiently considered how little there is in most men's ordinary life to give any largeness either to their conceptions or to their sentiments. Their work is a routine; not a labour of love, but of self-interest in the most elementary form, the satisfaction of daily wants; neither the thing done, nor the process of doing it, introduces the mind to thoughts or feelings extending beyond individuals; if instructive books are within their reach, there is no stimulus to read them; and in most cases the individual has no access to any person of cultivation much superior to his own. (*RG*, p. 411)

Both the savage and the worker are enthralled by the immediate satisfaction of need, subject to discipline, by need or force, which obliges them to perform a labor that is not of love. But there the similarity ends, though the terms of its interruption remain caught up with the figure of development. For the working class subject of nineteenth-century Britain lives in the conditions of an already developed society which affirms, if not the principle of representation, the principles of constitutional government and the "rule of law." There is in modern England a fully differentiated and articulated political sphere at every level of society, through participation in which working-class subjects can extend their narrow perspectives. Contact with that sphere, and with more cultivated minds within it, serves to raise them from their habitual and narrow considerations:

> It is by political discussion that the manual labourer, whose employment is a routine, and whose way of life brings him in contact with no variety of impressions, circumstances and ideas, is taught that remote causes, and events which take place far off, have a most sensible effect even on his personal interests; and it is

from political discussion, and collective political action, that one whose daily occupations concentrate his interests in a small circle round himself, learns to feel for and with his fellow citizens, and becomes consciously a member of a great community. (*RG*, p. 469)

The right to representation becomes, for Mill as for so many other reformers, dependent upon development, the simplest and most fundamental evidence of which is literacy and numeracy. Accordingly, as Mill succinctly puts it, "universal teaching must precede universal franchise" (*RG*, p. 470). There is perhaps no more reduced formulation of the mid-century belief in the intimate relation between education, as the elemental mode of cultivation, and the right to representation.

More directly concerned with "practical" measures, and more progressive in the extent to which he would apply those measures, Mill nonetheless shares with Arnold a common fundamental conception of culture and cultivation. At one in this with the principal bourgeois thinkers of the time, from Christian Socialists like F. D. Maurice and Charles Kingsley to John Ruskin and even Thomas Carlyle, Mill and Arnold elaborate a theoretical and practical understanding of culture that has less to do with the inculcation of a literary canon than with the larger and harmonious development of human powers, historically and individually. This much was already apparent in Williams's *Culture and Society*. But what they add that is less evident in other bourgeois thinkers of the time, with the possible exception of Ruskin, is the preoccupation with the link between the state and culture, one which is virtually genetic, according to Arnold, and intrinsic to the "ideal form of government," following Mill. The state of culture determines the form of the state.

Equally common to both thinkers is their hostility to what Mill terms "an inveterate spirit of locality" (*RG*, p. 417). For Mill this is at once an historically specific condition—one he attaches immediately to "the Asiatic village" and later to Europe's Celtic populations—and an instance of underdevelopment in the general sense, applicable to both historical and individual conditions.[11] For Arnold, it is figured rather in the "Alien," the man of culture who is estranged from whatever his class of origin as a cosmopolitan rather than a locally interested subject. Mill, indeed, envisages a similar figure in his argument for the weighting of representation towards the intellectuals as a class dispersed across the nation and unable to effect representation on the basis of local superiority of numbers.[12] In both, what is finally at stake is not the consideration of class or region in themselves, but the necessity to produce *abstract* citizens for a state which is, as idea, everywhere yet nowhere. The insistence on abstraction is directed at shaping a population that is less and less divided by differences of place and interest and more subject to a national "common sense." It is also informed by the view that the development and cultivation of the individual brings into being a disinterested and universal perspective. That is, abstraction of the citizen from his embeddedness in particularity produces the ethical subject for the state.

We would contend, then, that the work of Arnold and Mill, far from being peripheral or belated with regard to the work of the state, not only has a significant practical impact, but informs an emergent and increasingly dominant common sense regarding representation. Indeed, their work finally brings to bear the influence of Coleridge and of German thinkers like Schiller and Wilhelm von Humboldt on the somewhat incoherent interventions of earlier middle-class reformers. They theorize a "principled" and practical model that links a particular form of education to a new social imaginary, a rationalized civil society that represents the "end" of human history. The state, itself a kind of universalizing abstraction from society, is in this model far more deeply antagonistic to the social and political cultures of radical social movements, dependent as they are on the linking of local and particular practices into a mobile and decentered mass movement. Accordingly, the impact of Mill and Arnold is not "merely" ideological, in the sense of an ideational legitimation of a status quo, but material in its effects: the concept of development and its imbrication in the narrative of representation that we have discussed earlier in this book becomes in these writers encoded at the very heart of cultural, educational and political discourses and institutions. Their deep antagonism to the social logic of Chartism follows from the way in which their work consolidates and naturalizes a division of spheres of practice that determines the direction and dominance of specific emergent forms of modern society. It makes self-evident the distribution of social practices into spaces of education and culture, labor, and politics precisely at a time when the last possibilities of a resistance to this hegemonic division of the social were available. This we shall discuss further below.

In retrospect, of course, the force of these writings has entirely overshadowed the working-class discourse on education that was so vital and so radically alternative in the 1820s and 1830s and up through the waning of Chartism. Indeed, it proves even now difficult to read the alternative back through the saturation of our presuppositions with the self-evidence of propositions on culture and politics which were consolidated in Arnold, Mill and other middle-class liberals and radicals of the mid-nineteenth century. Chartists were concerned with the unity of the economic and the political in the same space, as with the necessity for an education that recognized and was part of that unity.[13] They insisted on the necessity for the autonomy of working-class institutions, as a means to protect the integrity of a working-class analysis of social and economic relations and of an alternative conception of culture and values. All these concerns were occluded with the ascendancy of the notion of a universal (state) education that was to be the precondition for representation. Above all, it is the very possibility of alternatives that seems to vanish from the discourse on education: educational practice is increasingly to be devoted, even for the most advanced liberals and radicals, to processes of normalization. Its function is to train the young for participation in forms and institutions which are already established and outside whose terms it is virtually impossible to imagine social relations and cultural forms that are not simply aberrant or primitive. To imagine or to exist otherwise flies in the face of a common sense which designates the alternative either to be violent, as in Arnold's working-class "mobs," or to be less than fully civilized, as in Mill's savages, colonial subjects and working classes. The question for us is, how it was possible for so powerful a hegemonic regime to emerge, and whether its possibility was in fact intrinsically bound up with the "failure" of the politicized working classes of the period to maintain the alternatives envisaged by their immediate forebears.[14]

INTELLIGENCE AND DISCIPLINE

Where the absence of any extensive discourse on cultivation in the radical papers of the 1830s was especially striking, equally so is the prominence of that discourse in the working-class journals of the 1860s. It must instantly be remarked that there is a huge difference between those radical papers and the working-class journals, one that can be summed up by saying that while the radical papers of the 1830s are largely produced by participants in emergent working-class movements, the working-class journals of the 1860s are predominantly *for* rather than *of* the working classes. They represent, in effect and sometimes even literally, the triumph of a very Coleridgean notion of the "clerisy," being on the one hand often written by clerics like Rev. H. Solly, a major contributor to *The Working Man*, or Rev. Charles Rogers, who "conducted" *The Workman's Friend*, and, on the other, performing throughout the function of the clerisy, that is, "to educe the citizen from the native of the soil." As Rev. John Anderson puts it in an article in *The Workman's Friend* entitled "Thoughts on Education":

> "Education" means to feed or foster—also a drawing out, or a leading forth—and you will never rightly educate any man unless you succeed in drawing out, and leading forth the powers of his mind, the dispositions of his heart, and the elements of reverence and of adoration that lie deeply buried in his soul.... Education is commonly taken to mean "schooling"—and even little of that.... But what about moral training? What about disposition and habits? What about educating the mind to give itself a better education than any schools can give?[15]

The echoes of Coleridge are clear here, as in the innumerable articles on education that saturate journals like this or the more lower-middle-class-oriented *Sixpenny Magazine*. The emphasis tends to fall on a new conception of working-class autonomy: education is regarded as a continuing process dependent on the primary formation of a *disposition* towards continual and ethical self-formation.

The autonomy thus granted lies less in the collective work of specifically working-class organizations, espousing a particular and class-oriented mode of social analysis and cultural forms, and more on the assumption that men and women of all classes can participate in a common ethical project. Not only the financial benevolence of the wealthy, but the exemplary function of the "parson," as in the instance of such writers or of the man of superior culture, enters into the core of working-class educational institutions. This assumes the beneficial effects on the formation of a national culture of a downward dissemination of knowledge and cultivation predicated on a class-unconscious set of educational institutions. A significant element of the radical autonomy of working-class institutions desired by figures like Robertson and Senex survived, however, and markedly inflected the way in which the middle class appropriated them. The educational associations of the working classes—clubs, Mechanics' Institutes, evening schools, and so forth—are ideally financially self-supporting and self-governing, even as they are subject to a patronization that is a far cry from that envisaged by Morrison for the Mechanics' Institute of the 1820s. Rev. Solly writes in 1866 of "the general principles that have guided the promoters of Working Men's Clubs and Institutes":

That working men should be led to do as much as possible for the undertaking themselves; to give as much, both in time and money, as it is right to afford; that they must be made to feel responsible for the good management and success of the society, and, therefore, be brought to feel that it is *their* club, and that they are their own masters there; that we have to help, but not to govern them— to supplement, in short, their efforts, not to supersede them.

   ... [T]hey must be made ... the means of improvement and elevation for those who seek, or will accept, such benefits, by giving a common meeting-ground in a sociable way, for working men and persons of higher culture and larger information—opportunities, in fact, to interchange ideas, either by chatting round the fire, or in more systematic form, in the class and lecture room.[16]

Under a new and less conspicuous form of patronage than the Mechanics' Institutes of a former generation, these institutions for working-class self-education are nonetheless to be subject to what is the familiar pedagogical trick of the Socratic method. The institutions are aimed at producing the desire for self-education, and thus continue to be distinct from government or religious schooling for children, but the conception of education seems no longer to be cast in class-specific terms. "Gentlemen" are encouraged to visit and to bring with them their knowledge and their examples and, accordingly, education which is *by* the gentlemen and *for* the worker must appear as the by-product of a combination of chance and the self-motivated curiosity of the working-class subject:

   a gentleman who, in a thoroughly unpresuming manner, with a kindly heart, drops in as a *guest*, not as an overlooker, can often set the talk a-going in a very pleasant, natural way. Perhaps he takes up a newspaper, and having read a paragraph, mentions some anecdote, or personal adventure of his own, bearing upon it, inviting his neighbour to do the same. Or he brings a map, engraving, or diagram to illustrate events referred to in the newspapers. Another evening he may bring a microscope, or stereoscopes; and in one corner of the room, so that nobody need come and look unless they like, he entertains and converses with those who have not found amusement elsewhere. Another evening somebody else brings the skeleton of a bird or of the human hand, and engages those who care to join in an interesting palaver on the structure and uses thereof. Another night, a bullock's eye may be dissected, and a highly amusing evening may be the result; decidedly more popular and attractive, as well as more promotive of the main object of the Club—viz., "good fellowship"—than any amount of mere lecturing.[17]

The unintentionally comic (yet somehow sinister) effect of such democratic subterfuges should not distract from their fundamental relation to the constitutive illusion of democratic pedagogy: the appearance of autonomy on the part of the learner subjected to the "positional superiority" of the pedagogue is preserved by the shared performance of a mutual project, of open-ended discovery. Unlike the work of the initial Mechanics' Institutes and the *Mechanic's Magazine* of forty years earlier, it is less the content than the *form* of education that now comes to count. We emphasize here the "shared" nature of the project in order to try to highlight the strangeness of the transformation, now so "self-evident" in the fully Althusserian sense of the term, from a suspicious and resistant radical discourse on education to an apparently willing, even deferential submission to pedagogy. For it is as if, at least within the purview of these journals, a new representation of the working-class subject, one that is primarily *moral* rather than political, is inseparable from a desire to be educated. It is also, in the words of Christian Socialist F. D. Maurice, an education directed at making "men know that they are persons," rousing the worker "to be a man."[18] This discourse is no longer only the property of the middle-class and aristocratic reformers; it is evidently embedded in working-class self-representation in both political and personal rhetoric.[19]

This transition is self-consciously marked as dating from a period "twenty years ago," that is, to the moment at which Chartism's peak has passed. Rossiter traces the formation of the Working Men's College under the direction of F. D. Maurice, precisely to the stalwart London tradesmen who sought to marshal the potential disorder of Chartist demonstrations.[20] But the same transitional moment is equally marked by self-described working-class writers. In one lengthy essay that runs through two issues of *The Working Man*, a "Lancashire Lad" narrates the foundation of the exemplary Royton Temperance Seminary, attributing it to the young men who stood aside from the activism of their fellow workers in the Chartist disturbances of 1842. His account is worth quoting at some length:

> After the first day [of "the plug drawing riot," designed to stop the operations of the mills] some few factory lads of Royton

determined that they would not go any further with the turn-outs,
but wait quietly in their own village, until they might be allowed
to go back to the mills. They met in the room in which they were
accustomed to hold their temperance meetings, and read and
talked over matters there.... The members [of the Temperance
Seminary] were all lads, some one or two of the dozen being, perhaps, twenty-two or twenty-three years old. Their subscription
was, of course, small. In a very short time they doubled their numbers, and when the mills were opened again, they determined to
continue the little educational work they had commenced.[21]

Here and elsewhere in the articles, the "Lancashire Lad" furnishes an
invaluable picture of working men's culture at the time, emphasizing
the hardship of their work at sixteen hours a day, yet at the same time
affirming both the survival of their "poetic" sensibilities towards their
environment and the insistence of a working-class literate culture that
drew them to find "occasional half-hours when we might steal away
to the boiler room ... or hide ourselves in the murk and steam
between the 'beeks' at which we laboured, and there enjoy such books
as we could then obtain." These books included Byron, Burns and
Scott as well as biographies of men like Isaac Newton or Benjamin
Franklin. The article also shows the ways in which working men's
institutes came to be disseminated: before long these lads hear of the
Temperance Seminary that had been established at the nearby village
of Royton and decide to take a pilgrimage there to get ideas for establishing their own institution. There they discover both the circumstances of its formation and the way it is organized, thus returning
"with a much better idea of how working men might educate themselves than we had before entertained."

But despite this glimpse of the continuities of working-class culture
and of its institutions, what is equally apparent is the distantiation of
the self-educating working classes from what, in their eyes, now appear as mobs. Before recounting the foundation of the Royton Temperance Seminary, the "Lancashire Lad" is at some pains to describe the
appearance of the "turn-outs" in which its founders declined to participate. That account is at once sympathetic and ambivalent:

[Given their wretchedness, one] cannot help wondering that want
should not have driven them to greater extremes than those to
which they resorted. What they did was to proclaim a grand holi-
day; even those for whom there was work should play; and so the

agitator, I suppose, hoped to find in the still gaunter, hungrier bodies of his clients speeches as moving in their eloquence as Marc
Antony found in the dead body of Caesar. Mobs formed, sometimes
five, sometimes ten, and sometimes twenty thousand strong, went
from one mill to another, demanded that the workers should turn
out, and join them in their pitiable designs.

As a rule, property was respected: where the demand of the mob
was not at once assented to there was some violence, a rush at the
boiler, the plug drawn, and so their design accomplished. It must
have been a sad sight to have stood somewhere and watched the
passing of one of these mobs. The gaunt looks of men and women;
their unkempt hair; the wild feverish excitement which kept them
together; the pikes and sticks, upon which loaves of bread and
huge lumps of bacon were hoisted aloft—the ironical banners of a
starving multitude—to have seen all these things would have
pained one's heart.[22]

In this portrait by one member of the working class of another seg-
ment of the working class as starving savages, we see a repetition of
middle-class or liberal constructions at the same time as we are presented with the possibility of understanding different aspects of the
"mob": the logic of its organization and its mobility; the practical non-
violence and "respect for property" which belies the aura of deliberate
violence and uncontrollable frenzy perceived by the non-participant
observer; the *ironic* carnivalesque that pervades the demonstration.

The historical narrative of the articles, however, tends toward a
reformist perspective: working-class self-education supersedes the
logic of the "mob." The final passage of the second article draws a
clear conclusion:

The fact that self-education is still pursued in Lancashire as I have
described; that even in the midst of that distress for which England
felt and did so much, there should be lads so resolute in their pursuit of knowledge under difficulties as even then to win their way
to college scholarships—these things deserve to be known, so that
a right knowledge may be had of the efforts and aspirations of the
best of our working men. This is not the place in which I might
properly allude to the political tendencies of the day; if it were, I
should like to remind certain statesmen whose voices are now and
then heard in the House of Commons, and certain journalists
whom I might name, that they could as easily do justice to the

great class from which the men I have described above have risen,
as they now do injustice.... [T]hey might encourage and help
where now they only embitter many who are conscious of their
own rectitude, and of the severe struggles which they have made
in the past, and are making still, to win for themselves the spoils
of knowledge, and so enable them to exercise wisely the rights and
privileges of citizens.[23]

In the midst of "political tendencies" leading to the second Reform
Act, and of the massive working-class demonstrations throughout the
country, the "Lancashire Lad's" comments are to the point. They are
also the staple of arguments for political reform and for extended,
national education for the working classes: a new conception emerges
of the working-class subject as sufficiently developed to receive the
franchise, not on account of absolute rights, but on account of his
transformation from "savagery" to morality through education. In
effect, education is the process which draws the subject from immediacy and particularism, from a class perspective, to a general perspective through which he can be united, not only with middle-class
reformers, but with the nation as a whole, as citizen.

Thus the very meaning of the mass demonstrations for reform
turns, from the reformists' perspective, away from that of the Chartist
mobilization which was deeply invested in a specifically working-
class culture and social organization. The specter and legacy of
Chartism certainly persist: the mass demonstrations not only owe
much of their organizational structure to the memory of Chartism,
they signify the potential of a politicization of class or trade movements. Conservative organs like *The Times* are made anxious by the
middle-class reformer John Bright's articulation of the political possibilities of mass organizations:

The burden of [Mr. Bright's] speech last night was that this organization [the Trade and Friendly Societies] should be strengthened
and made universal, so that all the power which the artisans are
able to use in industrial matters, in questions of labour or wages,
should be available for political action.... We must confess that
we hold the opinion Mr. BRIGHT stigmatizes, and believe it is not
desirable that the Trade or Friendly or Co-operative Societies
should be used as political machinery, either to obtain a Reform
Bill or for any other political purpose.... The chief cause of post-
ponement of Reform from year to year has been the tacit fear felt

by the middle class of this very organisation of the artisans. Their numbers, their docility, we might say their submission to their leaders, the ease with which they can be wielded, and the strength they possess to coerce both their employers and the recusant members of their own body, are the causes of the passive hostility with which their claims have been met, and which they may rest assured is stronger among the higher trading class which employs artisan labour than among country gentlemen or the members of professions who are popularly supposed to furnish the Tories of the country.[24]

The language and the reasoning may seem familiar in the wake of Thatcherism, but *The Times* misses the point that Bright, himself a member of the middle classes, is making in his speech, recorded verbatim on another page of the paper. Bright points to the political possibilities of Trades Unions and other such associations precisely to distinguish their peaceful, disciplined and constitutional agitation from the specter of "secret societies, and oaths and drilling, and arms and menace, and a threat of violence and insurrection."[25] Working-class "organisation" has already been inflected with a new meaning, one which combines discipline, order and patience with intelligence and education, constituting an ethical claim to citizenship.

That the correspondent to *The Working Man* on self-education goes under the name of a "Lancashire Lad" is not merely coincidental. Throughout both the debates on education and those on the extension of franchise, appeal is constantly made by advocates of the working classes to the exemplary docility of the Lancashire cotton workers during the economic crisis in their industry occasioned by the American Civil War and the Northern blockade of Southern cotton. One Mr. Leicester, a glassblower severely castigated in *The Times* editorial just quoted for inciting violence, in fact is reported in the same paper as having invoked precisely this example of moral self-discipline:

> When the people were described as unfit for the franchise the word "Lancashire" should be whispered. By their conduct during the cotton famine the people of Lancashire saved the country from sad dishonour, and prevented the Americans from venting their ire upon us.[26]

The Working Man had already made a similar point, equally connecting intelligence, morality and patriotism:

The old test of fitness for franchise was power. Like property, those got it who were able, and those kept it who could.... Now it transpires, in the great progress of the age, that rent does not represent mind, that patriotism lies deeper than rates, and that the highest qualities—those of intelligence and worth—exist among the common people as abundantly as among the uncommon; and the great experience of the cotton panic showed that the most needed qualities for self-government resided with the populace. The working classes of Lancashire acted well.... They acted as Englishmen and patriots should act, because they were intelligent. The cheap press had made them men of sense. The intelligence of the people now rules.[27]

The behavior of these workers during this crisis clearly betokens for sympathetic observers the waning of a threatening and radical working class and the emergence of a self-disciplined, "respectable" and patient working class. The turbulent worker has become a docile body in the fullest sense of the term "docile," that is, willing to be taught. Ultimately, this new figure of the docile, cultivated working class would indeed help to bring about the accession of a large number of working *men* to the franchise and therefore to full citizenship in consequence of the 1867 Reform Act. At the same time, it provided a strong motivating force in the passage of the 1870 Education Act.[28]

NEW TOPOGRAPHIES

Inevitably, we are struck by the regularity with which the matrix of concerns with the franchise and industrial discipline (the capacity for the one being reciprocally dependent on the capacity for the other) turns on the question of education. An apparently novel desire for education on the part of the working classes becomes at once the sign, the forge and the product of a new moral self-discipline which would be the ground for their political responsibility. This is not at all the same as Thomas Spence's or "Senex"'s arguments that the knowledge already in the hands and minds of the "producers of wealth" is quite adequate to the running of a factory, a parish or a state. On the contrary, it is deeply informed by a notion of knowledge as formation and of formation as a process preparatory to political responsibility. At the same time, as many thinkers on education were pointing out even then, the focus is nowhere, among capitalists or among workers, on the kind of technical education that characterized continental developments, especially in Germany and France. The emphasis is not on the need to produce a more skilled and technically-advanced working class for what was already the most advanced industrial nation in the world. It was, rather, on the regulation of a disciplined national citizenry. By 1860, accordingly, the discourse on working-class education is knowingly engaged with precisely the kind of Coleridgean principles of cultivation that were absent from radical thinking in the 1830s.

Less evident, but critical to our inquiry as to how working-class organizations moved from a radical critique to a widespread acceptance of educational provision, is the extent to which such thinking assumes the very differentiations of the social space that we found to be surprisingly absent in radical discourses of the 1830s. This is, of course, at one level an effect of the emergence of a skilled working class that is both generally better paid and, in consequence of a series of factory acts regulating hours and conditions of work, permitted considerably more extended leisure time. But that material difference is ideologically consolidated within the familiar discourse of culture which is in turn stabilized in relation to those domains of social or familial, economic and political activity from which it is resolutely distinguished. What has emerged is not simply a new working-class subject, the object of cultural pedagogy and moral self-representations, but a new set of social spaces that are increasingly differentiated and defined by both economic rationalization and legal interventions by the state. What we will argue in this section is that the emergence of the "respectable working-class subject," of whom the "Lancashire Lad" is a prime instance, is not simply explicable in terms of the receding radicalism of the Chartist movement and the co-optation of the "aristocracy of labor." Rather, these factors must be seen within the context of an unanticipated and unprecedented transformation of the social which normalizes the very division of spheres that 1830s radicalism resisted in its writings and its political practices. Within this new *socius*, the subject is divided into the political citizen and the economic worker, each operative in different social spaces.[29] What enables their suturing is the moral formation of the subject by a cultural rather than a technical pedagogy which, in turn, occupies its own distinct sphere. That pedagogical space becomes the site of a convergence between local and class-specific institutions for self-education, institutions which have their roots in an earlier radicalism, and the gradually expanding state project for universal education. The possibility of that convergence is given on the one hand by the congruence between the goals and forms of education that emerge in each kind of institution and, more importantly, by the need for working-class organizations that can address in their own terms a state that is increasingly the site of political formation and action. As in the simultaneously emergent trade unions, we can see the various forms of working-class education as engaging social and political struggle within the terms of an overarching hegemonic state. What those terms dictate is that docility or respectability replaces ownership as the condition for an extension of the franchise that will not threaten rights of property; yet, while this entails a considerably less radical agenda, moral formation is at the same time the condition for the recognition or interpellation of the worker as political subject. To understand this simply as a process of co-optation is to neglect the novelty both of the forms of hegemony that working-class movements confronted and of the differentiation of spheres within which they now had to operate.

Oscar Negt and Alexander Kluge have described the activism of the English working class leading up to and through the Chartists as "not merely the attempt at a political revolution but the beginnings of a social revolution." Crucial to this analysis is their observation that "[t]he forms of the public sphere associated with this did not exclude as backward any spheres of society. The movement spread from the industrial centers across the whole country."[30] Their analysis leads us to make two remarks on the radical work of the 1830s and the forms of the Chartist movement that we have already discussed. The first has relation to the spatial dimensions of the labor movements: rather than being concentrated in urban centers, as even those of the 1790s were, the social imagination that informs Chartist writings like Lovett's *Chartism: A New Organization of the People* includes rural as much as urban England. In doing so, however, it does not merely seek to found a nationally based mass movement; it refuses to assume a singular notion of material and historical progress in terms of the advance of a capitalist mode of production or its legal and political apparatuses. The conception of backwardness enters only with regard to the political institutions of the governing classes, and that with relation to their effects on social relations, not to their appositeness to given modes of production. The decentralized nature of Chartism is based on the principle that the question of production and its ownership and direction remains open, subject to economic and political transformation by the laboring classes; one sphere of production cannot therefore be envisaged as more advanced and therefore politically superior to others. If this is in part the influence of the historical experience of an artisanal intellectual class, it nonetheless answers to a moment at which a mass movement of working people believed that what was at stake was not merely political enfranchisement, but a fundamental transformation of an emergent mode of production.

Our second point is that not simply did the public sphere implied by English radicalism and Chartism not exclude particular social sites; it involved an autonomous public sphere in its media and, more importantly, in its implicit conception of social space. Nor is this public sphere "alternative," in the sense of opposing itself self-consciously to a previously formed and dominant one. For the bourgeois public sphere, despite its often analyzed roots in the eighteenth century, had still to reach its own specific forms and to consolidate its concomitant legal and political apparatuses. Moreover, its regulation of working-class social life was as yet sporadic and reactive and had not reached the degree of legal and "moral" penetration that it gradually achieved in the course of the century. As we have shown in relation to education, that process had far to go and the middle classes had yet to achieve sufficient political strength to be able to ensure success over aristocratic and conservative resistance to reform. Under these circumstances, it was still possible for the multiple forms of working-class social life to constitute a sphere of public activity that was not determined by incorporation into or reaction to the bourgeois public sphere.

Richard Johnson has argued that working-class movements had their own "radical repertoire": "They embraced, after all, a theory of economic exploitation, a theory of the class character of the state and a theory of social or cultural domination, understood as the formation of social character."[31] We have suggested in Chapter 2 that distinctive to that public sphere is an apprehension of social life as a unity: economic and political experience are one, as is the experience of education, and the notion of a separate and feminized domestic sphere, distinct from that of labor, is rarely evident in any modern sense. The very concept of culture is absent, as we discovered, precisely because such a differentiation of human practice into the reflective and the productive or interested was inconceivable within the terms of a working-class public sphere. By unity, of course, we do not mean to suggest what would be in any case necessarily a retrospective abstraction, a seamless and integrated totality. Rather we wish to define a social imagination that necessarily escapes both our experience and our conceptual framework, namely one in which what seem the proper and self-evident differentiations of spheres of practice, formal and analytic differentiations that constitute what we now understand and experience as "society," were absent, or at most emergent and by no means determinant. Within that imagination, a fluid and interrelated set of practices coexist and intersect, none of which can in any simple way be designated as economic, political, cultural, and so forth. As Johnson says of working-class educational projects at this moment:

> Typically, then, educational pursuits were not separated out and labelled "school" or "institute" or even "rational recreation." They did not typically occur in purpose-built premises or places appropriated for one purpose. The typical forms were improvised, haphazard and therefore ephemeral, having little permanent existence beyond the more immediate needs of individuals and groups. Educational forms were closely related to other activities or inserted within them, temporally and spatially. Men and women learned as they acted and were encouraged to teach their children, too, out of an accumulated experience. The distinction between "education" (i.e., school) and not-education-at-all (everything outside school) was certainly in the process of construction in this period, but radicals breached it all the time.[32]

The volatility and undecidability of discussions concerning representation, or the priority of education or politics, are symptomatic of the incommensurability of the experience of this kind of fluid social sphere with the other it comes to confront, the no less emergent public sphere of a consolidating bourgeoisie, for which notions like representation and development were crucial to the formation and differentiation of its subjects and institutions.

The moment of uncertainty in that confrontation does not last long. The various Factory and Poor Law Acts described in Chapter 3 marked, as we suggested, the consolidation of middle-class hegemony in its control of political legislation and the legal system, a hegemony that gradually extends into and shapes the whole sphere of education and culture. That hegemony was continually backed by a coercive force that even the largest of mass meetings could not hope to defeat— in the end, Chartism was defeated by a superior force that it could not confront without losing its essential popular form of public openness. Its brief turn towards military training and the hoarding of weapons could never have been in tune with the mode of politicization that had emerged among the people, any more than it could have overcome the military power arrayed against it. As the sympathetic General Charles

J. Napier remarked: "They talk of physical force. Fools! We have the physical force, not they. They talk of their 100,000 men.... What could 100,000 men accomplish with their pikes and flintlocks against my cannon shot . . . ?"[33]

The defeat of the Chartists by the legal and the violent means of the state may have spelt the end of the effectivity of the working-class public sphere through which they operated. That implies, however, only that a mass movement of this nature, with its transformative orientation, would be unable to access the public sphere that had consolidated in its wake and through which significant social power was articulated. It does not mean that its terms necessarily were erased entirely, perhaps only that they were occluded and misrecognized. Both the continuities and the force of occlusion can be traced. The continuities are clear, in the form of the emergence of a powerful association of trade unions and cooperative guilds whose possibilities were given both by the legislative regulation of employment and labor and by the emergence of a skilled "aristocracy of labor" which replaced the artisanal class and became the source of most of the movement's intellectuals. *The Times* certainly, if negatively, acknowledges the continuity with Chartism when it so baldly publishes its anxiety about the repoliticization of the unions. The continuities are no less clear in the persistent emphasis on the need for working-class education, wherein a Chartist and Owenite heritage inflects reform-oriented middle-class policy as well as informing the self-conception of workers themselves. A. E. Dobbs, indeed, regarded with some justice both elements of English labor movements as having a continually interwoven history:

> Two movements, whose relations to one another were not yet apparent, developed during the earlier half of the century; one consisting in an attempt to diffuse useful knowledge and to provide for the higher education of mechanics, the other connected with the growth of political and trade organisations which were a product of social unrest, and in which sections of the working class are found here and there struggling to evolve their own forms of instruction and to express their ideals. Both movements were experimental; and their breakdown, which became evident in the forties, formed the starting-point of a fresh series of developments which produced lasting results. A new phase of adult education commenced with the revival of co-operation at Rochdale in 1844, the appearance of an association formed by the Society of Friends

in 1847 which became the pioneer of modern Adult schools, the
rise of Working Men's Colleges during the next decade which was
followed by the Club and Institute Union of 1862, and the reform
movement stimulated at the oldest seats of learning by the
Commissions of 1850, which prepared the way, at least indirectly,
for University Extension.[34]

Our own conclusions tend to concur with Dobbs, rather than with the
more recent tendency to regard the Chartist movement as having
failed and what followed later as simply a retreat from the class antagonisms of the period leading up to 1850. The occlusion of Chartism's
legacy is intensified by a historiography which assumes the viability
and operability of one mode of class antagonism at all times and
regards any shift from that mode as a volitional error. But such a position depends on a retrospective assumption of political superiority and
represents an elementary failure of dialectical inquiry.

Most accounts of the emergence of state education in the second
half of the nineteenth century and of the extension of the franchise
that takes place during that period tend to emphasize the force of middle-class reformism and the intent to extend hegemony over an assim-
ilable working class. The forms of control of the bourgeois state were
by no means any more continuous than those of the working class,
and in fact involved, as we have already suggested, a considerable shift
from direct domination to hegemony. In the first half of the century, a
conflict is still manifest, usually along the Tory/Whig divide, between
those who continue to adhere to notions of direct domination and dis-
trust the advancement of working-class intelligence as potentially
subversive of order, and those who, to the contrary, see education as a
means to more effective social control over an increasingly mass society. These debates are manifest in a whole series of discussions concerning attempts to extend education to attempts merely to expand
the provision of libraries, just as they are in debates on the franchise.
Emphasis then falls on the major bourgeois figures in those debates
and their influence on their outcome in the form of state institutions
and legislation. What is seen as occurring in keeping with this model
is a gradual extension of middle-class ideology into an increasingly
well assimilated working class. Dobbs describes the nature of that ideology in his history of educational reform:

> Liberalism, in dealing with popular movements, relied in practice
> on middle-class leadership and introduced patronage in a new

guise. Insistence on the capacities common to all classes resulted in the hypothesis of a standard type of humanity, represented for all practical purposes by the business man of the period, to whom education was a means to "advancement in life." It would seem almost to follow that the distinctive characteristics of particular social groups signified little more than differences in degree of mental development; and the defect of certain forms of education addressed to adult artisans in the first half of the century may be explained, in some measure, with reference to this assumption, which overlooked essential differences of outlook and experience.[35]

We have outlined the developmental paradigm of liberal thinking above, and indicated the ways in which an "idea" or concept gradually came together with material institutional possibilities that it shaped and legitimated. Rather than extending discussion of this liberal intervention, we wish to explore here the exigencies on working-class organizations that determined their convergence with that paradigm and their virtual replication of its institutional forms.

Chartism was the product of a period of exceptional fluidity, even experimentalism, in an emergent industrial society which was, after all, the first of its kind. That fluidity attached both to the gradually consolidating bourgeois state and to the forms and principles of radical movements. On the cusp of a proletarianization whose tendencies were not yet clear, and in the wake of a "moral economy" whose assumptions had become inoperable in the face of wage labor and urbanization, social activism took place in as yet indeterminate spaces and in a mixture of familiar and ad hoc invented forms. In the period between the first and second Reform Acts, however, the principal endeavor of parliamentary domestic legislation was the regulation of social space. This ranged from the control of hygiene and urban design, the control of contagious diseases or the containment of working-class spaces of gathering and pleasure to the legislative regulation of factory conditions, hours of labor and restrictions on the employment of women and children. The intent was not only regulative, however. It combined regulation with the constitution of new institutions and spaces. The period accordingly saw the emergence of a modern police force and the expansion of reformatory institutions, of schools, and of medical institutions. It saw also, in consequence of an increased amount of leisure time due to the Factory Acts, spaces for working-class leisure which were at once closely monitored and licensed and productive of new forms of activity—public houses, music halls, clubs and, of course, educational institutes and union meetings and demonstrations. All of these were, to a large extent, transformations of existing practices, but took on a new meaning in differential relation to other reconstituted social spaces. Not least of those new spaces was the domestic space, slowly reconstituted as a feminized space of consumption and reproduction rather than production, and increasingly important as a site for the daily reproduction of ethical values and discipline.[36]

In the reconstitution of working-class social movements in the wake of Chartism's suppression and splintering, what had to be encountered was a materially different social terrain with marked divisions of the spheres within and by which subjects were constituted in particularized ways. Within the work we have been examining, these divisions are rarely analytically conceived; they appear rather as assumptions about conduct that are the traces of the ideological "material practices" embedded in particular sectors of the social space.[37] Their history is not legible as the consequence of the suppression of other forms of social life or, where that presses to the surface, the forms of life in question are seen as outmoded. The "Lancashire Lad" offers a most articulate instance of this in his alienated description of the Chartist mobs as belonging to an irrevocable past as well as in the self-evidence of his account of how the young men of Royton seized on a space and a time distinct from labor as the locus for self-education. Indeed, these assumptions seem strange to us only through the recovery of a prior social formation. But the new set of social spaces appears as self-evident not only within individual consciousnesses; it belongs with the very matrix of assumptions that structures the intentions of the journals and of the institutions they describe and promote. The clubs and institutes furnish spaces for working-class male recreation (and where women's institutions of this type exist, they offer quite distinct modes of domestic education).[38] The Rev. Solly is at pains to emphasize their recreational nature in his description of their functioning, and this role as sites of leisure sets them against both the work space of the factory and the no less recreational space of the home.[39] In that space of recreation, the "human" is free to develop in ways that succeed in unifying the divided economic and political aspects of the person at an always potentially higher level. The contradiction that prevents that unification lies in the fact that it is through a discrete sphere and its specific practice, cultivation, that the unification beyond spheres must be achieved.

That contradiction ensures that mass working-class movements in the 1860s cannot pass beyond the sphere of the political into a radical social transformation and as such can be seen to converge with bourgeois interests, constituting a fundamental element of the "ethical state." If the Chartists undertook a social revolution, the efforts of the 1860s by no means tended towards a political *revolution*, which would in any case, from a proletarian perspective, be a contradiction in terms. A revolution cannot be fought out on terms and in spaces constituted and defined by the dominant class. But what was occurring, what could only occur under the conditions of the 1850s and 1860s, was not an attempt at revolution but the effort to constitute some room for counterhegemonic maneuver within the now crystallizing bourgeois state.

In that effort it is not difficult to discern the legacy of Chartism: the hard-won capacity to organize mass movements and demonstrations, to seize public space dramatically, on the one hand, and on the other, the drive to cooperative self-education which leads ultimately to the desire for stable and perpetuable institutional structures that would preserve the precarious and often interrupted gains of the class. It is often assumed that the latter project was the work of William Lovett and his supporters and the sign of a moderate compromise with middle-class reform. But the same ideas are as ardently espoused by Chartist radicals like George Julian Harney and Ernest Jones, the latter of whom only half-ironically acknowledged from the dock that "the schoolmaster is the best policeman!"[40] There was no necessary reformist bent to the will to self-education; the cooperative principles of working-class institutions remained in opposition to the individualist drive of middle-class education and doctrines of "self-improvement." But what had been radically changed was the social sphere through which Chartism organized: the possibility of an unmediated intersection of educational, political and economic thought and practice was no longer available and working-class movements were obliged to reshape their forms and accordingly their contents to grapple with a social space dominated by bourgeois institutions and a public sphere saturated with the terms of liberal hegemony: culture, representation, and development. Even the most prescient of social analysts, Karl Marx—the first volume of whose *Capital* was published the same year as the second Reform Act (1867)—had yet to find a way to link his critique of capital fully to his earlier critique of political rights in "On the Jewish Question," a project in which, in any case, he made only sketchy progress and whose political aspects were unavailable to English speakers till the 1930s. Nineteenth-century debates were conducted in an "astounding ignorance" of what Marx had written.[41]

We have tried in these chapters to indicate the profound linkages between social spaces and ideological concepts that constitute the transformations and consolidations of hegemony. We have hoped above all to affirm the existence and significance of other social spaces and their material effects on the possibility of counterhegemonic forms of practice. Hard as such practices may be to read and comprehend from the vantage point of subjects formed under a very different mode of hegemony, difficult as it may be to read them without condescension and without relegating them to the junkyard of "prehistory," we have sought to read radical suspicion of culture, education and the state as part of a repertoire of historical possibilities. That social imaginary may have been defeated and forgotten in the triumphal procession of "progress," but its insights become available once more to a materialism concerned not to lose sight of the occluded openings and other spaces of a past never quite lost to history.

CONCLUSION

The Future Imperfect

Interests, Disinterest

Throughout this book, we have argued that in *Culture and Society*, Raymond Williams accepts the terms of the culture and society couplet inasmuch as he sees himself as the heir and transmitter of the cultural tradition, believing this to be capable of a socialist inflection. So close an identification led Williams to overlook the ironies of his placement as a radical intellectual within the "culture and society" tradition; some of these ironies are discussed further in the Epilogue. What should be indicated here is that Williams's predicament is a symptomatic not a personal one. In ways that Gramsci explored in detail, modern states lay claim to a "disinterested" transcendence of politics, while in practice operating through the articulation of these same interests. The tension that this contradiction creates can be relieved only by a dividing of the subject in general and not least of the intellectual critic of culture. This is to say that contradiction inheres not just *between* a traditionally-defined culture on the one hand and the dehumanizing effects of capitalism on the other; it also inheres *within* the intellectual, no matter how radical that intellectual may wish or claim to be.

Our more immediate concern with the argument and bearings of *Culture and Society*, however, is that its author's self-positioning in that couplet leads him to overlook the fact that some of the very thinkers to whom he awards places of honor within the tradition themselves connected culture not so much to society as to the state. They had good reasons for doing so, which we have been concerned to uncover. If our account carries conviction, then culture does not, or does not just, designate a discursive formation in opposition to

145

society. Increasingly, culture became charged, rather, with representing the fundamental common identity of human beings. By virtue of
its differentiation from the social and economic aspects of human
lives, it could become the agency and the site of citizen-formation.
Culture increasingly came to designate and to frame a set of institutions along the locus of society's intersection with the state. These
institutions occupy spaces of their own; for the very formulation of
the space or spaces of culture demands its actualization in pedagogical
institutions whose function is to transform the individual of civil society into the citizen of the modern state. In Williams's sense the axis
here is programmatic: culture can oppose society only in theory, and at
best with an anticipatory and ever-deferred utopianism, whereas in
practice culture can and does serve the state quite directly.

How it can do so is more readily seen once the state is understood
in Gramscian-Hegelian terms as the "ethical state." What had to take
place for the "ethical state" to emerge was a shift from a conception of
representation based on communities of interest to one based upon an
ethical, developmental narrative. As culture comes to represent the
fundamental common identity of human beings, so the state is conceived, ideally, as the disinterested ethical representative of this same
common humanity. The idea of culture produces the consensual
grounds for representative democracy and the liberal settlement by
annulling individual differences and drawing or eliciting the formal or
"representative" disposition in every person out of the real, particular
conditions of that person's life. The state came to be regarded as the
collective representative of an abstract ethical quality—the danger
implicit in Hegel, as Marx in the 1840s had recognized.[1] As to culture,
Schiller's influential argument posits a developmental narrative of
representability, in the course of which discernment and disinterest
can be internalized more or less effectively. Ethical formation makes
possible the approximation of individuals (who might otherwise be
unrepresentable) to the archetype of "humanity" the state is said
to represent.

What is practically required to effect this ideal is the moral formation of the citizen by an increasingly specialized cultural, not technical, pedagogy that occupies a separate space in its own right—a space
that is steadily delineated by the state for society.

The shift involved here is of enormous significance. The trajectory
memorably traced out by Albert Hirschmann,[2] for whom the (political)
play of the passions is displaced by the (social) articulation of interests
as capitalism kicks in and seeks legitimation, does not end but *only
begins* with the assertion of interests—an assertion which, after all,

cannot guarantee its own harmony or even unison (as Hegel was aware). Civil society is construed in the pages of Hegel's *Philosophy of Right* as the sphere of fragmentation, discontinuity, disruption and "immediacy." By its very nature it separates and disperses its human constituents, among whom blocked encounters are the only encounters possible. To see the problem with this ethical shortfall in mind is to see what has to be involved in its solution: reconnection, reconciliation, reunification, these being what the state is supposed to provide. But they are also and *at the same time* what culture is supposed to provide. In this sense, it is scarcely surprising that arguments about the state and arguments about culture underwent shifts at the same time. This is not of course to say that arguments about culture or the state are homologous or interchangeable. It is to say that they are complementary, that they work together and in tandem. Hirschmann's trajectory proceeds, once the state/civil society couplet is taken seriously, in the Gramscian-Hegelian direction of the "ethical state" that is founded and dependent precisely on the *dis*interest, or on what Arnold called the "best self," of the citizen, which it is the work of the state to educe in every subject. Culture elicits a particular form of subjectivity, a capacity for disinterested reflection which makes the state's mediation of conflicts among interests possible as well as necessary.

Our own arguments have tried, however, to counterpoint this intellectual and canonical history of culture and the state not only with a critique of its assumptions, but also with a study of the contestations that took place around the gradual institutionalization of its precepts. We have sought to demonstrate how the virtual self-evidence that underwrites the continuing if fragile influence of that cultural narrative was won only through the often violent suppression of alternatives. Disinterest and the social disengagement of the intellectual are rooted in violence and maintain their conditions of possibility through the alternating exercise of coercion and hegemony. Even when critique focuses on the practical investment of supposedly disinterested teaching and research in the armature of coercion—defense contracts, nuclear research, military and policing technologies—we must bear in mind no less the violence *always* implicit in the very foundations of the "liberal" institutions of intellectual life. This recognition of contradiction in no way contributes to the traditional politics of the alienated intellectual, a ruse directed at the disavowal of social power, but provides the conditions for a transformation of relations between intellectual workers and movements for social change. It offers possible grounds from which to rethink materialist solutions to the problem of the intellectuals that we broached in our introduction and will return to presently.

The collaboration that goes into this book originated, in large measure, from our common concern with Marx's political thought. Marx's writings from the 1842–3 period are particularly apposite here, for they set out, in admittedly sketchy fashion, what is involved in the political and social topography that has informed our account. In the introduction to his "Contribution to the Critique of Hegel's Philosophy of Law,: for example, Marx observed that it is only the modern bourgeois age that posits "the separation of civil society and political state as two different spheres, firmly opposed to each other."[3] Whereas among the ancient Greeks "civil society was a slave to political society," in modern, bourgeois society the opposite priorities obtain. In the Greek *polis*, no particularly or exclusively political sphere existed apart from the daily conduct of life and work. Public life was the "real content" of individual life; the person who had no political status was a slave, an *Unmensch*. "In Greece the *res publica* was the real, private concern, the real content of the citizen ... and the private man was slave, i.e. the political state as political was the true and sole content of the citizen's life and will."[4]

In the Middle Ages, by contrast, the "private sphere" came to acquire political status in its own right. "Property, commerce, society, man (i.e. private man, the serf) were all political: the material content of the state was given by its form; every private sphere had a political significance or was a political sphere" directly. If property was paramount in feudal society it was so because its distribution and transmission were directly political matters. To be sure, this congruence between "the life of the people" and "the life of the state" obtained because of the fundamentally unfree character of the former: the medieval world was the "democracy of unfreedom, accomplished alienation."[5] Nevertheless, a person's place within the overall division of labor appeared as an intrinsic, personal quality. People were held to relate to each other as the bearers of various social, political *and* personal qualities, various productive *and* individual characteristics. During the Middle Ages, "the classes of civil society and the political classes were identical because the organic principle of civil society was the principle of the state" at the same time. In medieval times, that is, "the political state in distinction from civil society was nothing but the representation of nationality."

On the one hand, then, "the old civil society [in the Middle Ages] had a directly political character" (if an unfree one): "the elements of civil life, such as property, the family, and types of association had been raised, in the form of lordship, caste and guilds, to being elements of political life." But on the other hand, what Marx calls "political emancipation" (read bourgeois revolution):

> released the political spirit, which had been broken, fragmented and lost, as it were in the various culs-de-sac of feudal society. [Political emancipation] gathered up this scattered spirit, liberated it from its entanglement with civil life, and turned it into a sphere of the community, the general concern of the people independent of these particular elements of civil life. A particular activity and situation in life sank into a merely individual significance, no longer forming the general relation of the individual to the whole.[6]

Marx's observation here is above all prescient: the separation of spheres which it identifies as being constitutive of modern bourgeois society was by no means consolidated by 1843. Still less had it been consolidated in Britain during the 1830s, as we have been at pains to show. In that decade, working-class radicals were operating on the assumption of the unity of the political and the economic within the same singular public space. (This does not, of course, make them in any way "medieval." It makes them transitional, and highly aware of their placement on the cusp of change.) Their concern, as we have seen, was with an education that recognized and was a constituent part of that same topographical unity. The differentiation of "the reflective," of "the productive," of "the interested," is a differentiation that was inconceivable within the terms of the working-class public sphere of the Chartist period. A fluid, interrelated set of practices coexisted and intersected to make up this public sphere, but none of these can be designated as exclusively "economic," "social," "cultural," or "educational." The working-class writings from this period were, to the contrary, severely critical of the assumption that knowledge is valid only when mediated through institutions defined by their distance from the conditions of labor. Such "validity," after all, disenfranchises knowledge from what would be termed the merely "local" conditions of oppression, while it simultaneously "emancipates" educational institutions from class positions. Working-class radicals of the Chartist period were not slow to see that there is, or ought to be no separation between economic, political, social and educational self-management. They tightly maintained their refusal to accept the division of education, politics and economics into separate, if inter-influential fields. Instead, education was understood as something that ought to be directed at the attainment of political knowledge of the kind that was to have enabled the transformation of the material conditions of the working class—a transformation that was to have freed them from oppression.

Modes of confrontation and contestation changed as what needed to be confronted and contested changed its form. The regulation of recreation in the wake of Acts controlling hours of labor becomes crucial to discourses on education and to discourses on the franchise alike. Conversely, the regulation of social and educational space in the 1832–67 period coincided with the institution from above of new spaces, new institutional forms that have been parts of our lives ever since. Sites of resistance were eroded, in large measure because state consolidation and regulation pushed politics, economics and their respective grievances apart, effectively uncoupling one from the other. Education itself became part of this process of differentiation by being officially redefined and imposed as an activity that took place in a designated set of separate institutions and specialized practices.

To this day our lives—as Marx foresaw over 150 years ago—are dominated by a kind of division of labor and a concomitant division between "the political," "the social," "the economic," "the cultural," "the educational," "the domestic." Nor are these equally weighted: the notion that "the personal is the political" can become a reflex of despair rather than an effective appraisal of our condition. The slogan holds only where it proposes the identity of the "personal" and the political, not where it effects a displacement of political discontent into the private sphere. In particular, it is according to the logic of what Marx, in "On the Jewish Question," called "political emancipation" that the state became the collective representative of an abstract ethical quality, a kind of distillate siphoned away from people's real differences in civil society. Division or difference itself becomes acutely problematic whenever equality or equivalence is asserted as a political value, and we still live in a world where this is so. On the one hand, the glaring contradiction between economic inequality and a supposed political freedom that is mostly the freedom of the market, obliges the state to use its coercive power more often and more openly in the service of "stability," international and domestic. This demands equally the eradication of vocal alternatives to capitalism of any kind. On the other hand, nationally and globally, ineradicable differences among social groups and their respective cultural formations continue and intensify both negatively and positively. Whether based in the perpetual forms of racialization in capitalist societies or on the persistence of national and local cultures, whether expressed through explicit ideological discourses or the dissonance of social domains that have never been completely assimilated, the insistence of difference everywhere challenges the regime of equivalence and "political emancipation."

THE INSTANCE OF WILLIAM MORRIS

It should not surprise us that oppositional echoes of a kind that recall Chartist contestations of this same division into exclusive spheres of activity can be traced later in the nineteenth century. Even in the tradition that Raymond Williams explored, echoes of the alternative are active but often overlooked. We have focused hitherto primarily on the oppositional modes of *working-class* activism; here we will focus on the critique of culture as it emerges from the contradictions between aesthetic and social interventions. We take as our example William Morris, a thinker and activist who seemed to Williams to fit neatly into the "culture and society" tradition. Williams's underestimation of the radical force of Morris's grasp of the function of culture is symptomatic of his failure to apprehend the differentiations of social space as anything but given. Thus he medievalizes and aestheticizes Morris's actual challenge to that space into the all-too familiar "arts and crafts" sanitization of his revolutionary socialism.

Carlyle and Ruskin, says Williams, "could find the 'organic' image only in a backwards look: this is the basis of their 'medievalism' and of that of others. It was not, in this tradition, until Morris that this image acquired a distinctly future reference—the image of socialism. Even in Morris ... the backward reference is still important and active."[7] Much hangs here on *which* of Morris's writings we are talking about. At a certain point in their history, after all, the "backward reference," however "important and active" it may have been up to that point, was *displaced* by the "future reference" of socialism (or, to use the term Morris himself increasingly preferred, communism). And it was displaced *in its entirety*. E. P. Thompson's central claim about Morris is very different from Williams's (and far closer to our own): "The Romantic critique of industrial capitalism, the work of Ruskin and Carlyle, assumes a new kind of significance in the light of William Morris's transformation of the tradition."[8]

Morris, far from reinflecting them, in fact overturned the central assumptions of his romantic precursors. Far from basing his argument on some notion of art or culture that either had been disrupted or was to attain its fruition in a new, more glorious future, Morris defined this future in political, not aesthetic terms, and for the sake of its attainment would not shrink from *abolishing* art. The word "visionary" does scant justice to so foundational a shift. "No, rather than art should live this poor, thin life among a few exceptional men, despising those beneath them for an ignorance for which they themselves are responsible, for a brutality that they will not struggle with—rather than this, I would that the world should indeed sweep away all art for a while. . . . [R]ather than the wheat should rot in the miser's granary, I would that the earth had it, that it might yet have a chance to quicken in the dark."[9]

In the 1880s Morris suggested more than once that the arts must die with capitalist society, and could only be reborn when socialist society had been established for many years. "The old art is no longer fertile," he wrote, "no longer yields us anything save elegantly poetical regrets: being barren it has but to die, and the matter of moment now is, how it shall die, with hope or without it."[10] If the source of art was "pleasure" in labor, then socialism is the necessary precondition of its rebirth. "It is possible," said Morris, "that all the old superstitions and conventionalities of art have got to be swept away before art can be born again; that before that new birth we shall have to be left bare of everything that has been called art; that we shall have nothing left us but the materials of art, that is the human race with its aspirations and passions and its home, the earth: on which materials we shall have to use these tools, leisure and desire."[11] Again

> [t]hese aspirations of the people can only be born from a condition
> of practical equality. . . . I am so confident that this equality will be
> gained, that I am prepared to accept as a consequence of the process
> of that gain, the seeming disappearance of what art is now left us;
> because I am sure that will be but a temporary loss, to be followed
> by a genuinely new birth of art, which will be the spontaneous
> experience of the pleasure of life innate in the whole people.[12]

In short, "Anyone who professes to think that the question of art and cultivation must go before that of knife and fork . . . does not understand what art means."[13] As to education, "it must of necessity cease to be a preparation for a life of commercial success on the one hand, or of irresponsible labour on the other. It will become rather a habit of making the best of the individual's powers in all directions to which he is led by his innate dispositions: so that no man will ever 'finish' his education while he is alive."[14] Morris's critique of education itself is deeply connected to his critique of the division of manual and intellectual labor: "The division between the intellectual and the worker, the man of 'genius' and the people, the manual and 'brain' worker, would be finally ended. . . . Just as physical labor would no longer carry with it any indignity, but rather the reverse, so intellectual labor at the expense of true exercise of bodily faculties would appear as an abuse of the fullness of life."[15] This is a key passage. Here, knowingly or not, Morris connects back his thinking with the working-class radical refusal during the long gone Chartist period to accept the bourgeois division of spheres as the basis of "education."

But Williams fails to acknowledge the specificity of Morris's intellectual and political leap. It is evidently more important to the Williams of *Culture and Society* to link Morris with Carlyle, Ruskin, and others than to do what Morris himself did, and separate him from the tradition they made up. It may even be that in linking Morris with Ruskin, in particular, Williams fails to acknowledge the specificity of either: it is at the very least noteworthy that none of Ruskin's authoritarianism or paternalism infected Morris.[16]

Williams quotes and glosses a passage from Morris's "How I Became a Socialist": "there were a few who were in open rebellion against . . . Whiggery . . . a few, say two, Carlyle and Ruskin. The latter, before my days of practical socialism, was my master towards the ideal." Morris's qualification, "before my days of practical socialism," is one that Williams effectively ignores. To Williams, "Morris acknowledges both the tradition and his extension of it."[17] This tradition appears to us, *per contra*, as something Morris, far from extending, actually repudiated. He self-consciously rejected, that is to say, that part of himself that had at earlier periods of his life subscribed to the tenets of Williams's "tradition." The Morris who appeals to Williams is the Morris who believed that "[i]t is the province of art to set the ideal of a full and reasonable life before [the workman]"[18] and not the Morris who, having recognized the fake-consolatory function of art so defined, intransigently went on to reject art. Not to put too fine a point on it, Williams tries to reinscribe Morris within a tradition of thinking about art that Morris himself had put behind him. "Morris," he insists, "uses the idea of culture, in particular in its embodiment in art, as a positive criterion: 'the true ideal of a full and reasonable life'."[19]

The result is that Williams glosses Morris's *Communism* out of all recognition. Socialism, Morris had written (quite reasonably), might "gain higher wages and shorter working hours for the working men themselves: industries may be worked by municipalities for the benefit both of producers and consumers. . . . In all this, I freely admit a great gain, and am glad to see schemes tried that would lead to it. But great as the gain would be, the ultimate good of it . . . would, I think, depend on how such reforms were done; in what spirit; or rather what else was being done, while these were going on." This, Williams insists, "is a familiar kind of argument, from the tradition, and Morris confirms it in its usual terms."[20] Again, "we realize the tradition behind Morris even as ... he gives a radically new application to its ideas. ... Morris is here announcing an extension of the tradition into our own century."[21] But, we must reiterate, Morris upon his conversion to revolutionary socialism was far less Janus-faced, and far more of a progenitor of twentieth-century and even contemporary developments, than such formulations would have us believe. He discarded a tradition Williams, perversely, would have him embody.

Williams's last reference to Morris in *Culture and Society*[22] contains an accurate statement for which nothing in the book's preceding account can have prepared us: that Morris's "socialism was of the revolutionary Marxist kind." This follows from nothing we have read about Morris up to this point. What should have been a central claim about Morris—it was one that Morris himself came to regard as central to his life and development—comes rather as a grudging admission, sandwiched into the bargain between two claims that are demonstrably untrue: that "Morris had linked the cause of art with the cause of socialism" (he had in fact severed the cause of socialism from the cause of art); and that "the terms of Morris's position were older (than Marxism), an inheritance from the general tradition which came down to him through Ruskin." Williams's next sentence, "The economic reasoning, and the political promise, came to [Morris] from Marxism; the general rebellion was in older terms," manages to sever "rebellion" from "political promise" in a manner that Morris himself, who linked the two by repudiating art, could not have found less congenial. He also reduces Morris's revolutionary arguments to mere aesthetic rebellion. The most that Williams will admit is that "Morris sometimes suggested that the cause of art must wait upon the success of socialism."[23] (Williams hastens to add that this suggestion "may well be wrong.") Williams's "sometimes," in any case, could be taken to suggest intermittency. Its usage here conceals the fact that once Morris had converted himself to this position, he held to it, with some tenacity, for the rest of his life. Williams writes that "the longing for identity of situation and feeling, which exerts so powerful an appeal in such writers as Morris, is merely a form of the regressive longing for a simpler, non-industrial society."[24] But why should this be so? As a statement not about "such writers as Morris" but about Morris himself, this is misleading enough to tell us much more about Williams. Even Williams's short discussion of Morris in *Resources of Hope* privileges the regressive, "medieval" aspect of Morris over the progressive, revolutionary aspect—which Morris himself, with no small flourish, espoused.[25]

Williams's misprision nonetheless allows us to reread William

Morris's writings as a moment in an ongoing dialectic of culture and politics within capitalist society, the dialectic not of culture and society, but an alternative movement of history that has been constantly marginalized by the apparatuses of the ethical state and its common sense. This movement, despite the occlusion that makes it appear discontinous and sporadic, has in fact a history that is both practically and theoretically traceable. If we reread Morris from this perspective, his work demands a rethinking of the place of culture within radical social movements rather than a confirmation of the "tradition." In this there are lessons that are instructive for the present as they are for the past.

Morris's communist writings are dialectical in their outlines, although Morris was himself no strict dialectician. Consistently, his negation of art or culture as a specialized activity taking place within a distinct sphere of production is sublated in its reemergence as an undifferentiated aspect of labor, a labor in turn reconceived as pleasure rather than constraint. This is as true of his essays as of his utopian fiction, *News from Nowhere*. In this, indeed, he is in accord with Marx's scattered reflections both on aesthetics and on post-revolutionary communist society. In this also are lodged both his difference from prior radical discourses and the conditions that limit his thinking, limits that have led a superficial reading to dismiss his writings as aestheticizing and medievalizing. His difference from the radical discourses of the first half of the century lies in the intervening consolidation of a theory and space of aesthetic culture from which, perforce, he had to depart but which was literally inconceivable before 1850. His vision of post-revolutionary society is very close to that of Thomas Spence but requires a far more extensive critique of the effects of the division of labor or "alienation" than Spence could possibly have envisaged. He shares with the Chartists and radicals of the 1830s and 1840s the conception of an undifferentiated social space, but unlike them must base it on a negation of differentiation rather than regard it as a still viable alternative. The end of the division of labor on which the integration of work and recreation and the end of politics are predicated is a post-revolutionary possibility rather than an alternative to still emergent capitalist social relations. At the same time, Morris is unstintingly opposed to reformist socialism, appositely termed "State Socialism" in *News from Nowhere*,[26] of the kind emerging in the 1860s. Precisely the kind of acceptance of state provision of education and cultivation that then came into being was anathema to him, however necessary that strategy may have appeared at the time. This antagonism to paternalist state intervention is no less what distinguishes him from Carlyle or Ruskin.

Morris's achievement, then, is to have proposed a dialectical movement, inseparable from social transformation, by which a now fully differentiated aesthetic culture, which at once displaces and specifies a category of human needs and pleasures, might rejoin the range of practices from which it had been separated. Such a dialectical movement is historical in itself and conditioned by an actual historical transformation of social spaces that we have discussed in previous chapters. Yet this condition also confines his social imaginary to a quasi-medieval negation of actual social relations. In part this is the personal and contingent result of his own formation among the pre-Raphaelite painters and poets who fetishized the attitude of medievalism. On another level, however, it is determined by an inevitable overestimation of aesthetic culture at a moment when it had appeared to many as the only practically available alternative space to capitalist social relations and the only imaginable analog for anticipating postrevolutionary conditions. And in this respect, Morris's imagination enacts a dialectical transmutation of Victorian medievalism from the authoritarian model of Carlyle, Ruskin or Tennyson, to one in which not only the abolition of alienated labor and capitalist modes of authority, but also the negation of industrial technology itself become the conditions for dereified social relations.

THE CULTURE OF SOCIAL MOVEMENTS

In the present moment, the anticipation of post-capitalist and post-patriarchal social relations is no less fraught with idealization, "nostalgic" or otherwise. Our own desire has been to undertake the task of contributing to opening the repertoire of historical possibilities rather than determining their proper ends, and we are not tempted to engage in utopian prognoses. We would suggest, however, that Morris's writings still constitute an extension of Marxist theory that has been largely ignored both within the "orthodox" Marxist traditions and by the majority of "cultural" Marxists from Lukács to Marcuse. Unlike Morris, whose argument for the abolition of art was aimed at destroying its masked instrumental function for the state and its compensatory role as autonomous space of freedom within capitalism, cultural Marxists have tended to view the aesthetic as the site for the affirmation of utopian desire or for the preservation of a residual subjective negation of capitalist social relations.[27] In effect, from Lukács on, cultural Marxism, in its emphasis on alienation, has preserved the function of art in bourgeois society. Orthodox revolutionary Marxism has tended, by the same token, to regard the end of the division of labor and the reduction of work as a deferred aim of post-capitalist society rather than the crucial means to the reconstitution of social relations, as Morris saw it. The fact that Communist societies did not address the issue of the division of labor concretely may have had as much to do with their eventual demise as their equally unrevolutionary centralization of production and political power, which, indeed, depended upon an entrenched division both of labor and of social spheres.

Arguments about the reasons not only for the demise of European socialist states and western revolutionary movements, but also for the simultaneous decline of the great institutions of "state socialism," the trade unions, are many and various. The latter arguments range from the corruption of union leadership and the unresponsiveness of their bureaucracies to workers' needs to the intensification of state assaults on labor organization and the accelerated mobility of transnational capital through the hyper-exploitation of "third world" labor pools or immigrant labor. To these arguments, all of which are crucial to the analysis of the present moment, we wish to add the contradictions embedded in the articulation of socialism with the projects of the ethical state.[28] We mean by this not only the assimilation of socialism to hegemony, but its structural reproduction of the social spaces of capitalism. The continued privileging—abstract as it has often been—of struggle in the economic sphere has not only subordinated other sites of struggle in the last few decades—feminist, anti-racist, ecological and so forth. It has continued to reify a concomitant mode of political subjectivity caught within the logic of representative democratic structures that emerged within the discourse on culture and the state that we have analyzed in nineteenth-century developments. The specific divisions within the modern citizen-subject that correspond to larger social divisions are confirmed rather than negated within these frameworks. Increasingly, this tendency has come into conflict with cultural and political movements that have not been primarily predicated upon economic analysis.

Thus far, our argument accords with a still indispensable work on social movements, Ernesto Laclau and Chantal Mouffe's *Hegemony and Socialist Strategy*, a work which has helped to clarify our understanding even where we disagree with its tenor. Our disagreement is, of course, in part historical: our work has shown that, far from displacing "*given* and relatively stable identities" within a context of clear antagonisms, the "democratic revolution" of the nineteenth century emerges from a highly fluid set of concepts and emergent social positions in which the boundaries of social space and subjectification were extremely "blurred." Indeed, we would argue that it was only out of the multiple possibilities of the early nineteenth century that the specific forms of representative democracy themselves became possible.[29] This is not to say, in reactionary fashion, that there is nothing new in the apparently unique conditions of the present, in which a destabilization of identities and a multiplication of politicized spaces tends towards the dissolution of "the differential positivity of the social" and the explosion of "the idea and reality itself of a unique space of constitution of the political."[30] On the contrary, we desire to extend the thinking of Laclau and Mouffe by bringing to bear our understanding of the historical dialectic of politics and culture on the theory of social movements and the practice of radical as opposed to representative democracy. This involves at once a set of theoretical, historical and practical considerations.

It is surprising to us that cultural forms play so small a role in Laclau and Mouffe's theorization of social movements, given the extent to which those movements have increasingly mobilized cultural antagonisms in their activism over the last decades. By social movements we intend, briefly, movements whose activism takes place across the ethical state rather than within the political state:[31] such movements are not determined by singular political or social issues, but multiply along the lines of intersection of various concerns or social spaces and forces; they are not regulated by any singular concept of political subjectivity or norms of practice, and accordingly do not occupy the space of "politics" as conventionally defined; they tend to branch rapidly onto contiguous issues, and may often seem, to programmatically informed theorists, to be sporadic and discontinuous. Such movements have been ubiquitous in decolonizing struggles globally and at every historical moment. But they have been critical in mobilizing opposition and alternative cultures within the major capitalist states also: mass movements like C.N.D. in Britain mobilized opposition to state nuclear programs, but intersected with and branched into contiguous environmental, anti-militarist and communitarian activism through the nineteen-sixties and seventies. Such activism was embedded in cultural forms of expression and in its turn contributed alongside socialist and feminist mobilization to the new formations of cultural resistance to Thatcherism and to racism through the eighties. In the United States, the history of the Civil Rights Movement and its legacy suggests a related dynamic of intersection and ramification, embodied in the continuous emergence of new modes and sites of struggle: feminist activism, the movements of racialized ethnic groups, radical environmentalism, each of which has to different degrees intersected with the others.[32]

In a peculiarly Leninist turn, such dynamics have been all too facilely interpreted as a destructive left-sectarianism or as particularism by New Left historians.[33] From our perspective, to the contrary, social movements gain their mobility and their dynamic from their transgression of the normative divisions of civil society and the state in capitalist society in ways exceedingly difficult for the hegemonic state to contain. Thus a prolonged engagement with state apparatuses may mean the "arrest" of social movements and their gradual incorporation, necessitating further transformation and reemergence at other sites in civil society. Consequently, the longevity of such movements is rarely grasped within conventional historiography, since their rhythm cannot be captured by narratives which emphasize punctual moments of victory and defeat within a progressive model of political history. As Paul Gilroy remarks, "[w]here the new movements keep their distance from the institutions of the political system," then the "distinction between human emancipation and the formal freedoms guaranteed by politics is constantly underlined."[34]

Throughout this work, we have emphasized the relation between radicalism and Chartism and the fluidity of an emerging state and civil society as against the later convergence of working-class discourse with a more powerfully hegemonic state wherein the divisions of civil society have begun to stabilize. We have also demonstrated how much those different conditions determined the acceptance of formal "political emancipation" and the retraction of democratic aspirations to the capacity to "be represented." That unique and unrepeatable period of transition has much to say now to oppositional politics at a moment when a new mode of production appears to be emerging and new transitions are taking place in the political sphere. But, unlike many contemporary social theorists, we would not overemphasize the degree to which a new mode of production itself determines the emergence of social movement politics.[35] Rather, we would argue, both civil society and the social movements that traverse it are in a more mediated relation to the new forms of capitalist production. The increasing porosity of the institutions of society to the inroads of both capitalist and state intervention, quite as much as the decline of older modes of labor organization, multiplies the openings for social movements as well as heightening the necessity to fight to maintain diverse spaces for alternative cultural formations that have little to do with class or formal political subjectivity.

But the logic of social movements also seems more comprehensible on account of the distinct intellectual history of theories of culture within which, indeed, our own project has been embedded.

Theoretically, the possibility of conceiving culture, not as a specialized activity of either aesthetics or recreation, but as a mode of articulation of practices that cuts across all the differentiated spheres of society, has been given by post-nineteenth-century disciplinary developments. Once again, as with Morris, these developments involve a conceptual dialectic which transforms both the meaning and the practice of culture as a set of signifying acts. Just as the concept of culture in its aesthetic sense was reaching its apogee and beginning to displace the general sense of "harmonious cultivation of the individual," an anthropological definition of culture as the "complex whole" of primitive societies was emerging. In effect, this division of the concept underwrites the distinction between non-modern "cultures," which are undifferentiated, and modern societies which are highly and progressively more differentiated.[36] This distinction is supplemented by a further distinction in the twentieth-century emergence of the concept of mass culture. Relegated by left-wing thinkers such as the Frankfurt School to the status of mass ideological delusion, "mass culture" (popular culture or the products of the "culture industry") is initially subordinated to the increasingly negative critical value of a residual aesthetic work: they are, as Adorno puts it, "separated halves."[37] But this double set of distinctions can be seen to undergo dialectical transformation as the concepts of ethnographic culture are drawn into relation with aesthetic concepts in the service of retrieving and reevaluating working-class or popular forms. Williams's own shift in *Culture and Society* from the concept of the whole person to that of culture as a "whole way of life" is one signal and influential instance of this process, despite his momentary inability to grasp the need to rethink the modes of aesthetic judgment that cannot actually accommodate the latter concept. Out of this dialectic emerges the conceptual vocabulary of contemporary cultural studies which has, in every possible sense, displaced and dispersed the aesthetic conception of the "whole" or "representative man."[38]

In much the same way that modern anthropology could not have emerged as a disciplinary practice outside of the global extension of imperial power and colonization, cultural studies as an interdisciplinary practice could not have coalesced without a corresponding historical shift. Rather than a simple dichotomization of "high" and "low" culture,[39] cultural studies increasingly takes as its object the highly differentiated forms of cultural production *and* reception that have emerged in time with the increasing intervention of capitalism in civil society, in the domain of "values" and recreation, and through the intensification of a commodification of culture that is indifferent to aesthetic distinction except in the instrumental form of audience and consumer stratification. While much cultural critique, from the Frankfurt School to Guy Debord's *Society of the Spectacle* and contemporary studies of transnational culture, has tended to regard this as an homogenizing extension of hegemony into the very recesses of the imaginary, we concur rather with those who would view this process as performing a dissolution of the distinct spaces of a hierarchical tradition of cultural practice and judgment. This cultural dispersion corresponds to the dispersion of the political sphere that Laclau and Mouffe theorize in *Hegemony and Socialist Strategy*. Culture can no longer be practically addressed in terms of a proper space, whether aesthetic or recreationary, that is distinct from other social spaces.

What we envisage, however, is a collapse of the culture/politics distinction that would extend Laclau and Mouffe's conception of social movements and of the passage to "radical democracy." As we have remarked, *Hegemony and Socialist Strategy* largely ignores the cultural dynamics of social movement practices. We do not mean by this simply the elements of cultural expression (songs, theater, murals, etc.) that supplement direct "political action" as distinct practices; nor do we mean the politicizing function of cultural interventions that interpellate and form subjects for a political struggle, as, for example, in nationalist movements. We seek to designate a dynamic wherein the formerly discrete practices of culture and politics, with their distinct modes of subjectivity, are dissolved into the very texture of social movements that cut across the differentiated spaces of liberal society and representative democracy. The social movement responds to the ideological divisions of space in civil society that are themselves increasingly inadequate to a capitalism that unfolds through every dimension of the social structure. Take for example the emergent environmental movements whose object is no longer a distinct category, "nature" in its residual externality to capitalist depredation, but the multiple effects of industrial pollution on urban as well as rural communities defined by racial and class status. For such movements, the antagonism to the economic exploitation of capitalism is inseparable from questions of domestic environment, health and child-rearing, racism and cultural difference, access to political power and the public sphere, and so forth. In such cases, social movements are not defined by pre-established subject positions but by the very dynamic of a counterhegemonic practice which defies differentiation into any given social space or direction by any singular end. What occurs here is not

the *articulation* of distinct social formations or modes of subjectification, which implies prior and discrete formations within the given differentiations of liberal society, but the insistence on a fluid and
resistant phenomenology of historically constituted intersections of
the effects of power and exploitation.

Our emphasis on the historical constitution of such intersections
refers to the evidence we find for the historical continuities that link
contemporary struggles across the appearance of a discontinuity that is
the product of a *historiographical* occlusion. Dominant historiogra-
phies, shaped on the left and the right by the logic of progress and differentiation, declare the successive extinction or incorporation of
counterhegemonic social movements.[40] Our contention, to the contrary, is that the counterhegemonic force of these movements has lain
as much in their refusal to succumb to differentiation as in their actual
discursive and material resistance to specific forms of domination.

Contemporary social movements preserve and are articulated
around their insistence on an undifferentiated space of practice that is
far more effectively counterhegemonic than any socialist project based,
as Laclau and Mouffe argue, on the "renunciation of the category of the
subject as a unitary, transparent and sutured entity" and its replacement by "antagonisms constituted on the basis of different subject
positions."[41] Their own belief that the path to radical democracy lies
not in "the abandonment of the democratic terrain, but, on the contrary, in the extension of the field of democratic struggles to the whole
of civil society and the state" ties them to an articulation of the already
constituted political and social subject positions of liberal or representative democracy. This leads to a rather static conception of the "articulation" of struggles which follow pre-given lines of distinction such as
race, gender and class, and are represented in corresponding and "equivalent" movements: "anti-racism, antisexism, and anti-capitalism."
The theory misses what we have shown to be the transgressive relation
of social movements to the fixed spaces and subject categories of liberal
civil society.[42] Our research suggests rather that any path through the
categories defined within the concept of representative democracy to
the alternative forms of radical democracy is at best improbable. In
other words, Laclau and Mouffe remain enmeshed within what Marx
termed "mere political emancipation"; to move beyond that to the
condition of "human emancipation" demands more even than what
Marx envisaged in the form of economic or class struggle; it demands
the dissolution of both categories, an economic and political dissolution striven for by an earlier radical tradition and dialectically re-
embodied in the potential of contemporary social movements.

Raymond Williams
and George Orwell

Nineteen Eighty-Four, says Anthony Burgess in his much lesser novel, *1985*, was "Orwell's revenge on the workers of 1948. They had let him down." This is an exaggerated, misleading claim. If anyone had let Orwell down, in 1948 or earlier, it was not the workers but the intelligentsia: the same intelligentsia that has "let him down" ever since, just as he might have foreseen. It is common to find Orwell regarded or portrayed as "the voice of political disillusion, of the inevitable failure of revolution and of socialism."[1] The words are those of Raymond Williams, although views similar to these have been expressed by any number of political and literary commentators, including E. P. Thompson and Isaac Deutscher, as well as Anthony Burgess.[2] The breadth of this consensus is cause for suspicion, but its strength has been such that anyone who would indicate that Orwell's "disillusion" was in fact less than complete, and that his admittedly idiosyncratic commitment to socialism was nonetheless genuine, is obliged to take the high road and painstakingly reconstruct Orwell's politics. This task is complicated by Orwell's own complications, as well as those of his critics. Raymond Williams, whose hostility to Orwell is a matter of record, and who will be used as a touchstone in what follows, is a case in point; but his views of Orwell strike chords and echoes in the unlikeliest places. The question of how Orwell came to be seen as the voice of political world-weariness is connected in significant ways with other, broader questions: how did he come to be regarded as the prophet or avatar of "totalitarianism," a construct used by cold-war

163

ideologues (though not by Orwell himself) to indicate the congruence of fascism and Stalinism? How did Orwell after his death get slotted into a bipolar view of the world, a cold-war rhetoric into which he signally fails to fit? There is considerable and bitter irony in the fact that *Animal Farm* and *Nineteen Eighty-Four,* the books for which Orwell is best remembered, particularly today, are still commonly thought of as signs of an opposition to *socialism* that Orwell manifestly did not express—however disillusioned he may have become with some of its intellectual proponents (and they with him, as the instance of Raymond Williams once again indicates).

Orwell continued to insist, after *Nineteen Eighty-Four* just as before it, on his commitment to democratic socialism as an alternative to capitalism as well as to Stalinism. In March, 1947, when work on *Nineteen Eighty-Four* was in full progress, Orwell published in *The New Leader* a lengthy review of James Burnham's *The Struggle for the World,* in the course of which he insisted that there is a "third way" between and beyond Burnham's stridently over-drawn alternatives of capitalism and collectivism.[3] He wrote of *Nineteen Eighty-Four* to an American reader (Francis A. Henson of the United Auto Workers) that "My recent novel is NOT intended as an attack on socialism . . . but as a show-up of the perversions to which a centralized economy is liable and which have already been partly realized in communism and fascism."[4] T. R. Fyvels's memoir of Orwell insists, rightly, that *Nineteen Eighty-Four,* whatever its shortcomings and ambiguities, "was not [the] savage attack on socialism" its publisher, Frederic Warburg, considered it to be, but a warning about a possible type of state tyranny that called itself socialist." In "Writers and Leviathan," Fyvel aptly reminds us, "Orwell had written that it was a weakness of the Left to suppose that with the overthrow of capitalism, something like democratic socialism would inevitably take its place. There was no such inevitability . . . *Nineteen Eighty-Four* was an allegorical warning about the worst possible consequences."[5] As such, it is a correlate of, not a corrective to, the political convictions Orwell expressed in his 1948 essay "In Defense of Comrade Zilliacus":

> Social democracy, unlike capitalism, offers an alternative to communism, and if somewhere or other it can be made to work on a big scale, if it turns out that after all it *is* possible to introduce socialism without secret police forces, mass deportations and so forth, then the excuse for dictatorship vanishes.[6]

Orwell's political creed had already been summed up in his 1947 essay on F. A. von Hayek. "Our present predicament," Orwell wrote, is that "capitalism leads to dole queues, the scramble for markets and war. Collectivism leads to concentration camps, leader-worship and war. There is no way out of this unless a planned economy can somehow be combined with freedom of intellect."[7] Such a combination may not be the likeliest outcome of the practice of politics, but Orwell neverthe-less believed it to be the preeminent political project of his generation if further collective insanity were to be avoided. Orwell's reasons for writing *Nineteen Eighty-Four*, a hypothetical picture projected into a future he had the temerity to pin down with a date, should be under-stood with reference to the political task of steering us away from the world the book portrays. Orwell's letter to Francis A. Henson goes on to make this clear:

> I do not believe that the kind of society I describe necessarily will arrive, but I believe (allowing of course for the fact that the book is a satire) that something resembling it *could* arrive. I believe also that totalitarian ideas have taken root in the minds of intellectuals everywhere, and I have tried to draw these ideas out to their logi-cal consequences. The scene of the book is laid in Britain in order to emphasize that the English-speaking races are not innately bet-ter than anyone else and that totalitarianism, *if not fought against*, could triumph anywhere.[8]

There is of course buried in this admonition the question of agency: just who is going to do the fighting, and in the name of what? Orwell is less clear about groups and group values that are fit to take on the task than about those that oppose it. These, in George Kateb's words, included, "the old-fashioned reactionaries, capital, the military, the church; there was the fascist movement culminating in Hitler, 'the criminal lunatic', as Orwell called him in an essay on H. G. Wells written in 1941; there were the Bolsheviks who, in some ways better than the Fascists and Nazis, had nevertheless destroyed revolutionary idealism in the course of consolidating their power. There was, finally, the curse of ideology: the unreasoning attachment to the views of one's group, whatever the group, the blind loyalty to the group at the expense of the truth, at the expense of sanity itself." Kateb quotes Orwell's "Notes on Nationalism" (1945): "the habit of identifying oneself with a single nation or other unit, placing it beyond good and

evil and recognizing no other duty than that of advancing its interests,"[9] this—the obverse, not the expression of what Orwell understood by patriotism—is the enemy to be combated.

All of this on the face of it seems unexceptional enough. But Orwell
—who was fond of needling his largely left-wing readers by champi-
oning writers like Wodehouse or Kipling, who could scarcely be
expected to endear themselves to the left—went further. He insisted
that the authentic socialism he had encountered in Barcelona during
the Spanish Civil War had precious little in common with the socialism of that "huge tribe of party-hacks and sleek little professors" at
home who were intent on proving that socialism meant nothing more
than "a planned state capitalism with the grab-motive left intact."[10]
Orwell's understanding of democratic socialism, in George Kateb's
paraphrase, is that "socialism is not in any important sense the quest
for abundance and a life of self-indulgence, with all the state control
and planning that that would necessitate. Orwell was always more
interested in abolishing extreme suffering than in imagining total
felicity. In fact, Orwell thought that it was only after the abolition of
extreme suffering that the real problems of humanity—the moral and
spiritual ones—could fully disclose themselves."[11]

Orwell's thought has a Rousseauean as well as a socialist side to it,
and in more than one sense. His hostility to a left-intelligentsia (of
which he was a characteristic product) bears comparison with Rousseau's hostility towards the *philosophes* of the French Enlightenment
(among whom he too should nevertheless be numbered). Yet this comparison implies its own limits. Orwell, in George Woodcock's words,
was "not very adept at close political discussion, and had a temperamental reluctance to think in terms of elaborate social plans or clearly
defined party platforms. . . . [W]hat concerned him much more deeply
than political programs were the general principles of conduct, particularly conduct affecting other men, which had been developed in the
long tradition of English radical dissent, and which were quickly losing ground in modern political life." Nevertheless, "Orwell hated
political doctrinaires, professional do-gooders and faddists of all kinds.
. . . [T]he less a writer had to do with any organized body, the better for
him and his work."[12] Woodcock identifies something very important
about Orwell: a hostility towards the intelligentsia, a group into
which the left made inroads during the 1930s in Britain out of all pro-
portion to their electoral influence. Orwell often set out deliberately
and with no small flourish to rile and irritate the very people who
were most likely to read him. The description of the Left Book Club

meeting in *Coming Up for Air* (one of Orwell's rare stabs at humor), and the second part of *The Road to Wigan Pier* (a far less rare stab at invective) are cases in point.

Orwell was convinced, rightly or wrongly, that "the English in 1943 were allowing their admiration for the military heroism of the Russians to blind them to the faults of the Communist regime, and [that] the Communists were using their position as unofficial representatives of Russia in England to prevent the truth from being known, as they had done in Spain." But Orwell in 1944, after completing *Animal Farm*, distinguished the comparatively healthy Russophilia of the working class—"they feel Russia is the working class country where the common man is in control"—from the Russophilia of the intellectuals, which he associated, problematically, with "power-worship." George Woodcock goes on to indicate that, while "Orwell loathed ... Nazism" it remains true that, "if he devoted more time to the exposure of the rival creed of communism, it was only because he felt that there was more danger of the communists' being able to deceive and dominate the left in democratic countries."[13] The truth is a little more complicated, not least by Orwell's evident conviction that deceit and domination, to be effective, would have to be refracted through the medium of the intelligentsia.

It is this stress on the *trahison des clercs* that links *Animal Farm* retrospectively with *Homage to Catalonia* and prospectively with *Nineteen Eighty-Four*. The extent to which Newspeak and Ingsoc itself are *direct* examples or expressions of a *trahison des clercs* has rarely been acknowledged. Intellectual treason is nevertheless an unmistakable leitmotiv of *Nineteen Eighty-Four*, as it had been of *Animal Farm* and of *Homage to Catalonia* (Orwell indeed considered it a theme of the publication histories of these three books). The proles in *Nineteen Eighty-Four*, whatever Anthony Burgess and others may think, are not the betrayers but the betrayed. ("We didn't ought to 'ave trusted the buggers," Winston Smith remembers an old man saying as the bombs fell outside the air-raid shelter.) The proles are more pointedly victims of their *ongoing*, institutionalized betrayal by the intelligentsia, the Inner Party, with all their power-worship and sadism. Winston Smith's defeat by and submergence within it is intended to indicate that the world of *Nineteen Eighty-Four* is in the fullest sense insane. The Party élite who are in power gain nothing from Ingsoc but power, power that is exercised almost entirely and always most directly over other members of the same elite, those in the Outer Party. The Party, whose members have sacrificed every human quality for power, lives within its own circle of fantasy and counter-fantasy. The Party's circle is one that by definition excludes the proles, 85 per cent of the population of Airship One, whose lives proceed not unaffected by the Party—they presumably fight as well as cheer its wars, for one thing—but who are nevertheless immunized to a remarkable extent against whatever goes on at the rarefied levels occupied by the angels and archangels of the Inner and Outer Parties. Official society in *Nineteen Eighty-Four* excludes the proles, just as their informal society—ignored, despised and sealed off from the élite—operates without regard to the gyrations of the Empyrean legions above them.

Nineteen Eighty-Four is not a betrayal of socialism, but a depiction of such a betrayal. It is a statement of what socialism could become if it loses what in Orwell's view were its moorings, if the ordinary, everyday values of the people—which Orwell continued in his way to cherish—are relinquished for the sake of the extraordinary "values" of the intelligentsia, as exemplified by those of O'Brien. Yet what he also did in this book, as George Kateb points out, "was to imagine a world in which everything he hated had coalesced and become omnipotent." He sacrificed a simple, straightforward line to achieve an intensity of vision, and "he desired to achieve an intensity of vision in order to rouse [people] to danger."[14] Orwell is honest enough to entertain doubts as well as hopes about the regenerative potential of the proles, and obsessive, perhaps perverse, enough to have no doubts about what motivates their would-be betrayers, the socialist intelligentsia.

Could this perhaps be why Orwell's espousal of democratic socialism has not endeared him to Raymond Williams, even though (or precisely because) it is close to what Williams himself has advocated? The question reveals a deeper paradox. Williams's various efforts to distance himself critically from Orwell are not reducible to hard-and-fast, obvious differences separating the two, but have something to do with their very proximity. This paradox can be stated in another way. Williams is not generally disdainful of or impatient with (let alone bitter about) writers with whose views he disagrees. It is important to Williams's entire enterprise that such writers are in a certain sense grist to his mill. He has repeatedly and convincingly proved himself adept at digesting and explaining views he would admit to regarding as repellent. But while his sympathy extends to those he regards as fundamentally unsympathetic, Williams does not finally extend it to Orwell, whose views—not least those about democratic socialism—are surely far less distasteful to him than those of, say, Carlyle.

Orwell and Williams have a great deal in common. We have to bear in mind that comparisons between an academic literary and cultural critic and a resolutely non-academic novelist and essayist become strained if we try and push them too far. Nevertheless, points of similarity and areas of overlap do emerge, and these are largely political. Both Orwell and Williams have disagreed openly with the vulgar-Marxist contention that the economic base defines or determines the political (or cultural) superstructure of society—Orwell because he never thought of himself as a Marxist, Williams because as a Marxist he finds such reductionism unwarranted. While this feature may push both Orwell and Williams in a more "British," less doctrinaire direction, it also makes them British socialists of a particular type. Their socialism is at one level very British in its Tawneyite concern with removing class barriers to equality and democratizing society at the level of perception. Orwell's notorious diatribe against middle-class socialists in the second half of *The Road to Wigan Pier* has as its final point the admonition that socialism should broaden its appeal to induce the lower middle class, who in turn have "nothing to lose but their aitches," to make common cause with the workers in overthrowing the "plutocracy."[15] But this concern is quite remote from another, no less characteristic strand of British socialism. It is a far cry from the Webbs, Shaw, and G. D. H. Cole. Orwell and Williams are alike indifferent to the mechanics of "parliamentary socialism." While each of them has condemned the class betrayal that "parliamentary socialism" has been said (by Ralph Miliband and others) to involve, even this is not really at the center of their concerns. Orwell and Williams share a preoccupation that cuts across questions of parliamentary politics and economic or industrial policy, and of the nuts and bolts of public administration, trade union structure, and local government. Their focus is on questions of culture, language, attitude, perception, value, and consciousness—consciousness of the kind that is not *always* class consciousness. Orwell and Williams share a fundamental desire to emphasize human relationships rather than numerical social aggregates, people and their lived experiences and circumstances rather than the statistical methods other people use to "explain" them. In this sense, Orwell and Williams position themselves a long way away from Fabian Socialism and Bernsteinian Revisionism alike.

This concern with human relationships and lived experience—which is also an academic concern to Williams, having to do with the imprint of F. R. Leavis—also encompasses the personal. Orwell and Williams frequently refer or appeal to their own experiences, perceptions, and recollections and inscribe these within accounts of social, cultural, or political events and processes that are much more general. Each has a sense of being, or wanting to be, part of what he is writing about, and each habitually gives expression to this sense as a way of pointing up more generalized processes and giving them greater immediacy.

Orwell's well-known decision to "go native" in his own country, for the sake of revealing one half of it to the other, had a personal side he was in no way reluctant to reveal, but that nevertheless needs careful appraisal. Orwell says in *The Road to Wigan Pier*:

> I could go among these people, see what their lives were like and feel myself temporarily part of their world. Once I had been among them and accepted by them, I should have touched bottom, and—this is what I felt: I was aware even then that it was irrational—part of my guilt would drop from me.[16]

On the one hand, Orwell, in the words of George Woodcock "rarely tells of his own experience except to make a point illustrating some general argument, usually of a political or social nature"; and much the same could be said of Raymond Williams. On the other hand, Orwell's "impulse to render his own experiences into some meaningful form was . . . much stronger in him than the impulse to invent original situations and sequences of events." Woodcock is surely quite right in saying of Orwell, whose "way of reacting to experience" was indeed to write about it, that "he found it hard to create a fictional character, observed from within, who was not filled with Orwellian attitudes, even to the point of breaking at times into his creator's language and expressing his most characteristic thoughts."[17] Examples— Gordon Comstock, George Bowling, even Dorothy Hare and certainly Winston Smith—are not hard to come by.

Raymond Williams also reacts to experience, to the "surface of life" (as Orwell would have called it) in his semi-autobiographical novels, and even, occasionally, in academic works of literary and cultural criticism. When he inserts the first person singular he too does so for the sake of revealing one part of society to another, though not for the sake of assuaging guilt as Orwell sometimes did. (It is not incidental to what follows that Williams is conscious of not needing to descend into the lower depths in the same way). This means that, despite temperamental as well as social differences, Orwell and Williams have in common a desire to break down barriers in perception and recognition, which leads us into another area of overlap. In Woodcock's words, a "group of Orwellian essays"—"Boys' Weeklies," "The Art of Donald McGill," "Raffles and Miss Blandish," and others—"have formed the

foundation for a whole branch of contemporary British criticism represented particularly by Raymond Williams and Richard Hoggart
devoted to the study of popular culture at various social levels."[18]
However much he may or may not have shared in the spirit of the
age—the age here being the British 1930s, with its Mass Observation
Surveys, its Grierson documentary movement in film, and so forth—
Orwell surely was "one of the first writers with a literary sensibility to
take popular culture seriously and to show that the attempt to understand it could be an absorbing and revealing discipline," just as Alex
Zwerdling says. Moreover, "in his refusal to ignore or dismiss popular
culture, in his willingness to read the wrong books and look at the
wrong pictures, [Orwell's] influence was certainly liberating and indirectly revealed the unsuspected limitations of more fastidious taste
and more rigorous aesthetic doctrine,"[19] even though his reasons for
undertaking these investigations were not at all academic, and more
immediately political.

While the political and the academic cannot be separated with anything approaching such neatness in the case of Williams, this difference
from Orwell does not obliterate yet another area of shared concern that
is quite possibly the most important, and the most problematic, of all.
This is the question of language. Orwell and Williams share a direct
and politically charged preoccupation with the use and meaning of
words, a preoccupation that links Williams's book *Keywords* with
Orwell's essays on language, particularly "Politics and the English
Language" and "Why I Write." This fairly obvious point of similarity is
more far-reaching than might initially be supposed. Williams is in a
certain sense vulnerable by virtue of the self-conscious reflexivity by
which and with which he inscribes himself within the "culture and
society" tradition he commemorates, resuscitates and (in a way) invents, this tradition being for Williams both a platform and a refuge.
Orwell is vulnerable not so much for the same reason as for a different
one. He believes in *language itself* as the desired refuge. Since this, it
can be argued, is both a strength and a weakness in Orwell, it should be
positioned a little more precisely. Language as Orwell understands it
would be a refuge of the required kind if its transparency could be preserved from its willful obfuscators. Newspeak in *Nineteen Eighty-Four*
blocks off access to this transparency of meaning that Orwell thinks
characterizes good prose, a transparency that gives it its critical as well
as its consolatory force. This is largely the reason why Newspeak was
such a nightmarish construct to Orwell. In his best-known formulation, "good prose is like a window-pane"[20]—that is, it is what New-

speak cannot be, a clear window through which we might see or find a securely familiar world (instead of what Winston Smith sees in his telescreen). This world out there is not so much reflected back to us—language is a window-pane, not a mirror—as simply revealed to our gaze.

Orwell's "transparency" image is of course meant to work inwardly as well as outwardly: good, transparent prose is the best, indeed the only way of directly expressing the beliefs, ideas, positions, and self of the writer. Even so, Orwell was aware of at least some of the dangers, which he described in terms that are not just political but actually military.

"In prose," he says, "the worst thing one can do with words is surrender to them." Stock phrases and clichés are particularly dangerous antagonists; unless you are "constantly on guard" they will "[invade] your mind."[21] When you think you are using them, they are in fact using you; worse still, you are not choosing your words for yourself, but supporting the various élites whose interests are served by clichés and stock phrases, by lack of thought, and who (like it or not) shape the language we use. Orwell's point, in other words, has political resonance: he claimed to be attacking the intelligentsia "not because they were intellectuals but precisely because they were not what [he meant] by true intellectuals."[22] True intellectuals think independently and speak out fearlessly; what Orwell held against the "shock-headed Marxists chewing polysyllables" of his day was that they—like many of their antagonists—took their ideas and their language prefabricated.

Raymond Williams is clearly not an intellectual of this type. Yet he is more concerned to distance himself from Orwell than to agree with him. His various treatments of Orwell contain two main lines of criticism, which have to do with Orwell's path to socialism and, following from this, his understanding of socialism. Williams stresses Orwell's socialism as something he had to come to or arrive at, always a terminus or destination, never a starting point. Orwell's original exteriority to the socialism he came to espouse is stressed throughout: "he thought of himself as an anti-imperialist and an anti-fascist, as a believer in equality, and only through these positions as a socialist." Socialism, on this rather ungenerous view—most people, after all, arrive at it (if they arrive at it at all) through some other thing or things they experience—is a political creed that was never immediate to Orwell. Orwell himself frequently acknowledged that socialism was something he worked toward and finally adopted by working through other, related creeds. It was not something he imbibed from an early age or was born into. But what does not follow from this is Williams's further point that "socialism as such was *always* secondary in [Orwell's] mind, to the struggle against fascism, imperialism and inequality." It may be true that socialism to Orwell was among other things "a general idea, a general name against these evils." It may also be true that "before he left England [for Spain, not Burma] it had little positive content."[23] Orwell himself freely admitted as much on several occasions. But Williams has some sort of interest in regarding Orwell's understanding of socialism as skin-deep *because* it is a second-order, residual, catch-all category. Yet there is no good reason why Orwell's understanding of socialism should be explained simply by reference to his indirect path to socialism. Socialism was not part of the "lived experience" Orwell was born to—"to me in my early boyhood, to nearly all children of families like mine, 'common' people seemed almost inhuman,"[24] Orwell recalled—but the fact remains that he made it part of the experience he proceeded duly to live. Nobody forced Orwell to go "down and out," or obliged him to go to Wigan or fight in Spain. Orwell did these things very deliberately; he went against the grain of his upbringing and background each time.

Even so, there is a sense in which Orwell remains unforgiven by Williams either for the choices he made or for the way he made them. Orwell's various quests seem irredeemably stamped by their lack of authenticity. If Orwell audaciously became a tramp, thereby temporarily joining what were arguably the most *déclassé* elements in England during the 1930s, it is because, Williams sniffs, "the absence of roots is also the absence of barriers." Orwell was always the outside observer, never the true participant. He had, in Williams's words, "his own idea of what the working class was like";[25] and, moreover, to the extent that this idea might be complicated by the "reality" of working-class experience, Orwell according to Williams ignored the sources of temptation—as when he overlooked the preexisting "social and political network" of Northern working-class communities and omitted this network from his description of their poverty and culture in *The Road to Wigan Pier.*[26] But whether or not this accusation is true—and Orwell's own recollections cast a rather different light on the circumstances of the omission—Williams has surely made the kind of claim that cuts both ways. Who, after all, *doesn't* have his or her own idea of what the working class is like? Certainly not Williams himself, who was, as he tells us, born into it. But it does not follow that the authenticity this gives him is of one voice or view, or that his background in the working class precludes a certain selectivity in what he too later chose to say about it.

Williams has repeatedly accused Orwell of falsification of the record in the case of *The Road to Wigan Pier*. He refers in *Politics and Letters* to Orwell's "suppression of how he got to go down the [coal]-mine, and how he stayed in the homes of working-class socialists, who he then denied ever existed." He excoriates "Orwell's choice of the working-class areas he went to, the deliberate neglect of the families who were coping—although he acknowledged their existence in the abstract—in favour of the characteristic imagery of squalor: people poking at drains with sticks."[27] In *Writing in Society* Williams summarily lambastes *Wigan Pier* as an example of how documentary reportage should not be written.

> When [Orwell] wrote *The Road to Wigan Pier*, he sought out the lowest doss-house in town, even though he had arrived with introductions from leaders of the Unemployed Workers' Movement and trade unionists and had stayed with educated working-class socialists. He then "proved" that socialism is just a middle-class idea.[28]

While Orwell no doubt was selective in what he considered memorable reportage, just as he was, at times, condescending about working people in ways Williams is right to find offensive, Williams's criticism is nevertheless, in a certain sense, wide of the mark. This is not because of Orwell's documented embarrassment at being addressed as "comrade" by those who induced feelings of guilt in him, but because of something fundamental about *Wigan Pier* that Williams misprizes. There is a reflexivity to Orwell's honesty and to his views on language that Williams seems determined not to allow. The problem with the book has to do with its division into two parts: the one Victor Gollancz and the Left Book Club commissioned, and with which they were pleased, and the unexpected and embarrassing second part, to which Gollancz felt obliged to write an apologetic foreword, disassociating himself and his colleagues from some of Orwell's remarks about middle-class socialists. Raymond Williams is right to perceive (in his way) that these two parts are connected. What he misprises is the character of their connection. Orwell never intended *Wigan Pier* as flat documentary reportage, let alone "realism" as this term was understood in the thirties. Samuel Hynes has acutely pointed out that not only did Orwell "get his feelings into the story" in the *first* as well as the second part of the book; "these feelings *are* the story." A passage ostensibly about the poor "is not so much about poverty as it is about middle-class feelings about poverty, how poverty degraded the poor, and how one draws back instinctively from such degradation." A passage about the miners "is not about the working class but about middle-class feelings about the workers, feelings which sentimentally elevate working men to the level of heroes." Unlike Williams, Hynes hits the nail on the head:

> *Wigan Pier* is ostensibly about poverty, but it is more profoundly a book about class. The primary subject is Orwell himself, as a representative of his own middle-class generation repelled by poverty but sentimentally impressed by workers, preaching universal socialism but despising middle-class converts, desiring a classless society but separated from the working class by his bourgeois background, his accent and his ingrained prejudices.... [I]t was in passages ... [where] Orwell was writing about himself and his prejudices, and demonstrating his prejudices in operation, that he wrote most brilliantly and most imaginatively—more brilliantly than in any of his thirties novels.[29]

Whether Orwell is correct in his beliefs about immediate perception seems to depend on whether socially-unmediated perception of culture (or culturally-unmediated scrutiny of society) is even possible, let alone desirable. Williams has pointed out, apropos of Cobbett as well as Orwell, that "the key point about the convention of the plain observer with no axes to grind, who simply tells the truth, is that it cancels the social situation of the writer and cancels his stance toward the social situation he is observing."[30] Orwell, however, did have "axes to grind" (as did Cobbett, for that matter), which he did not disdain to reveal; one of them is that plain writing and absence of "humbug" would come closest to conveying the truth of a situation. There is more substance to this conviction than Williams allows. Hanna Pitkin has persuasively indicated (in an unpublished talk) that the power of Orwell's reportage, which is frequently polemical as well as autobiographical, is never meant to involve the "objectivity" of a detached, neutral, dispassionate observer. Instead Orwell conveys a most personal, sometimes painfully personal account—but not *of* his state of mind or subjectivity. He cares about communicating the truth or reality of a social situation, but recognizes that reality by its very nature calls for judgment, not registration. Orwell's concern, in Hanna Pitkin's formulation, is with "the truth of witness." He takes responsibility for the claims he makes about a social situation. He puts himself as witness into the report. This introduces not bias but veracity. A witness knows only what he or she saw or heard or felt; he or she is bound to have personal biases, and might embroider, or even have some reason to lie. Yet the presence of a witness allows and is meant to allow us to form our own judgments about what has been witnessed, about what kind of person the witness is, and about the trust we should place in what the witness says. And this is to say that while impersonal, objective distancing does not enter into a witness's account, truthfulness, of the kind that invites the reader into Orwell's witnessed world, most certainly does. It is striking that Raymond Williams, who should not on the face of it be hostile to this notion of "witnessed truth," does not characterize Orwell as a witness but as an outsider.

According to the chapter on Orwell in *Culture and Society*, all Orwell's paradoxes are collapsible into one, central paradox, which Williams terms "the paradox of the exile" and sees as Orwell's isolation from and exteriority to whatever he happens to be observing. While "the substance of community is lacking" even in the exile, "Orwell, in different parts of his career, is both exile and vagrant. The vagrant, in literary terms, is the 'reporter'.... [T]he reporter is an observer, an intermediary; it is unlikely that he will understand, in any depth, the life about which he is writing," Williams goes on, since he is looking "invariably from the outside." What this means is that Orwell's "principal failure was inevitable: he observed what was evident, the external factors, and only guessed at what was not evident, the inherent patterns of feeling." While this is a drawback even in his early works of reportage, by the time of *Nineteen Eighty-Four* Orwell's "way of seeing the working people is not from fact and observation, but from the pressures of feeling exiled."[31]

While the implied progression—from exile to vagrant "reporter" to reporter to observer to the exile who is no longer capable of observing adequately—may make a certain amount of sense as a way of characterizing Orwell's successive vantage points, this should not obscure the fact that Williams is also using them as a means of shifting his own ground, and of doing so more rapidly than adroitly. However muffled it may be by the characteristic woolliness of Williams's prose, his argument is nevertheless so slippery that we should have no difficulty in turning it inside out. Why is it that Williams cannot afford to admit that Orwell might have been right even for a moment? Why does he not grant that Orwell's exteriority might once in a while have provided a vantage point from which examination, and not mere observation, is possible? What does Orwell's exteriority really represent to Williams?

Orwell is isolated from a certain class background (seen by Williams as involving a "substance of community" and "inherent patterns of feelings," Leavisite terms that toll like minute bells through his exposition). He is isolated from Marxism (seen, again vaguely, by Williams as part of this class background as well as informing the intelligentsia). And he is isolated from the intellectuals themselves, particularly as these have a place in the academy. From Williams's point of view, Orwell has no place to stand. This is one of the reasons Williams provides such a good touchstone for the left's reception of Orwell. These three refuges—the proletarian, the Marxist, the academic—triangulate Raymond Williams's career, and Orwell either was isolated or isolated himself from all three. Because his socialism owes nothing to any of them, his example raises the question, to Williams and to us, of how much anybody's socialism owes, or should owe, or must owe to these sources.

The other reason why Williams is such a good touchstone emerges when we consider that Orwell did in fact have a place to stand. It was called England (as opposed to Airstrip One), and there is a sense in which Orwell's tendency to extol an idealized England of the none-too-distant past—a tendency that seems to many readers (including the present writers) to have a straightforwardly reactionary side—is particularly irritating to Williams. It cuts close to the bone. Orwell's socialism, however we are to appraise it, manifestly owes something, and something significant, to the "culture and society" tradition that has proved so important to Williams. Yet Orwell never used "culture and society" speculation, as Williams did for a long time, in an attempt to bracket together class, Marxism, and the academy. He believed to the contrary that culture and society could be looked at, retrospectively to be sure, but unmediated by and unrefracted through these three categories, categories Williams could not afford to relinquish or to regard as extraneous.

Orwell touches a nerve. What he and his much-maligned exteriority represent, most pointedly to Williams but also by extension to other avatars of the left, could reasonably, and without undue drama, be construed as a threat. The threat is on the one hand that democratic socialism could be espoused, and could indeed be advanced with reference to the "culture and society" tradition cherished at one time by Williams, but without recourse to anything within Williams's no less cherished triangle of class, Marxism, and the academy. Perhaps these props and struts are not really necessary after all. Perhaps what they are propping up is not democratic socialism at all, but merely each other.

This query helps put into perspective Williams's last and most critical reflections on Orwell, which are contained in a series of interviews with members of the *New Left Review*'s Editorial Board, published in

1979 as *Politics and Letters.* The interview about Orwell[32] exhibits a dramatic structure that it is instructive to delineate. The members of the Board seem determined from the outset not to let Williams off the hook for his indulgent treatment of Orwell—not so much (to be sure) in *Culture and Society* but in his short "Modern Masters" survey, *George Orwell.* Williams's earlier position as the members of the Board paraphrase it is that "while the sum effect of Orwell's work has been on the whole very reactionary . . . nonetheless Orwell was a man who became a revolutionary socialist for a significant period of his life and then tragically and perhaps inevitably went wrong." It is for this reason that the Board thinks Williams's "book is very controlled and sympathetic in tone towards Orwell." *George Orwell* is indeed more nuanced, sympathetic and differentiated, and less one-sided than *Culture and Society* (which resorts at one point to a two-page parade of quotes out of context) had been, but this does nothing to endear it to the Board, whose point of view is that Orwell, after all (unlike Deutscher and Trotsky, but like—inevitably—Koestler) broke under the pressure of Stalinism, became a social patriot and a violent anti-communist; and that the "pathos" of Williams's account, which is far too sympathetic an account, is wasted on such a figure.

The sheer viciousness of this opening salvo is such that Williams seems momentarily taken aback. He sputters out the rather weak observation that there was during the Second World War a widespread belief that "British society could be transformed through the conduct of the war," and that "there was then a crucial slippage from that position to social patriotism," a slippage that can be regarded sympathetically. Not, however, by the members of the Board. Yet by now even these inquisitors feel the need to shift the grounds of their interrogation, by deciding at this point to pose Three Big Questions, all of them rhetorical, about Orwell. "Did he produce new theoretical knowledge about society or history?" "Did he produce first-rank works of creative imagination—novels of major literary value?" The answer to these questions is a resounding if unsurprising "no" (along with the rather unfortunate prediction that *"Nineteen Eighty-Four* will be a curio in 1984"). "Did he provide faithful accounts of what he witnessed or experienced?" This, "the most frequent claim for Orwell's achievement as a writer," is less of a straw man, and gives the Board pause. It dismisses *The Road to Wigan Pier* because of the "elements of suppression and manipulation" Williams had identified in its reportage, though not because of Orwell's uncharitable remarks about middle-class socialists. (These perhaps provide a target that had simply been

hit too many times before.) And *Homage to Catalonia* fares rather better: "a very fine reportage, whatever its limitations as a general view of
the Spanish Civil War." But this faint praise is merely a case of *reculer
pour mieux sauter*, for the Board then immediately proceeds to ask: "if
Orwell had few or no original ideas, a limited creative imagination and
an unreliable capacity to recount information, what remains of his
achievement?" This loaded question turns into an accusation not just
against Orwell but also against Williams. If the answer to it is Orwell's
creation of "Orwell" as a character—and the Board entertains no other
view—then Williams can (bizarrely enough) be accused of "[abstain-
ing] from any judgment of this figure," despite Orwell's (or "Orwell's")
evident "lack of literary scruple."

At this point in Williams's interrogation, the Board seems to have
gone off the rails entirely. But it draws itself back and makes what
appears to be an interesting, even accurate, observation. "What
[Orwell's] writing seems to suggest is an active predisposition from the
start to see ... the dark side of his subject. ... Orwell seems to have
been temperamentally in his element when he was vituperating
causes which in another part of himself he hoped to advance. His very
tense and ambiguous relationship with socialism is the most obvious,
but not the only example of this strain," which in fact "was not specifically about socialism in the first instance" at all. Not only does this
statement strike an unexpectedly sympathetic note, it is even augmented by the (correct) observation that "Orwell himself never voluntarily accommodated" the "political demand ... for parables of the
cold war."

But such observations are too positive for Williams, who by now
has found his feet and quite possibly senses a trap. He admits apropos
of *Animal Farm* that "there was an oppositional element in [Orwell]
which made him first in the field," which of course insinuates Orwell
back into the cold war again even though *Animal Farm* was written in
1943; he insists that "Orwell's later works ... had to be written by an
ex-socialist. It also had to be someone who shared the discouragement
of the generation; an ex-socialist who had become an enthusiast for
capitalism could not have had the same effect." Even though we could
grant Williams his last point (as a way of taking care of Norman
Podhoretz,[33] perhaps), this still emerges as an extraordinary statement.
It seems to salvage "disillusion," but only at the cost of an illegitimate
use of the imperative voice (why should these works have "had to be"
anything?), and of a no less illegitimate confounding of Orwell's intentions with the presumed effects of what he wrote. But there is worse to

come, since Williams—accompanied no doubt by a nodding of the heads of the members of the Board—has by now built his bridge to *Nineteen Eighty-Four*. His line on this novel makes it unrecognizable. "The recruitment of very private feelings against socialism becomes intolerable by *Nineteen Eighty-Four*. It is profoundly offensive to state as a general truth, as Orwell does, that people will always betray one another. If human beings are like that, what could be the meaning of a democratic socialism?" The answer to this question is, of course, that, since Orwell does not state that people will always betray each other as a general truth, but does state that under the circumstances depicted in *Nineteen Eighty-Four* people can be coerced into betraying each other, democratic socialism would have to look very different from these circumstances, circumstances that are designed to prevent democratic socialism from arising. But this point seems not to have occurred either to Williams or to his interlocutors. And by the time we find Williams denouncing *Nineteen Eighty-Four*'s "projections of ugliness and hatred, often quite arbitrarily and inconsequentially on to the difficulties of revolutionary or political change," we are entitled to shake our heads in disbelief and wonder whether he has read the same book as we have. Since there is no revolutionary or political change—there is for that matter no politics, properly so-called, at all—in Ingsoc, we are also entitled to conclude that the arbitrariness is all Williams's.

The trouble is however that it isn't *all* Williams's, and that the left at large has long been just as unfair to Orwell as Orwell was to it. As we have seen, all sorts of reasons can readily be adduced for the left's dislike of Orwell: his rejection of Marxism, and of Marxists; his condescending references to workers, counterbalanced by his sentimentalizing about them; his lack of a systematic theory combined with a sometimes cloying nostalgia for the recently vanished English past; and, not least, his frequent, perverse desire to bite the hand that fed him, and needle his audience. These characteristics do not make for popularity: no one likes a self-appointed conscience that dredges up inconvenient facts, revives uncherished memories and raises awkward questions in public. The left's response has often been the no less spiteful one of casting Orwell in a cold-warrior mold, of placing him in a position he fails to fit but where he can more easily be assailed. This happened during Orwell's lifetime and has happened ever since.

There are of course reasons why some people on the right sought to extract ammunition from Orwell's writings, reasons that cannot be entered into here even though they too are important to the left's rejection of him. But the motivations of those who have been content, even relieved, to disown Orwell, for these and other reasons, are more convenient than convincing. The left has colluded with the right in shunting off Orwell to the inappropriate and inhospitable sidelines staking out the cold war, which means that Orwell needled them all too effectively. Orwell's needling of Raymond Williams is particularly interesting in this regard, which is why Williams is so apt a touchstone for the left at large in its uncomfortable dismissal of Orwell. In his wartime essays, and elsewhere, Orwell happily acknowledges the reactionary aspect of a "culture and society" tradition Williams was later to trace and even cherish. Orwell does not attempt to deny or conceal its reactionary side. He subscribes to it, and thus sees no need to explain it away. It poses him no problems for this reason. But because Orwell identifies something about this tradition that is not easy for Williams to digest, Williams has his own reasons to strike back, reasons that add to the reasons already listed for Orwell's unpopularity and that in a certain sense point them up.

The key fact about the "culture and society" tradition in England, with which Raymond Williams has long associated himself, is that in its origins, and in its articulation, it had very little to do with the working class *per se* and still less with socialism. Latterly, socialism has helped to keep it alive, and may indeed have done more for "culture and society" than the tradition ever did for socialism. The "culture and society" movement had its early-nineteenth-century origins in a series of always horrified, generally literary responses to the onset of the Industrial Revolution. These responses were at once regressive, in their desire to keep in play various traditional and newly-threatened, cultural forms and organic values, and also exemplary in that a minority of literati were charged with the task of their preservation. Opinions varied about the exact extent, nature, and value of the artifacts to be preserved, and about the credentials of the keepers of the flame; but all the movement's avatars were in basic agreement about the beleaguered, defensive character of its task, which was above all one of recuperation and preservation, against the grain of historical development. In this sense the lineage from Wordsworth and Coleridge, through Matthew Arnold and T. S. Eliot to F. R. Leavis, is clear enough. Leavis in particular may be taken to have encapsulated a crucial stage in the development of the movement in both its regressive and its élitist dimensions. The traditional relationship between "civilization" (the totality of social relations) and "culture" (the values on which "fine living" depended), he believed, had been strained to the point of rupture by "the advance of the machine." Society to Leavis was now threatened by a "breach in continuity," the best defense against which is a certain kind of concern with language.

Industrialization and commercialization on this influential view of them destroy an older order and despoil its "natural" setting; the now pervasive spirit of "mechanism" and calculative rationality atrophies all traces of organic wholeness in individual and society alike. Against these clear and present dangers, *Scrutiny* continued (and continually redefined) a line of response and protest that included Cobbett and Shelley, Ruskin and William Morris, Carlyle and Lawrence, as well as Leavis himself, whose idea of the "clerisy" as cultural guardian resumes an argument initiated by Coleridge and developed by Arnold, as we have seen. As Francis Mulhern points out, *Scrutiny* "opened up an educational space within which the cultural institutions of bourgeois-democratic capitalism could be subjected to critical analysis—a space which was to be utilized to remarkable effect, most noticeably by Raymond Williams and the Center for Contemporary Cultural Studies [at Birmingham University] founded by Richard Hoggart." Two points are worth stressing in estimating this achievement. First, even if the educational themes and practices it involves were never anything more than a "radical-romantic counterpoint to the conventional wisdom of Liberal-Fabian educational policy, a latter-day variation on the romantic/utilitarian antinomy that constitutes one of the abiding structures of industrial capitalist culture," as Mulhern suggests, it did not lack force for this reason. It was much more successful on any measure, as Mulhern also points out, than its most immediate rival during the 1930s, the reductionist-Marxist school represented most noticeably (and almost entirely) by Christopher Caudwell's *Studies in a Dying Culture* and Cecil Day Lewis's symposium, *The Mind in Chains*.[34]

The second point about the movement brings it joltingly up to date. This is that the decisive shift, the change of valency within the tradition, comes not so much with Orwell (who contributed to it, but from the outside) as with writers like Raymond Williams and Richard Hoggart who took it upon themselves to democratize a response, still a response of the time-honored kind, to the unsettling, disastrous, and above all continuous irruption of capitalist social relations into daily life. Williams, Hoggart, and others charged themselves with the task of rescuing or resuscitating specifically working-class forms of response to the onset and persistence of capitalist industrialization, and the commercialization of everyday patterns of life. And they pointedly did so within the terms set by the "culture and society" tradition of which they became heirs and transmitters.

The relative autonomy (as we now say) and specificity of cultural forms was throughout these exercises necessarily acknowledged, respected, even revered; and in respecting them Raymond Williams, in particular, had to fight on two fronts, against the reductionist Marxism of the period and against his teacher at Cambridge, Leavis. Williams's *Culture and Society, 1780-1950* was written in response to the élitist, high-culture programs of Leavis and T. S. Eliot, whose *Notes Toward the Definition of Culture* had appeared a decade or so earlier. Williams's book could be seen as bringing together or systematizing Orwell's scattered remarks on culture (e.g. in his *Critical Essays* of 1946, published in the United States as *Dickens, Dali, and Others*), and as culminating in a separate chapter on Orwell himself. Richard Hoggart's *The Uses of Literacy*,[35] which was also in the style and spirit of Orwell's social-cultural criticism, valiantly plumbed the depths of working-class culture as lived experience, expressed in the forms of daily life of working-class people—forms that, he insisted (and as George Orwell would have liked to believe), were creative, exemplary responses to deprivation and want, responses that contained within themselves the seeds of opposition and social regeneration. This enterprise of reappraisal of working-class life, action, and response was then extended backwards to the emergence of the English working class, with all its distinctive attributes, by E. P. Thompson in his monumental study, *The Making of the English Working Class*.[36]

All these various re-readings were obviously valuable in their own right, as attempts to set the record straight. But in appraising this value we nevertheless need to bear in mind that the terms by which an indigenous, authentic working-class culture was assessed and recaptured were, in their origins, terms set by an intellectual movement that had little of socialism, and much less of Marxism, about it. The working-class culture that Orwell, among others, was so concerned to explore, revalue, and recuperate is a peculiarly English construct, largely for this very reason. It is striking that elsewhere the cultural task the left took upon itself was not at all a matter of recuperation in this sense. It was often concerned instead with deliberate, programmatic cultural creation. It was a matter not of raking through the debris in the hope of finding something valuable, but of the construction of an alternative that was to be original, new, and forward-looking. It is not hard to think of other, non-English, examples of recognizably working-class cultures that were not historical artifacts but the creations in the here and now of political parties; we have only to consider the French PCF in the 1940s and 1950s, the Italian PCI somewhat later, the SPD in Wilhelmine Germany (which modernist leftists of the interwar era admittedly hated), or the heroic period of Lunacharsky and Mayakovsky in the fledgling Soviet Union, to see the difference. Even later, the attempts by Brecht and Piscator to form a people's theater, and the very different efforts of Georg Lukács to sustain and preserve a "high culture" that was admitted to be bourgeois, were alike predicated upon the belief that the working class, like it or not, was a deracinated mass whose cultural teeth had been pulled by capitalism, and for whom cultural provision had to be made for political purposes. In England, by contrast, there was (and still is) a dogged determination not to make the same assumption, and indeed to deny it its medium of existence.

This "peculiarity of the English" helps explain the characteristic vulnerability of English "culture and society" Marxism in more recent times to the threat posed by Althusserian structuralist Marxism. It is no accident that E. P. Thompson, having just revised and reissued his long book about William Morris, then entered the lists against Althusser in a polemical book, *The Poverty of Theory*, which became celebrated in English (or *some* English) left-wing circles. For the Althusserian attack had been frontal and direct. It hit where it hurts. During the 1970s, at a time of almost institutionalized class conflict, of unregenerate strike activity carried on in the absence of anything remotely resembling a Marxist vanguard, Althusserians, with an almost ridiculous ease, were able to strike at the central presuppositions of "culture and society" Marxism by pointing to the *results* of working-class culture, the *outcomes* of the "authenticity" so cherished by the literati. They pointed to the ways in which expressions of the indigenous working-class milieu, its agencies and institutions, its forms of daily life and cultural artifacts, far from counterposing themselves critically to the prevailing status quo, in fact lent themselves to absorption by a prevailing system that was Protean. It sopped them up like a sponge. The Althusserians raised the question whether even forms of working-class *resistance*, far from embodying the promise of any alternative, were *in effect* the ideological props and struts of the status quo. How do we know whether they are not forms of ideology in action? How are we to know whether these expressions of ostensible resistance do not amount in practice to a serial demonstration of the hidden complexity and force of ideology, ideology which instead of obstructing the workings of capitalism actually allows it to function smoothly? To put it in a nutshell: what does it matter if school children crucify their teachers if they go on to work in factories? The educational system will have done its work well enough.[37]

The Althusserian critique was of course more thoroughgoing, more extreme, than Orwell's honest and painful doubts could have been. According to Althusserian theory, indeed, the more "creativity" (of the kind Thompson, Hoggart, et al., had been concerned unproblematically to celebrate) gets expressed, the greater the degree of ideological "interpellation" that will take place. Those who celebrate the "authenticity" of working-class responses are on this argument the dupes of a structured system ensuring that the working class cannot emancipate or even situate itself by dint of its own efforts; the assumption of transparency in cultural forms can no longer be sustained. What comes out is not transcendence of the status quo but submission (which only *appears* not to be abject) to it.

Our point here is not to push Orwell and the Althusserians—people he would no doubt have found wholly unsympathetic—artificially close together. It is simply to indicate an unexpected area of overlap between two vastly dissimilar ways of thinking, an unlikely penumbra whose delineation poses a serious question about working-class radicalism and culture in Britain. Orwell comes into it because, while he wanted to discover and believe in an authentic, indigenous working-class culture as the basis of political change, he found this culture not in England but in Spain. In England it existed—it had a kind of permanence—but Orwell entertained honest doubts about its regenerative potential. In Spain it was liberating in a much more evanescent way, and Orwell never doubted its regenerative potential at all.

This is a point of some importance that has frequently been overlooked or disregarded. Raymond Williams is quite right to insist that "nothing could be more false than the quite general idea that Orwell returned from Spain a disillusioned socialist, who then gave his energy to warnings against a totalitarian socialist future."[38] But what, then, is the connection between Williams's attempted displacement of Orwell's disillusionment, its displacement forward into the era of the cold war, and what Orwell had said, not just about the communists' and intelligentsia's betrayal of socialism, but also about the true character of what they betrayed? "I have seen wonderful things," said Orwell of his experiences in Spain, "and at last really believe in socialism, which I never did before."[39] The socialist culture Orwell experienced and celebrated has very little in common with the culture Williams was later to extol. It was not an "organic" outgrowth or presupposition of the "lived experience" or communal values of the Barcelona workers. It was not something woven into the fabric of everyday life, nor yet something partaking of licensed opposition to the status quo. It was oppositional in a quite different, and much more fundamental sense. It was cast up to the surface in the turmoil of revolution. It pointed forward, not backward, and was liberating, indeed exhilarating, for this very reason. In testifying to the galvanizing effect of being for the first (and only) time in his life in a town, Barcelona, "where the working class is in the saddle," Orwell was at pains to contrast the shock of deciding that fighting the fascists "seemed the only conceivable thing to do"[40] with anything he had experienced in England. In the militia, he says,

> many of the normal motives of civilized life—snobbishness, money-grubbing, fear of the boss, etc.—had simply ceased to exist. The ordinary class divisions or society had disappeared to an extent that is almost unthinkable in the money-tainted air of England. . . . In that community [in Spain] . . . one got, perhaps, a crude foretaste of what the opening stages or socialism might be like. And, after all, instead of disillusioning me, it deeply attracted me. The effect was to make my desire to see socialism established much more actual than it had been before.[41]

Yet how different it was from England. Think of the final words of *Homage to Catalonia*, describing Southern England as it struck him on his return (as one of the few English writers of his generation who had crossed the Franco-Spanish frontier as a wanted suspect). Orwell refers to "the deep, deep sleep of England, from which I sometimes fear that we shall never wake till we are jerked out of it by the roar of bombs,"[42] the very roar of bombs Orwell was concerned to prophesy. *Coming Up for Air*, Orwell's next book after *Homage to Catalonia*, is not just a forlorn idyll dealing with the "loss, disillusion, disenchantment" of the "old England [of Orwell's] childhood,"[43] as Raymond Williams thinks. It is also a prediction of the world of *Nineteen Eighty-Four*, treating fascism and terror as a kind of home-front destiny. In both novels the colorless decrepitude of a present which is able to make time itself synthetic is broken by an almost tangible and iconic past and by a future almost too terrible to contemplate.

Orwell, as is well known, changed his mind about the inevitability of fascism and about the final uselessness of war as a means of com-

bating it. By the time the Second World War had broken out, Orwell
had become what Raymond Williams and others like to term a "social
patriot." His writings of this period, early in the war, particularly *The
Lion and the Unicorn,* once again needled, antagonized, and embarrassed his readers on the left, thanks to what Woodcock calls
their "extraordinary mingling of conservative and revolutionary concepts."[44] This, we may surmise, is why Raymond Williams, whose
own writings mingle conservative and revolutionary concepts in a different way, finds these writings among the most objectionable of all.
Once again, Orwell cuts too close to the bone. He calls into question
something Williams has no desire to relinquish. In this way, Orwell in
effect points up the self-defeating nature of a characteristic feature of
the British left intelligentsia. This is its recurrent yearning for an
"authentic," radical proletarian autarchy, for a truer and ever less
compromised source of opposition to bourgeois hegemony. Orwell had
Winston Smith's diary pose the (Lukácsian) conundrum about the proles: "Until they have become conscious they will never rebel, and
until after they have rebelled they cannot become conscious." This
conundrum, which he derived from his experience in Spain as well as
England, led Orwell to despair; and perhaps what bothers Orwell's critics on the left when they despair of him is the nagging fear that he may
be right. Orwell was in his own way victim as well as critic of the
yearning for proletarian autonomy. Yet his doubts about the regenerative (as opposed to regressive) potential of working-class culture and
"lived experience" point up in advance the dangers involved in trying
to hang on this particular hook more weight than it can reasonably be
expected to bear.

There is a problem with the left's recurrent quest for an "authenti-
cally" oppositional force that is always presumed to be out there,
somewhere. It lies in the fugitive nature of the quest itself. The search
for successive Archimedean points within society from which society
might be regenerated may be the search of a concept for an object.
There is no shortage of examples of such elusive *points d'appui.*
Raymond Williams, who is by no means the worst offender, was wont
to describe himself latterly not as British (an ideological construct) but
rather as a "Welsh European" ("I want the Welsh people—still a radical and cultured people—to defeat, override or bypass bourgeois
England").[45] Consider even Terry Eagleton, whose *Literature and
Ideology* had provided a sharp, persuasive critique of Raymond
Williams.[46] Eagleton's *Literary Theory* contains the following parable:

We know that the lion is stronger than the lion-tamer, and so does the lion-tamer. The problem is that the lion does not know it. It is not out of the question that the death of literature might help the lion to awaken.[47]

The lion is that slumbering giant, the people who, we are given to understand, have been prevented by their own literature, imposed on them by a cultural élite, from becoming conscious of themselves. Literature, a bourgeois concept, must be abolished as "literature" if social regeneration is to be achieved. At one level the wheel, Raymond Williams's wheel, has turned full circle. But at another level it is still the same wheel. The agency of regeneration has not changed at all. Orwell alone despairingly dared to imagine that the lion of Eagleton (and Williams) might be nothing more than the iconic counterpart to the unicorn, that the sleeping lion might be declawed as well as supine. But since he did have the courage to advance it, the last word should perhaps be his beloved Shakespeare's:

> *Glendower* [a Welsh European]: I can call spirits from the vasty deep.
> *Hotspur*: Why, so can I, or so can any man; But will they come when you do call for them?[48]

Notes

NOTES TO INTRODUCTION

1. Matthew Arnold, *Culture and Anarchy, with Friendship's Garland and some Literary Essays*, ed. R. H. Super (Ann Arbor: Michigan University Press, 1965), p. 135.

2. We will not address here other concepts of culture that emerge later than our period: ethnographic concepts of culture, "that complex whole which includes knowledge, belief, art, morals, law, custom," etc., or that of "cultural studies" which combines aesthetic and ethnographic definitions, "high" and "low" culture. The citation is from A. B. Taylor's *Primitive Culture* (1871), cited in Christopher Herbert, *Culture and Anomie: Ethnographic Imagination in the Nineteenth Century* (Chicago: University of Chicago Press, 1991), p. 6. We do address the distinctions in passing throughout the book, and have drawn freely from Herbert and from John Brenkman, *Culture and Domination* (Ithaca, NY: Cornell University Press, 1987) and from chap. 1, "Culture," of Raymond Williams, *Marxism and Literature* (Oxford: Oxford University Press, 1977).

3. See Part II, "Critique of Teleological Judgement," First Division, #4, of Immanuel Kant, *Critique of Judgement*, trans. James Creed Meredith (Oxford: Oxford University Press, 1952), p. 23n for a succinct definition of the state as an "organization."

4. Michel Foucault, "Governmentality," in *The Foucault Effect: Studies in Governmentality*, ed. Graham Burchell, Colin Gordon, and Peter Miller (Chicago: University of Chicago Press, 1991).

5. See Williams, *Marxism and Literature*, pp. 83–89 and "Base and Superstructure in Marxist Cultural Theory," in *Problems in Materialism and Culture* (London: Verso, 1980), pp. 31–49. Foucault's earlier *Discipline and Punish*, a work far closer to Marx than his more recent ones, expresses the necessity for transfer impeccably:

> [The Panopticon] is polivalent in its applications; it serves to reform prisoners, but also to treat patients, to instruct schoolchildren, to confine the insane, to supervise workers, to put beggars and idlers to work. It is a type of location of bodies in space, of distributions of individuals in relation to one another, of hierarchical organization, of disposition of centres and channels of power, of definition of the instruments and modes of intervention of power, which can be implemented in hospitals, workshops, schools,

189

> prisons.... These disciplines ... Bentham dreamt of transforming into a
> network of mechanisms that would be everywhere and always alert, run-
> ning through society without interruption in space or in time. The panoptic
> arrangement provides the formula for this generalization. It programmes, at
> the level of an elementary and easily transferable mechanism, the basic
> functioning of a society penetrated through and through with disciplinary
> mechanisms.

See Foucault, *Discipline and Punish: The Birth of the Prison*, trans. Alan Sheridan
(New York: Vintage, 1979), pp. 205 and 209.

6. Althusser, "Ideology and Ideological State Apparatuses: Notes towards an
Investigation," in *Lenin and Philosophy and Other Essays*, trans. Ben Brewster (New
York: Monthly Review Press, 1971), p. 181.

7. Karl Marx, *The Eighteenth Brumaire of Louis Bonaparte*, 3rd ed. (Moscow:
Progress Publishers, 1954), p. 106.

8. On the link between Kant's aesthetic and political philosophy, see Hannah
Arendt, *Lectures on Kant's Political Philosophy*, ed. with an interpretive essay by
Ronald Beiner (Chicago: University of Chicago Press, 1982), pp. 58–72. See also
David Lloyd, "Kant's Examples," in *Unruly Examples: On the Rhetoric of Exemplarity*, ed. Alexander Gelley (Stanford: Stanford University Press, 1995), pp. 255–76,
for a more critical reading of Kant's *sensus communis* in relation to pedagogy and
subject formation.

9. That such powerfully precursive statements of the function of aesthetic culture vis à vis the state should have emerged in late-eighteenth-century Germany is
perhaps attributable to the comparatively weak position of a national bourgeoisie
hampered by the economic and political fragmentation that attended *Kleinstaaterei*.
Hence Marx's ironic remark on the *theoretical* strengths of the Germans as opposed
to the industrial or political discoveries of the English and French respectively. See
Karl Marx, "Contribution to the Critique of Hegel's Philosophy of Law, Introduction" in Marx and Engels, *Collected Works*, vol. 3 (New York: International Pub-
lishers, 1975), pp. 175–87. For discussions, see Paul Thomas, *Alien Politics: Marxist
State Theory Retrieved* (New York and London: Routledge, 1994), chap. 8, and
Harold Mah, "The French Revolution and the Problem of German Modernity: Hegel,
Heine and Marx," *New German Critique*, no. 50 (Spring–Summer 1990), pp. 3–20.

10. For this concept, see Thomas, *Alien Politics*.

11. See Karl Marx and Friedrich Engels, *The Communist Manifesto*, intro. by A.
J. P. Taylor (Harmondsworth: Penguin, 1967), p. 105, where the "Combination of
education with industrial production" is proposed; and Karl Marx, *Critique of the
Gotha Program*, in *The Marx–Engels Reader*, ed. Robert Tucker, 2nd ed. (New York:
Norton, 1978), p. 541, where it is proposed that "an early combination of productive
labor with education is one of the most potent means for the transformation of present day society."

12. Raymond Williams, *Culture and Society, 1780–1950* (New York: Columbia
University Press, 1983).

13. Raymond Williams, *Politics and Letters: Interviews with New Left Review*
(London: New Left Books, 1979), pp. 99–100.

14. Williams, *Politics and Letters*, p. 97.

15. It is fair to point out that Williams, reflecting later on *Culture and Society* in
Politics and Letters, recognizes the lack of any sustained discussion of the state in
the earlier volume. See *Politics and Letters*, pp. 119–20. In general, we should stress
here that our critique of *Culture and Society* in this essay does not constitute a critique of Williams's later revisions and intellectual developments. What we have
sought to isolate is a critical moment in cultural materialism which continues to
exert considerable influence quite apart from Williams's later revisions. (As he puts

it in *Politics and Letters*, p. 100, "it is the very success of the book that has created the conditions for its critique.") We are not convinced, however, that even these later self-criticisms and transformations constitute a rethinking of the fundamental commitment to culture as defined in *Culture and Society*, a rethinking which, we argue here, would require a rearticulation of the social spaces differentiated historically as well as conceptually as the economic, the political, the cultural, etc. In the terms of "A Hundred Years of Culture and Anarchy," *Problems in Materialism and Culture*, (London: Verso, 1980) pp. 3–10, the concepts invoked are still the "known" rather than the "knowable" of much cultural theory, the separate sphere of culture continuing to provide a self-evident basis for even radical cultural critique.

16. See Rousseau, *The Social Contract* (1762), trans. Maurice Cranston (Harmondsworth: Penguin, 1971), Book 3, chap. 15, p. 141: "The idea of representation is a modern one. It comes to us from feudal government, from that iniquitous and absurd system under which the human race is degraded and which dishonors the name of man. In the republics and even in the monarchies of the ancient world, the people never had representatives: the very word was unknown."

17. For some background to this intellectual moment, see Williams's own discussion in *Politics and Letters*, pp. 61–3, and Alan Sinfield, *Literature, Politics and Culture in Postwar Britain* (Berkeley: University of California Press, 1989), pp. 6–22.

18. "Structures of feeling" is, of course, a later theoretical concept introduced by Williams to deal in many respects with precisely the kind of problem we are indicating here in the earlier work. It has the advantage of addressing the social construction of emotion while allowing the importance of "feeling" as a crucial site for hegemonic and counterhegemonic struggles. With regard to the recurrent opposition between socialist enlightenment and feeling, Williams reveals his continuing sensitivity to this debate in defending *Culture and Society* in the Introduction to the Morningside Edition, where he remarks that along with Hoggart's and Thompson's works of the same period, *Culture and Society* had been "assigned to a kind of cultural radicalism which had since been outdistanced by a clearer, harder and indeed more traditional kind of socialism" (*Culture and Society*, p. xi).

19. Williams, *Culture and Society*, pp. 4–5.

20. Ibid., p. 316.

21. Ibid., p. 333.

22. Ibid., p. 333.

23. Ibid., p. 123.

24. Ibid., p. 320.

25. The relationship between our critique of Williams here and current critiques of American pluralism from the perspective of "minority discourse" could be elaborated. The political force of *minority* (as distinct from particular ethnic) cultures derives from their historically damaged position, which obliges a critical take on dominant cultural formations. See Abdul JanMohamed and David Lloyd, Introduction to *The Nature and Context of Minority Discourse* (Oxford: Oxford University Press, 1990), pp. 4–11. Lisa Lowe has given a very powerful critique of current cultural pluralisms in "Imagining Los Angeles in the Production of Multiculturalism," chap. 4 of *Immigrant Acts: On Asian-American Cultural Politics* (Durham, NC: Duke University Press, 1996).

26. Ian Hunter, *Culture and Government: The Emergence of Literary Education* (London: Macmillan, 1988).

27. Ibid., p. 262.

28. Ibid., p. 37.

29. Ibid., p. 39.

30. Hunter's lengthy invocation of Thomas Laqueur's work on Sunday Schools, and his assertion that since such schools were statistically distributed equally in rural and urban locations, there was no evident correlation with "the spread of

factory production" is simply absurd. Capitalization of agriculture and industrialization affected the rural as much as the urban poor, and were certainly recognized by the Chartists as continuous issues.

31. Thomas Babington, Lord Macaulay, "Education," in *Selected Writings*, ed. John Clive and Thomas Pinney (Chicago: University of Chicago Press, 1972), p. 214.

32. Hunter, *Culture and Government*, p. 56.

33. Richard Johnson, quoted in Michael Sanderson, *Education, Economic Change and Society in England, 1780–1870* (London: Macmillan, 1983), p. 17. See also John Lawson and Harold Silver, *A Social History of Education in England* (London: Methuen, 1973), chap. 8; Paul Richards, "State Formation and Class Struggle, 1832–48," in *Capitalism, State Formation and Marxist Theory: Historical Investigations*, ed. Philip Corrigan (London: Quartet Books, 1980), pp. 74–6, as well as our own survey in Chapter 3.

34. Hunter, *Culture and Government*, p. 49.

35. Ibid., p. 58.

36. Ibid., p. 59.

37. On this constitutive pedagogical pun, see Lloyd, "Kant's Examples," pp. 263–5.

38. Louis Althusser, "Ideology and Ideological State Apparatuses," p. 169. Unfortunately, Althusser's brief analysis of the school as material ideological apparatus is truncated by his swerve to the Church as paradigm, a swerve which underwrites his assertion of the transhistorical nature of ideology and obscures the central hegemonic function of education.

39. In the different context of the U.S. racial state, Omi and Winant express the conundrum succinctly:

> Despite all the forces working at cross-purposes within the state—disparate demands of constituents, distinct agency mandates and prerogatives, unintended and cross-cutting consequences of policy, etc.—the state still preserves an overall unity.

Michael Omi and Howard Winant, *Racial Formation in the United States: From the 1960s to the 1980s* (New York: Routledge, 1986), p. 78.

40. Antonio Gramsci, *Selections from the Prison Notebooks*, ed. and trans. Quintin Hoare and Geoffrey Nowell-Smith (New York: International Publishers, 1971), p. 263.

41. Gramsci, *Prison Notebooks*, pp. 242, 247.

42. Renate Holub maintains that "Without the intellectual ... there is perhaps no Gramscian critical theory." *Antonio Gramsci: Beyond Marxism and Postmodernism* (New York: Routledge, 1992), pp. 151–2.

43. Perry Anderson's important essay, "The Antinomies of Antonio Gramsci" (*New Left Review*, no. 100 [Nov. 1976–Jan 1977], pp. 5–78), is sadly typical in regarding the distinction in question as original, foundational, and persuasive—and therefore refusing to interrogate it.

44. Gramsci, *Prison Notebooks*, p. 3.

45. Ibid., p. 323.

46. Ibid., pp. 26–43.

47. Richard Johnson, "'Really Useful Knowledge': Radical Education and Working Class Culture, 1790–1848," in *Working Class Culture: Studies in History and Theory*, ed. John Clarke, Chas Critcher and Richard Johnson, Centre for Contemporary Cultural Studies, University of Birmingham (London: Hutchinson, 1979), p. 89.

48. Gramsci, *Prison Notebooks*, p. 5.

49. Walter A. Adamson, *Hegemony and Revolution: A Study of Antonio Gramsci's Political and Cultural Theory* (Berkeley and Los Angeles: University of California Press, 1980), p. 143. Adamson's text is one of the few interpretations (as opposed to outlines or accounts which are content to take Gramsci at his own word) in any of the secondary literature on Gramsci.

50. Gramsci, *Prison Notebooks*, p. 5.
51. See Adamson, *Hegemony and Revolution*, p. 143.
52. Gramsci, *Prison Notebooks*, p. 7.
53. Ibid., p. 341.
54. Ibid., p. 3.
55. Ibid., pp. 10–11.
56. Ibid., p. 334.
57. Ibid., pp. 334–5.
58. Ibid., pp. 332–3.
59. Ibid., p. 418.
60. Ibid., p. 332.
61. Ibid., p. 173.
62. Ibid., p. 3

63. Our criticism of Gramsci here is equally relevant to his discussions of intellectuals in "Americanism and Fordism," where the actual transformation of university and schooling institutions into organic elements of the capitalist structure was unavailable to him. See *Prison Notebooks*, pp. 285–6. For more recent work on these transformations, see Clyde W. Barrow, *Universities and the Capitalist State: Corporate Liberalism and the Reconstruction of American Higher Education, 1894–1928* (Madison: University of Wisconsin Press, 1990); and, more generally, Samuel Bowles and Herbert Gintis, *Schooling in Capitalist America: Educational Reform and the Contradictions of Economic Life* (New York: Basic Books, 1976).

64. For texts on decolonization and the formation of the nationalist intellectual, see Frantz Fanon, "On National Culture," *The Wretched of the Earth*, trans. Constance Farrington (New York: Grove Press, 1965); Ngugi Wa Thiong'o, *Decolonizing the Mind: The Politics of Language in African Literature* (London: J. Currey, 1986); Benedict Anderson, *Imagined Communities: Reflections on the Origin and Spread of Nationalism*, rev. and extended ed. (London: Verso, 1991). Homi K. Bhabha comments extensively on the phrase cited from Fanon in "DissemiNation: Time, Narrative and the Margins of the Modern Nation," *The Location of Culture* (London: Routledge, 1994), pp. 152–3.

NOTES TO CHAPTER 1

1. See Terry Eagleton, *The Ideology of the Aesthetic* (Oxford: Blackwell, 1990), esp. chap. 2.

2. Immanuel Kant, *The Conflict of the Faculties* (1798), trans. and ed. Mary T. Gregor (New York: Abaris, 1979), pp. 154–5.

3. Hannah Arendt, *Lectures on Kant's Political Philosophy*, ed. Ronald Beiner (Chicago: University of Chicago Press, 1982), p. 52.

4. Reinhart Koselleck, *Kritik und Krise: Ein Beitrag zur Pathogenese der bürgerlichen Welt* (Freiburg and München: Alber, 1959). Page references will be to the English translation of Koselleck's text, *Critique and Crisis: Enlightenment and the Pathogenesis of Modern Society* (Cambridge, MA: MIT Press, 1988).

5. On the formality of the political subject, see Paul Thomas, *Alien Politics: Marxist State Theory Retrieved* (New York and London: Routledge, 1994); on the political significance of the aesthetic subject, see David Lloyd, "Analogies of the Aesthetic: The Politics of Culture and the Limits of Materialist Aesthetics," *New Formations*, no. 10 (Spring 1990), pp. 109–26.

6. Jean-Jacques Rousseau, "First Discourse" (1750), in *The First and Second Discourses*, trans. Roger D. Masters (New York: St. Martin's Press, 1964), p. 37.

7. Jean Starobinski, *Jean-Jacques Rousseau: Transparency and Obstruction*, trans. Arthur Goldhammer (Chicago: University of Chicago Press, 1988), p. 182.

8. Jean-Jacques Rousseau, *Politics and the Arts: Letter to M. D'Alembert on the Theater* (1758), trans. Allan Bloom (Ithaca, NY: Cornell University Press, 1960), p. 61.

9. Rousseau, *Letter to D'Alembert*, p. 80.

10. Rousseau, "First Discourse," *First and Second Discourses*, p. 59.

11. Friedrich Schiller, *On the Aesthetic Education of Man, In a Series of Letters* (1795), ed. and trans. Elizabeth M. Wilkinson and L. A. Willoughby (Oxford: Clarendon Press, 1967), p. 43. Future references will be made parenthetically, accompanied by the abbreviation *AEM*.

12. Rousseau, *Letter to D'Alembert*, pp. 16–17.

13. Rousseau, Ibid., p. 25.

14. See Starobinski, *Transparency and Obstruction*, pp. 95–6.

15. Starobinski, *Transparency and Obstruction*, pp. 93–4.

16. Ibid., pp. 92–93.

17. Ibid., p. 96.

18. Wokler, "Rousseau and Marx," in *The Nature of Political Theory: Essay in Honour of John Plamenatz*, eds. David Miller and Larry Siedentop (Oxford: Oxford University Press, 1983), p. 236. The Rousseau reference is to *Essai sur l'origine des langues*, ed. Ch. Porset (Bordeaux: Ducros, 1970), p. 199.

19. Wokler, "Rousseau and Marx," p. 243.

20. Koselleck, *Critique and Crisis*, pp. 163–6. *Kritik und Krise*, pp. 136–8.

21. Walter Benjamin, *Illuminations: Essays and Reflections*, ed. Hannah Arendt, trans. Harry Zohn (New York: Schocken, 1968), p. 241.

22. For the critique of Rousseau in these terms, see Edmund Burke, *Reflections on the Revolution in France* (1790), ed. L. G. Mitchell (Oxford: Oxford University Press, 1993), pp. 264–75.

23. Mona Ozouf, *Festivals and the French Revolution*, trans. Alan Sheridan (Cambridge, MA: Harvard University Press, 1988), p. 54.

24. Cf. Ozouf, *Festivals, passim*. See also Bronislaw Baczko, *Utopian Lights*, trans. Judith N. Greenberg (New York: Paragon House, 1989), *passim*, and Paule-Monique Vernès, *La ville, la fête, la démocratie: Rousseau et les illusions de la communauté* (Paris: Payot, 1978), *passim*.

25. *Emile, or On Education* (1762), trans. Allan Bloom (New York: Basic Books, 1979), pp. 82, 81.

26. On the structure of Kantian pedagogy, see David Lloyd, "Kant's Examples," in *Unruly Examples: On the Rhetoric of Exemplarity*, ed. Alexander Gelley (Stanford: Stanford University Press, 1995), pp. 255–76.

27. Louis Althusser, *Lenin and Philosophy and Other Essays*, trans. Ben Brewster (New York: Monthly Review Press, 1971), pp. 170 ff.

28. See Friedrich Schiller, *Essays Aesthetical and Philosophical* (London: George Bell & Sons, 1879). References to the essay will be made parenthetically, accompanied by the abbreviation *SMI*.

29. We owe to Stallybrass and White a remarkable account of the gradual containment of the very different spaces of popular assembly, especially the fair, as the condition of emergence for modern manifestations of "the public." It is striking that virtually all the institutions that for Gramsci constitute "the ethical state" and for Habermas "the public sphere" take the form of theatrical and moral sites. See Peter Stallybrass and Allon White, *The Politics and Poetics of Transgression* (Ithaca, NY: Cornell University Press, 1986), esp. chap. 1.

30. E. P. Thompson, "The Moral Economy of the English Crowd in the Eighteenth Century," *Past and Present*, no. 50 (Feb. 1971), pp. 76–136.

NOTES TO CHAPTER 2

1. On the genealogy of English radicalism in the 1890s, see E. P. Thompson, *The Making of the English Working Class* (New York: Vintage, 1966), Part One, "The Liberty Tree."

2. For a brief biographical note on Spence, his political activism and frequent arrests, as well as on his posthumous contribution to English radical thought, see Marilyn Butler, ed., *Burke, Paine, Godwin and the Revolution Controversy* (Cambridge: Cambridge University Press, 1984), pp. 189–90. On p. 190, Butler writes:

> An eccentric and a 'loner', he lived on in London in great poverty. His cause and his personal example made him a hero to a small band of devoted Spensonians, headed by Thomas Evans, through whom his ideas became part of the stock of nineteenth-century radicalism.

3. Thomas Spence, *The End of Oppression*, Cambridge University Library Rare Books.

4. Williams, *Culture and Society, 1780–1950* (New York: Columbia University Press, 1983), p. 70.

5. Ibid., p. 32.

6. Ibid., p. 42.

7. Ibid., p. 43.

8. Ibid.

9. For a discussion of Shelley's relation to emergent political society, see Stephen Goldsmith, *Unbuilding Themselves: Apocalypse and Romantic Representation* (Ithaca, NY: Cornell University Press, 1993), chap. 4.

10. See Alexander Pope, *An Essay on Man*, in *Alexander Pope: A Critical Edition of the Major Works*, ed. Pat Rodgers (Oxford: Oxford University Press, 1993), pp. 270–308.

11. Coleridge, *On the Constitution of the Church and State*, ed. John Colmer (Princeton, NJ: Princeton University Press, 1976), pp. 42–3. Emphases in the original. Future references will appear parenthetically, abbreviated *CCS*. Williams quotes most of this and other related passages in *Culture and Society*, pp. 61–3.

12. On those debates, see especially John Lawson and Harold Silver, *A Social History of Education in England* (London: Methuen, 1973), and J. M. Godstrom, "The Content of Education and the Socialisation of the Working Class Child, 1830–1860," in *Popular Education and Socialisation in the Nineteenth Century*, ed. Philip McCann (London: Methuen, 1977), pp. 93–109. It is important to note that these debates may have been most intense, as well as earlier articulated, in the colonies, just as the forms of British national education seem to have emerged first away from the metropolis. For some account of the debates and on imperial formations of educational institutions see D. H. Akenson, *The Irish Education Experiment: The National System of Education in the Nineteenth Century* (London: Routledge and Kegan Paul, 1970) and Gauri Viswanathan, *Masks of Conquest: Literary Study and British Rule in India* (New York: Columbia University Press, 1983).

13. We may recall here how, in *Biographia Literaria*, Coleridge remarks on the effect of the dissemination of the King James Bible not in relation to the inculcation of religious sentiment but rather in terms of its improvement of the syntax and vocabulary of rural individuals. Its cultivating effect refers to the forms of speech rather than to Christian dogma. See *Biographia Literaria*, vol. 2, eds. James Engell and W. Jackson Bate (Princeton, NJ: Princeton University Press, 1983), p. 44.

14. William Wordsworth, *Poetical Works*, ed. Thomas Hutchinson, rev. Ernest de Selincourt (Oxford: Oxford University Press, 1969), p. 735. Future references will appear parenthetically, abbreviated as *PW*.

15. Cf. Coleridge, *Biographia*, vol. 1, p. 304.

16. For Wordsworth's discussion of this at the level of meter in the 1800 "Preface," see *PW*, p. 740.

17. See especially such "ballads" as "Simon Lee" or "An Anecdote for Fathers" in *Lyrical Ballads*, and the numerous "poems on the naming of places," *PW*, pp. 116–21.

18. We transcribe the 1815 version of the poem from *PW*, p. 448, and the 1798 version from Wordsworth and Coleridge, *Lyrical Ballads 1798*, ed. W. J. B. Owen (Oxford: Oxford University Press, 1969), pp. 105–6. Cited in the text as *LB*.

19. The 1798 version of the poem presents us with a short-lived heteroglossic lyric at the very moment of Romantic restructuring of the genre. It is not an *impossible* phenomenon, merely one "improbable" in the emergent canon. Wordsworth in 1815 would have agreed with Mikhail Bakhtin's insistence that *poetry* depends on "the unity of a voice" and that with the introduction of another voice "the poetic plane is destroyed." The Wordsworth of 1798 provides room to disagree with such assumptions and highlights what is excluded by the monology that overtakes poetry with and after Romanticism. See M. M. Bakhtin, "Discourse in the Novel," *The Dialogic Imagination: Four Essays*, ed. Michael Holquist, trans. Michael Holquist and Caryl Emerson (Austin: University of Texas Press, 1981), p. 328.

20. See Terry Eagleton, *The Ideology of the Aesthetic* (Oxford: Blackwell, 1990), chap. 2, for a discussion of the political function of taste in the eighteenth century.

21. See Thomas Robert Malthus, *An Essay on the Principle of Population*, ed. Antony Flew (Harmondsworth: Penguin, 1970), p. 175.

22. *The Prose Works of William Wordsworth*, eds. W. J. B. Owen and Jayne Worthington Smyser, vol. 2 (Oxford: Clarendon Press, 1974), p. 24.

23. Franco Moretti, in *The Way of the World* (London: Verso, 1987), pp. 5–6, remarks on the nineteenth century's preoccupation with "youth" as the index of a modernity which is predicated on change and development.

24. *Penny Papers for the People*, 18 Mar. 1831.

25. *Mechanic's Magazine*, 12, 15 Nov. 1823, pp. 190–1.

26. *Penny Papers*, 23 Apr. 1831.

27. *Mechanic's Magazine*, 7, 11 Oct. 1823, pp. 99–100.

28. *Penny Papers*, 26 Mar. 1831.

29. As Brian Simon has argued in *The Two Nations and the Educational Structure, 1780–1870* (London: Lawrence and Wishart, 1974), the history of the London Mechanics' Institute "provides an instructive example of the way in which Radicals, industrialists and Whig politicians combined to turn what originated chiefly as a working class institution to their own purposes" (p. 153). The Institute was set up by Hodgkin and Robertson, and was conceived from the start as an Institute fully under workers' control. Under material and other pressures, however, Hodgkin approached Francis Place for assistance which, though forthcoming, came at a price. The middle-class reformer George Birkbeck loaned £3,000 to the Institute from his own pocket and was installed as its President (pp. 153–4). Hodgkin and Robertson, "outmaneuvered and outfinanced," were not re-elected as secretaries in 1823, when the Institute was formally set up; "the Institute of which they were the originators slipped from their control" (p. 154).

30. *Mechanic's Magazine*, 99, 16 July 1825, pp. 238–40.

31. For the critique of Hodgkin's book, see *Mechanic's Magazine*, (New Series) 7, 16 June 1827, p. 378. Simon quotes some relevant passages in his *Two Nations* (p. 156, n.3).

32. Quoted in Simon, *Two Nations*, p. 159.

33. J. W. Hudson, *History of Adult Education* (1851), pp. 54–5. Quoted in Simon, *Two Nations*, p. 158.

Notes to Chapter 3

1. Gareth Stedman Jones, *Languages of Class: Studies in Working Class History 1832–1982* (Cambridge: Cambridge University Press, 1983), *passim*. For critiques of Stedman Jones, see Richard Ashcraft, "Liberal Political Theory and Working Class Radicalism in Nineteenth-Century England," *Political Theory*, vol. 21, no. 2 (May 1993), pp. 249–72; Neville Kirk, "In Defence of Class," *International Review of*

Social History, vol. 32 (1987), pp. 2–47; John C. Belchem, "Radical Language and Ideology in Early Nineteenth-Century England: The Challenge of the Platform," *Albion*, no. 20 (Summer 1988), pp. 247–59; and Robert Grey, "The Deconstruction of the English Working Class," *Social History*, no. 11 (Oct. 1986), pp. 363–73. In anticipation of our critique of their work in our Conclusion, we should note here that Ernesto Laclau and Chantal Mouffe rely all-too heavily on Stedman Jones in their historical remarks on the nature of Chartism as a *political* movement. See their *Hegemony and Socialist Strategy: Towards a Radical Democratic Politics* (London: Verso, 1985), pp. 155–156.

2. Dorothy Thompson, *The Chartists: Popular Politics in the Industrial Revolution* (New York: Pantheon, 1984), p. 301.

3. See Ralph Miliband, *Parliamentary Socialism* (London: Merlin, 1972), passim.

4. E. P. Thompson, *The Making of the English Working Class* (New York: Vintage, 1966), p. 12.

5. Ellen Meiksins Wood, *The Retreat from Class* (London: Verso, 1986), p. 111; emphasis added.

6. E. P. Thompson, *Making of the English Working Class*, p. 807.

7. See Eric Hobsbawm and George Rudé, *Captain Swing: A Social History of the Great English Agricultural Uprising of 1830* (New York: Pantheon, 1968), passim.

8. See Thompson, "The Peculiarities of the English," in *The Socialist Register* no. 2 (1965), eds. Ralph Miliband and John Saville; repr. in *The Poverty of Theory and Other Essays* (London: Merlin Press, 1979), pp. 35–91.

9. "Peculiarities," p. 70.

10. Thompson, "Peculiarities," p. 71.

11. E. P. Thompson, *Making of the English Working Class*, p. 198; cf. also p. 181.

12. For a good summary, see Eric Foner, *Tom Paine and Revolutionary America* (Oxford: Oxford University Press, 1976), pp. 7–8. Thomas Spence was a singular and prefigurative exception to this rule of thumb.

13. Gregory Claeys, *Citizens and Saints: Politics and Anti-Politics in Early British Socialism* (Cambridge: Cambridge University Press, 1989), p. 4; cf. D. Thompson, *Chartists*, pp. 276–7.

14. Benjamin Wilson, "The Struggles of Old Chartism," *Testaments of Radicalism*, ed. David Vincent (Frankfurt: Europa, 1977), p. 210; Claeys, *Citizens*, pp. 216–17.

15. Claeys, *Citizens*, p. 224.

16. Joan Wallach Scott, *Gender and the Politics of History* (New York: Columbia University Press, 1988), p. 58.

17. Eileen Yeo, "Practices and Problems of Chartist Democracy," in *The Chartist Experience: Studies in Working-Class Radicalism and Culture*, eds. James Epstein and Dorothy Thompson (London: Macmillan, 1982), pp. 373–374.

18. Claeys, *Citizens*, p. 283.

19. Asa Briggs, ed., *Chartist Studies* (London: Macmillan, 1960), p. 295.

20. D. Thompson, *Chartists*, pp. 16–17.

21. Richard Johnson, "Educational Policy and Social Control in Early Victorian England," *Past and Present*, no. 49 (Nov. 1970), p. 97.

22. *Form of Report for Her Majesty's Inspectors of Schools, Minutes of the Committee on Education, 1840–41*.

23. Johnson, "Educational Policy," p. 119.

24. Hunter, *Culture and Government: The Emergence of Literary Education* (London: Macmillan 1988), passim. See also our Introduction above.

25. Simon, *The Two Nations and the Educational Structure, 1780–1870* (London: Lawrence and Wishart, 1974), p. 159.

26. Simon, *Two Nations*, p. 160.

27. See Hobsbawm and Rudé, *Captain Swing*, passim.

28. See Claeys, *Citizens*, passim.

29. In R. K. Webb, ed., *The British Working Class Reader, 1790–1848: Literacy and Social Tension* (London: Allen & Unwin, 1955), p. 93.

30. *Westminster Review*, vol. XIV, no. 28 (Apr. 1831), p. 372. Quoted in Simon, *Two Nations*, p. 161.

31. Henry Brougham, *Practical Observations upon the Education of the People, Addressed to the Working Classes and their Employers* (London, 1825); quoted in Trygve Tholfson, *Working Class Radicalism in Mid-Victorian England* (New York: Columbia University Press, 1977), p. 130.

32. Charles Knight, *Passages of a Working Life During Half a Century: With a Prelude of Early Reminiscences*, vol. 2 (London: Bradbury & Evans, 1864), p. 310.

33. Knight, *Passages*, p. 171.

34. See Simon, *Two Nations*, pp. 162–3.

35. J. E. G. de Montmorency, *State Intervention in English Education: A Short History from Earliest Times Down to 1833* (Cambridge: Cambridge University Press, 1902), p. 300.

36. Simon, *Two Nations*, p. 163.

37. Ibid., pp. 138–39.

38. Ibid., p. 166.

39. Ibid., pp. 165–66.

40. Ibid., p. 164.

41. *Moral and Physical Education*, repr. in *Four Periods of Public Education, As Reviewed in 1832, 1839, 1846, 1862* (London: Longman, Green, Longman, and Roberts, 1862), p. 39. Quoted in Simon, *Two Nations*, p. 169.

42. "The tradition of mutual study, disputation and improvement" was "firmly established as an aspect of working class life . . . by the time of the Chartist decade." Tholfson, *Working Class Radicalism*, pp. 62–3.

43. See Tholfson, *Working Class Radicalism*, pp. 64–8.

44. Quoted in Simon, *Two Nations*, p. 215.

45. Ibid., p. 215.

46. *The Poor Man's Advocate and People's Library*, 25 Feb. 1832, p. 44. Quoted in Simon, *Two Nations*, p. 220.

47. Simon, *Two Nations*, p. 221.

48. *Northern Star*, 29 Jan. 1848. Quoted in Simon, *Two Nations*, p. 223.

49. Simon, *Two Nations*, p. 223.

50. A. Aspinall, *Politics and the Press, c. 1780–1850* (London: Home & Van Thal, 1949), p. 60; Simon, *Two Nations*, p. 223.

51. Simon, *Two Nations*, pp. 223–4.

52. See John Foster, *Class Struggle and the Industrial Revolution: Early Industrial Capitalism in Three English Towns* (New York: St. Martin's Press, 1974), pp. 62–4.

53. E. P. Thompson, *Making of the English Working Class*, p. 549.

54. Dorothy Thompson, *Chartists*, pp. 243–4.

55. In Webb, ed., *British Working Class Reader*, p. 144; Simon, *Two Nations*, p. 229.

56. *Proceedings of the Third Co-operative Congress*, 23 Apr. 1832, ed. W. Carpenter, pp. 70–1; Simon, *Two Nations*, pp. 229–30.

57. *Poor Man's Guardian*, 28 Feb. 1835, p. 448. Quoted in Simon, *Two Nations*, p. 231.

58. William Lovett, *The Life and Struggles of William Lovett, in His Pursuit of Bread, Knowledge, and Freedom* (1876), vol. 1 (New York: Knopf, 1920), p. 99. Quoted in Simon, *Two Nations*, pp. 233–4.

59. *New Moral World* (Third Series), vol. 1, no. 17, 24 Oct. 1840, p. 265. Quoted in Simon, *Two Nations*, p. 235.

60. *New Moral World* (Third Series), vol. 1, no. 23, 5 Dec. 1840, p. 360; no. 3, 18 July 1840, p. 41. Quoted in Simon, *Two Nations*, p. 235.

61. Lovett, *Life and Struggles*, vol. 1, p. 137. Quoted in Simon, *Two Nations*, p. 243.

62. *Northern Star*, 17 Oct. 1840. Quoted in Simon, *Two Nations*, p. 244.

63. Quoted in Asa Briggs, Introduction to William Lovett and John Collins, *Chartism: a New Organization of the People* (1840; New York: Humanities Press, 1969), p. 14.

64. "The Right of Universal Suffrage: The Principle of the People's Charter, Part Two," *The Red Republican*, vol. 1 (1848), p. 144.

65. "Morality of the Working Classes," *Chartist Circular*, 2 Nov. 1839.

66. "Progress of Democracy, Part Two," *Chartist Circular*, 1 Oct. 1841; "Popular Legislation—its Effects," *Chartist Circular*, 14 Mar. 1840.

67. "National Education," *Chartist Circular*, 28 Sept. 1839; "Chartist Schools," *Chartist Circular*, 21 Mar. 1841.

68. "The Popular Education of the People," *Chartist Circular*, 21 Dec. 1839.

69. "Address of the Democratic Chartist Association of Manchester to the Lovers of Truth and Liberty," *Poor Man's Guardian and Repealer's Friend*, no. 2, p. 14.

70. Simon, *Two Nations*, p. 271.

71. Ibid., p. 251.

72. D. Thompson, *Chartists*, pp. 46–51.

73. Simon, *Two Nations*, p. 172.

74. Ibid., p. 171.

75. Ibid., p. 173.

76. Karl Marx, *Capital: A Critical Analysis of Capitalist Production*, vol. 1, trans. Samuel Moore and Edward Aveling, ed. Frederick Engels. With a Supplement, ed. & trans. Dona Torr (New York: International Publishers, 1947), p. 397.

77. Simon, *Two Nations*, p. 273.

78. *Northern Star*, 30 Jan. 1847. Quoted in Simon, *Two Nations*, pp. 273–4.

79. Howe, *The Cotton Masters, 1830–1860* (Oxford: Clarendon Press, 1984), p. 243.

80. Howe, *Cotton Masters*, p. 284.

81. Ibid., pp. 284–85.

82. Ibid., p. 286.

83. Ibid.,

84. *The Speeches of Charles Dickens*, ed. K. J. Fielding (Oxford: Clarendon Press, 1960), p. 153. Quoted in Howe, *Cotton Masters*, p. 287.

85. Howe, *Cotton Masters*, p. 290.

86. Ibid., p. 298. The internal citations are from "Working Men and the Art Treasures," *Art Treasures Examiner* (Manchester, 1857), p. 40.

87. Howe, *Cotton Masters*, p. 301.

88. John Ruskin, *A Joy for Ever*, p. 95, 114. Quoted in Howe, *Cotton Masters*, p. 300.

89. John K. Walton, *Lancashire, A Social History, 1758–1939* (Manchester: Manchester University Press, 1987), p. 244.

90. Claeys, *Citizens*, p. 244.

91. E. P. Thompson, *Whigs and Hunters* (New York: Pantheon, 1975).

92. See Robert Sykes, "Early Chartism and Trade Unionism," in *The Chartist Experience*, p. 157 and *passim*; Walton, *Lancashire*, p. 161.

93. Walton, *Lancashire*, p. 268.

94. Ibid., p. 275.

Notes to Chapter 4

1. We would trace the theoretical components of the notion of common sense as an at once cultural and political exigency at least to Kant's *Third Critique*; see Hannah Arendt, *Lectures on Kant's Political Philosophy*, ed. Ronald Beiner (Chicago:

University of Chicago Press, 1982) and David Lloyd, "Kant's Examples," in Alexander Gelley, ed., *Unruly Examples: On the Rhetoric of Exemplarity* (Stanford, CA: Stanford University Press, 1995), pp. 255–76. Our previous chapter has discussed the initial practical as well as theoretical contestability of the emergent concept of representation in the 1830s. The self-evidence of that concept is only later established.

2. Matthew Arnold, *Culture and Anarchy, with Friendship's Garland and some Literary Essays*, ed. R. H. Super (Ann Arbor: Michigan University Press, 1965), p. 143. For Arnold's strictures on Mill and others, see *Culture and Anarchy*, p. 111. For Mill's comments on the Hyde Park riots, and Arnold's reaction, see John Stuart Mill, *Public and Parliamentary Speeches, November 1850–November 1868*, Volume 28 of *The Collected Works of John Stuart Mill*, ed. John M. Robson and Bruce L. Kinzer (Toronto: University of Toronto Press, 1988), pp. xxxii-xxxiii, and xxxii, n.

3. Arnold, *Culture and Anarchy*, pp. 134-5. The emphases are Arnold's.

4. In addition to Williams's *Culture and Society, 1780-1950* (New York: Columbia University Press, 1983), see for example Michael Loewy's useful essay on nineteenth-century European critiques of capitalist social relations, *Marxisme et romantisme révolutionnaire* (Paris: Sycomore, 1980), as well as Loewy and Robert Sayre, *Révolte et mélancholie: le romantisme à contre-courant de la modernité* (Paris: Payot, 1992).

5. Matthew Arnold, *The Popular Education of France*, in *Democratic Education*, ed. R. H. Super, vol. 2 of *The Complete Prose Works of Matthew Arnold* (Ann Arbor: University of Michigan Press, 1962), pp. 26-7; 28-9. The term "State-power" suggests Arnold's knowledge of Wilhelm von Humboldt's *Individuum und Staatsgewalt* (1792; Leipzig: Reklam, 1985): the term is a literal translation, if an uncolloquial one, of the German *Staatsgewalt*. The eventual Prussian Minister of Education, an early friend of Schiller and other German intellectuals, and exponent of self-cultivation, von Humboldt had wide influence on Victorian thinkers: on this, see further below.

6. See John Stuart Mill, "Coleridge," in *Essays on Ethics, Religion and Society*, ed. J. M Robson, intro. by F. E. L. Priestley, vol. 10 of the *Collected Works of John Stuart Mill* (Toronto: University of Toronto Press, 1969), esp. pp. 133-6, 140-1 and 147-50. F. R. Leavis and Raymond Williams both grasp well Coleridge's influence on Mill. See *Culture and Society*, p. 50, and *Mill on Bentham and Coleridge*, ed. F. R. Leavis (London, 1950).

But Mill's essay "Civilization" (1836) is no less insistent on the necessity for education for the "strengthening and enlarging of . . . intellect and character" and for "strengthening the weaker side of Civilization by the support of a higher Cultivation." See Mill, "Civilization," in *Essays on Politics and Society*, I, *Collected Works*, vol. 18, ed. J. M. Robson, intro. by Alexander Brady (Toronto: University of Toronto Press, 1977), pp. 139 and 143.

7. Mill, *On Liberty*, in *Essays on Politics and Society*, I, *Collected Works*, vol. 18, p. 261.

8. John Stuart Mill, *Considerations on Representative Government* (1861), in *Essays on Politics and Society*, II, ed. J. M. Robson, intro. Alexander Brady, vol. 19 of *Collected Works* (Toronto: University of Toronto Press, 1977), p. 394. Cited in the text hereafter as *RG*.

9. In her rich and important essay "Rethinking Imperial Histories: The Reform Act of 1867" (*New Left Review*, no. 208 [Nov./Dec. 1994], pp. 3–29], Catherine Hall demonstrates how practically, and in ways in line with Mill's *Consideration on Representative Government*, the enfranchisement of white, male working-class subjects involved a redefinition of citizenship around the exclusion of both women and Caribbean (and of course more widely colonial) "subjects" of the Empire. This exclusion permitted the formation of the British male subject as citizen of imperial Britain. One can read Mill's work as critically self-contradictory, even baffled, by the ways in which his developmental assumptions meet their limits in essays like "On the Subjection of Women" or "On the Negro Question."

10. Mill's own involvement as a civil servant at India House in the formation of British policy is relevant here. In another essay we would want to provide a fuller critique of Mill's ethnological and world-historical assumptions, though this is not the space to do so. For some work towards the critique of liberal developmental histories and racialization, see Lloyd, "Race under Representation" in *Culture/Contexture: Explorations in Anthropology and Literary Study*, eds. E. Valentine Daniel and Jeffrey M. Peck (Berkeley: University of California Press, 1996) and "Genet's Genealogy: European Minorities and the Ends of the Canon," in *The Nature and Context of Minority Discourse*, ed. Abdul JanMohamed and David Lloyd (Oxford: Oxford University Press, 1991), pp. 369-93. For further on Mill and his racial theories, see David Theo Goldberg, *Racist Culture: Philosophy and the Politics of Meaning* (Oxford: Blackwell, 1993), pp. 33-6. It's also worth remarking that, in the passage quoted, Mill's claim that the "improvement" of "the slaves" "cannot come from themselves, but must be superinduced from without" is eerily reminiscent of Marx: "They cannot represent themselves, They must be represented." (*The Eighteenth Brumaire of Louis Bonaparte*, 3rd ed. [Moscow: Progress Publishers, 1954], p. 106.) Marx, of course, was being ironic; Mill was not.

11. Mill, discussing the limits of the principle of national feeling, later argues that:

> Experience proves, that it is possible for one nationality to merge and be absorbed into another: and when it was originally an inferior and more backward portion of the human race, the absorption is greatly to its advantage. Nobody can suppose that it is not more beneficial to a Breton, or a Basque of French Navarre, to be brought into the current of the ideas and feelings of a highly civilized and cultivated people ... than to sulk on his own rocks, the half savage relic of past times, revolving in his own little mental orbit, without interest or participation in the general movement of the world. The same remark applies equally to the Welshman or the Scottish Highlander, as members of the British nation. (RG, p. 549)

The significant omission of Ireland in this remark points to the uncertainty of the benefits of assimilation: either in the context of the failure of British administration in the relatively recent famine or in the fact that the continuing need for military coercion would demand another scenario than "merging and absorption," one that would highlight the founding violence of state formation and extension.

12. See *RG*, pp. 473-9. For further discussion on the topic of Mill's reconception of minorities as the "instructed," see Lloyd, "Genet's Genealogy," pp. 373-4. Mill's notion of the necessary influence of the dispersed intellectual classes is continuous with, and doubtless influenced by, Coleridge's notion of the "clerisy." See Chapter 2, p. 68.

13. The merest vestige of the notion that labor and learning should be converged activities survives, paradoxically, in the notion of "half-time education" that originated as a compromise formation, enabling employers to employ child labor at the price of providing some hours of formal education to the children daily. This mode of education is retrieved by Marx and other radical thinkers in the 1850s and 1860s as an alternative preferable to separate schooling and as already a "potent means for the transformation of present day society." Marx, *Critique of the Gotha Program*, in *The Marx–Engels Reader*, ed. Robert Tucker, 2nd ed. (New York: Norton, 1978), p. 541; see also Harold Silver, "Ideology and the Factory Child: Attitudes to Half-time Education," in *Popular Education and Socialization in the Nineteenth Century*, ed. Philip McCann (London: Methuen, 1977), p. 155. According to Silver, Marx is drawing from but also diverging from Owenite ideas on labor and education. He is also foreshadowing Gramsci's later understanding of the relation between industrial and mental labor for the organic working-class intellectual.

14. Trygve R. Tholfsen argues that working class movements for reform by the 1850s and 1860s were virtually indistinguishable from middle-class reformism:

> Lodged in a culture that prized rational reform and renovation to remedy demonstrated grievances, working-class radicalism was vulnerable to assimilation; the whole apparatus of protest and agitation could easily be co-opted and assigned an appropriate role along with other movements devoted to the cause of progress. In this situation, demonstrations and demands were liable to lose their edge, and lapse into the blandness, if not the banality of mid-Victorianism.

See Tholfsen, *Working Class Radicalism in mid-Victorian England* (New York: Columbia University Press, 1977), p. 314. While we agree to a certain degree with his characterization of radicalism as participating in a wider culture of consensus, we will attempt to give a fuller picture of the structural constraints on radicalism at this moment.

15. John Anderson, "Thoughts on Education," no. 1, in *The Workman's Friend*, vol. 1, no. 1 (1 Feb. 1862), p.7. Compare his remarks to those by "R. W. C. T." in "The Education of the Young," *Sixpenny Magazine*, vol. 9 (1 Mar. 1865), p. 370:

> There are few words in the English language more commonly confounded than *education* and *instruction*.... [W]hereas education of its nature signifies to "lead forth", to "bring out", instruction, on the contrary, means to "prepare," to "instil": the one developing the germs of what already exists, and as a corollary giving them a right direction; the other supplying new principles, planting fresh seed, laying a foundation, as it were, for future structure, but always "in" *into* from without, as the former "e" *out of* from within.

16. Rev. H. Solly, "The Working Men's Clubs and Institutes Movement. Their Origin and Progress," *The Working Man*, 30 Jan. 1866, p. 51. Solly interestingly recounts the history of the "movement" in the philanthropic efforts of middle-class and clerical reformers to provide forms of recreation for working men other than the public house and eventually to extend their individual and dispersed efforts on a national basis. The figure of the infamous Lord Brougham emerges again, this time as the first President of the Working Men's Club and Institute Union. Solly was a minister in the English Presbyterian chapel in Lancaster, prior to giving up his place to become the first Secretary of the Union in 1862.

17. Rev. H. Solly, letter to Lord Lyttleton, 6 Dec. 1866, printed in *Occasional Papers of the Working Men's Club and Institute Union*, No. 9 (Feb. 1866), p. 3.

18. F. D. Maurice, cited in William Rossiter, "History of the Working Men's College, II," *The Working Man*, 20 Jan. 1866, p. 34. To give a full account of the Christian Socialist movement would lead us to too long a digression here. It was founded by F. D. Maurice and others, as was the Working Men's College in London, in the wake of their reflections on the potential violence of the Chartist Movement in 1848. The College included among its "Council of Teachers" not only Maurice but other figures as influential as John Ruskin, and most were graduates of Oxford and Cambridge. Its founding principles were profoundly influenced by Coleridge's philosophy, through Maurice who counted Coleridge as his principal philosophical mentor, and devoted to the principle of "cultivation" in the broad sense we have outlined above. Though the number of active participants was relatively small, Christian Socialism may have had considerable influence on the processes of reform leading up to the Reform Bill and the Education Act.

19. Marx said that "theory itself becomes a material force when it has seized the masses" ("Contribution to a Critique of Hegel's Philosophy of Law. Introduction"

(1844), in Karl Marx and Frederick Engels, *Collected Works*, vol. 3 (New York: International Publishers, 1975), p. 182. There is more than one sense in which this statement is true.

20. Rossiter, "History of the Working Men's College, I," *The Working Man*, 13 Jan. 1866, p.19.

21. "Letters from Lancashire, by a Lancashire Lad. I.—Something of Self-Education in Lancashire," *The Working Man*, 27 Jan. 1866, p. 58.

22. "Letters from Lancashire," p. 58.

23. "Letters from Lancashire, II," *The Working Man*, 3 Feb. 1866, p. 69.

24. *The Times*, 5 Dec. 1866, p. 7.

25. Ibid. It is difficult to deduce from Bright's phrase "across the channel," whether he is referring to the Irish populist movement, the Fenian Brotherhood, or the insurrectionary movements in France that led to the establishment of the Paris Commune in 1871.

26. Joseph Leicester, *The Times*, 5 Dec. 1866, p. 7.

27. "Political Intelligence," editorial, *The Working Man*, 16 June 1866, p. 376.

28. Regrettably, perhaps, this claim for the moral conduct of the Lancashire working classes turns out to be legend or myth. Recent historical work has largely dismantled the grounds for believing the tale of their ethical endurance and support for abolition, which may have been true only of John Bright's constituency and a few other relatively small locations. Even Karl Marx, who promoted the idea in the name of the international solidarity of the oppressed and working-class fervor for American democracy, regarded the workers finally as sheeplike rather than class-conscious. See Norman Longmate, *The Hungry Mills* (London: Temple Smith, 1978), chap. 19 and Mary Ellison, *Support for Secession: Lancashire and the American Civil War* (Chicago: University of Chicago Press, 1972); Peter d'A. Jones's Epilogue to this work summarizes its argument and gives a succinct account of Marx's gradual disillusion. Catherine Hall, in her essay "Rethinking Imperial Histories," does not question the legend, but does demonstrate the effect it had on turning the opinion of significant figures concerning reform, not the least of which was Gladstone.

29. As Marx had put it in 1843, "Political emancipation is a reduction of man, on the one hand to a member of civil society, an *independent* and *egoistic* individual, and on the other hand, to a *citizen*, to a moral person." "On the Jewish Question," in Marx and Engels, *Collected Works*, vol. 3 (New York: International Publishers, 1975), p. 168. For further discussion, see Thomas, *Alien Politics* (New York and London: Routledge, 1994), *passim*.

30. Oskar Negt and Alexander Kluge, *Public Sphere and Experience: Toward an Analysis of the Bourgeois and Proletarian Public Sphere*, foreword by Miriam Hansen, trans. Peter Labanyi, Jamie Owen Daniel, and Assenka Oskiloff; Theory and History of Literature, vol. 85 (Minneapolis: University of Minnesota Press, 1993), p. 197. Their work draws extensively from Michael Vester, *Die Entstehung des Proletariats als Lernprozess* (Frankfurt-am-Main: Europäische Verlagsanst, 1970).

31. Richard Johnson, "'Really Useful Knowledge': Radical Education and Working Class Culture, 1790-1848," in *Working Class Culture: Studies in History and Theory*, ed. John Clarke, Chas Critcher and Richard Johnson, Centre for Contemporary Cultural Studies, University of Birmingham (London: Hutchinson, 1979), p. 88.

32. Johnson, "Really Useful Knowledge," p. 79.

33. See Vester, *Die Entstehung des Proletariats*, as cited at length in Kluge and Negt, *Public Sphere and Experience*, pp. 191-5.

34. A. E. Dobbs, *Education and Social Movements, 1700-1850* (London: Longmans, Green and Co., 1919), pp. 240-1.

35. Ibid., p. 242.

36. For a general account of the bourgeois transformation of space, see Donald Lowe, *History of Bourgeois Perception* (Chicago: University of Chicago Press, 1982), esp. chap. 4. For accounts of the confinement of working-class space, see Peter

Stallybrass and Allon White, *The Politics and Poetics of Transgression* (Ithaca, NY: Cornell University Press, 1986) and Patrick Brantlinger, *Bread and Circuses: Theories of Mass Culture as Social Decay* (Ithaca, NY: Cornell University Press, 1983).

It should not be ignored, however, that many of the interventions that transformed social space were under the partial impetus of working-class demands for reform.

37. We derive the notion of the "material practices" of ideology from Althusser, "Ideology and Ideological State Apparatuses," in *Lenin and Philosophy and Other Essays,* trans. Ben Brewster (New York: Monthly Review Press, 1971), p. 169.

38. See, for example, "The Value of Knowledge to Working Women," *The Working Man,* 28 Apr. 1866, p. 263. While commencing with an assertion that the indubitable equality of the sexes "will arrive as general intelligence proceeds," the article goes on to discuss the need for women's education:

> People who used to trust in ignorance for security and comfort, have now found out their mistake and their danger. Intelligence is the only thing that can be trusted, and everybody who is intelligent knows it. To the wives of working men it is no less important. The humblest knowledge is not only power, it is also property. It is economy as well as pleasure.... An intelligent wife, who gives her mind to household duties, and takes pride in them, will better feed her family, and give more pleasure at table, upon twenty shillings a week, than an ignorant woman upon two pounds.

One might say that, just as the spheres of culture and home are distinct if related, women's education thus defined can never be "for itself," but is always "applied" insofar as her sphere is relegated to the domestic.

39. We might say, after Negt and Kluge's use of the term from Reimut Reiche, that the institute or club forms a means to escape "the permanent terrorizing function of the family": *Public Sphere and Experience,* p. 30 and n. 49. It provides the appearance of a space open to self-improvement or uncoerced comradeship, untrammeled by the dismal recognition that even the most intimate spaces of personal life are already given over to functions and contradictions that reinforce domination's hold. This appearance of course in turn belies the functioning of both purposive and playful recreation for capital.

40. Ernest Jones, "Political Prisoners," the text of a letter written at the Old Bailey, 10 July 1848, to Lord Truro, then Chief Justice, reprinted in *Notes to the People,* vol I, no. 11 (1851), p. 208. Tholfsen discusses at length the educational thinking of Harney and other radical Chartists in the 1850s as a step towards the "assimilation of popular radicalism to the forms of mid-Victorian culture," in *Working Class Radicalism,* pp. 308-15.

41. See Paul Thomas, "Critical Reception: Marx Then and Now," in *The Cambridge Companion to Marx,* ed. Terrell Carver (Cambridge: Cambridge University Press, 1991), pp. 23-54, esp. p. 34.

NOTES TO CONCLUSION

1. See Paul Thomas, *Alien Politics: Marxist State Theory Retrieved* (New York and London: Routledge, 1994), esp. pp. 27–49.

2. Albert Hirschman, *The Passions and the Interests: Political Arguments for Capitalism before its Triumph* (Princeton, NJ: Princeton University Press, 1977), *passim.*

3. Karl Marx, "Contribution to the Critique of Hegel's *Philosophy of Law: Introduction,*" in Marx and Engels, *Collected Works,* vol. 3 (New York: International Publishers, 1975), p. 176. See Thomas, *Alien Politics,* p. 69.

4. Marx "Contribution to the Critique of Hegel's Philosophy of Law," p. 32. *Alien Politics*, p. 70.

5. Ibid., p. 32. Cf. also p. 165.

6. Marx, "On the Jewish Question," in *Collected Works*, vol. 3, p. 166.

7. Raymond Williams, *Culture and Society 1780–1950* (New York: Columbia University Press, 1983), pp. 140–1.

8. E. P. Thompson, *William Morris: From Romantic to Revolutionary* (London: Merlin Press, 1977), p. 728.

9. Morris, "The Lesser Arts," in *The Collected Works of William Morris*, vol. 22 (London: Longmans, 1910–1915), p. 25.

10. "The Aims of Art," *Signs of Change*, p. 134. Quoted in Thompson, *William Morris*, p. 664.

11. *Commonweal*, April Supplement, 1885. Quoted in Thompson, *William Morris*, p. 664.

12. *The Letters of William Morris to His Family and Friends*, ed. Philip Henderson (Longmans, Green & Co., 1950), pp. 355–7. Thompson, *William Morris*, pp. 664–5.

13. Morris, "How I Became a Socialist," *Justice*, 6 June 1894. Quoted in Thompson, *William Morris*, p. 665. See also Williams, *Culture and Society*, p. 150.

14. William Morris and Belfort Bax, *Socialism: Its Growth and Outcome* (1893), p. 317. Quoted in Thompson, *William Morris*, p. 690.

15. Quoted in Thompson, *William Morris*, pp. 690–1.

16. See Michael Loewy and Robert Sayre, *Révolte et mélancolie: Le romantisme à contre-courant de la modernité* (Paris: Payot, 1992), p. 199.

17. *Culture and Society*, p. 149.

18. Williams italicizes this sentence from "How I Became a Socialist" when he cites it in *Culture and Society* (p. 150).

19. Ibid.

20. Ibid., p. 156.

21. Ibid., p. 158.

22. Ibid., p. 265; see also *Problems in Materialism and Culture* (London: Verso, 1980), pp. 204–5.

23. Williams, *Culture and Society*, p. 273.

24. Ibid., p. 238.

25. Williams, *Resources of Hope: Culture, Democracy, Socialism* (London: Verso, 1989), pp. 215–18.

26. See William Morris, *News from Nowhere*, in *News from Nowhere and Selected Writings and Designs* (Harmondsworth: Penguin, 1984), p. 275.

27. Herbert Marcuse's *The Aesthetic Dimension: Toward a Critique of Marxist Aesthetics*, trans. and rev. Herbert Marcuse and Erica Sherover (Boston: Beacon Press, 1978), is an exemplary instance of the former tendency; Theodor W. Adorno's *Aesthetic Theory*, ed. Gretel Adorno and Rolf Tiedeman, trans. C. Lenhardt (New York: Routledge and Kegan Paul, 1984) instantiates the latter. We are not directly concerned here with Maoist cultural politics, within which cultural work is viewed as performing the clarification and propagation of popular revolutionary ideas; for its classic statement, see Mao Zedong, "Speech to the Yenan Forum" in *Selected Works of Mao Tse-Tung* (Beijing: International Press).

28. On the state and socialism, see Stuart Hall, "The State—Socialism's Old Caretaker," in Stuart Hall, *The Hard Road to Renewal* (London: Verso, 1988), pp. 220–32.

29. See Laclau and Mouffe, *Hegemony and Socialist Strategy*, p.171. Emphasis in the original text.

30. Ibid., p.181.

31. We use Gramsci's terms here to emphasize that even as Laclau and Mouffe recognize that the terrain of new struggles is principally civil society (*Hegemony and Socialist Strategy*, pp. 179–85), they lose sight of the constitutive relation between

civil and political society while at the same time, as we shall see, retaining the subjects formed within that differentiation.

32. On the intersection of anti-racist and anti-Thatcherite movements in the early 1980s, See Paul Gilroy, *'There Ain't No Black in the Union Jack': The Cultural Politics of Race and Nation*, foreword, Houston A. Baker (Chicago: University of Chicago Press, 1988), chap. 4. On C.N.D. and other social movements, see Williams, *Resources of Hope*, pp. 187–244. For the dialectic between civil rights struggle and the emergence of an alternative cultural politics and a "new political subject" in contradiction with the democratic subject of rights, see Lisa Lowe, *Immigrant Acts: On Asian American Cultural Politics* (Durham, NC: Duke University Press, 1995), pp. 22–4; 163–5; and 170. And for the importance of "hybrid cultures" in the critique of representation and the practice of movement politics, see Arturo Escobar, *Encountering Development: The Making and Unmaking of the Third World* (Princeton, NJ: Princeton University Press, 1995), chap. 6. Though these last two works concern fields quite remote to our historical and geographic area, their arguments have been critical to our understanding of the potential relevance of our argument to contemporary issues.

33. See, for example, Todd Gitlin, *The Twilight of Common Dreams: Why America is Wracked by Culture Wars* (New York: Metropolitan Press, 1995).

34. See Gilroy, *'Ain't No Black'*, p. 231.

35. See Ibid., pp. 224–27, for an excellent summary of social-movement theory.

36. For some sources, see our Introduction, n. 2. The distinction made here is inseparable from the extension and rationalization of European imperialism and the necessity to codify non-western practices in order that the "natives" could be educated into docile colonial subjects. On the relations between anthropology and imperialism, see Talal Asad, ed., *Anthropology and the Colonial Encounter* (New York: Humanities Press, 1973); George W. Stocking, Jr., ed., *Colonial Situations: Essays on the Contextualization of Ethnographic Knowledge* (Madison: University of Wisconsin Press, 1991); and James Clifford and George Marcus, eds., *Writing Culture: The Poetics and Politics of Ethnography* (Berkeley and Los Angeles: University of California Press, 1986). On the differentiation between "cultures" and "societies," and for its further implications for a contemporary redefinition of culture, see Lisa Lowe and David Lloyd, eds., *The Politics of Culture in the Shadow of Capital* (Durham, NC: Duke University Press, 1997).

37. Theodor W. Adorno, "On the Fetish-Character in Music and the Regression of Listening," in *The Essential Frankfurt School Reader*, eds. Andrew Arato and Eike Gebhardt (New York: Urizen, 1978), pp. 275.

38. Given the terrain of *Culture and the State*, we are taking as our paradigm the emergence of British cultural studies. Other developments have taken place within both a U.S. cultural studies based on the contradictions between racialized and national cultures and international work that studies the dialectics of subaltern and anti-colonial or nationalist conceptions and practices of culture. Rather than exhaust the reader with an extensive bibliography, let us just indicate the work that leads in the U.S.A. from counterethnographic work like Zora Neale Hurston's in the 1930s to contemporary work by a variety of scholars including Sterling Stuckey, Patricia Rose, George Lipsitz, Lisa Lowe, Rosalinda Fregoso, Herman Gray, Robin Kelly, Charles Payne, or José Saldivar; and in the colonial context from early theoreticians of national culture to contemporary scholars like Ngugi Wa Thiong'o, Ranajit Guha, Dipesh Chakrabarty, Partha Chatterjee, Reynaldo C. Ileto, KumKum Sangari, Susie Tharu and Luke Gibbons. Stuart Hall and Paul Gilroy represent important syntheses of both currents.

39. See *Zur Dichotomisierung von hoher und niederer Literatur*, eds. Christa Burger, Peter Burger and Jochen Schulte-Sasse (Frankfurt-am-Main: Suhrkamp, 1982).

40. For a parallel argument on the "common sense" that founds the continuity of

such historiography, see Laclau and Mouffe, *Hegemony and Socialist Strategy*, p. 160.

41. Ibid., p. 166.

42. Ibid., pp. 166 and 176.

NOTES TO EPILOGUE

1. Raymond Williams, *George Orwell* (New York: Viking Press, Modern Masters Series, 1971), p. 59. This book was reissued in 1984 by Columbia University Press; the pagination remains the same.

2. See E. P. Thompson, "Outside the Whale," in *Out of Apathy* (London: Stevens and Sons, 1960), pp. 158-65; Isaac Deutscher "1984—the Mysticism Of Cruelty," in *Heretics and Renegades* (New York: Bobbs-Merrill, 1969), pp. 35-50.

3. George Orwell, "Burnham's View of the Contemporary World Struggle" (first published in the *New Leader*, New York [29 March, 1947]), in *The Collected Essays, Journalism and Letters of George Orwell*, ed. Sonia Orwell and Ian Angus (Harmondsworth: Penguin Books, 1970), vol. 4, pp. 360-74. This work will hereafter be cited as *Collected Essays*.

4. Orwell, *Collected Essays*, vol. 4, p. 564.

5. T. R. Fyvel, *George Orwell: A Personal Memoir* (London: Weidenfeld and Nicholson, 1982), p. 161.

6. Orwell, *Collected Essays*, vol. 4, p. 451. Konni Zilliacus was a left-wing Labor MP widely suspected of having "fellow-traveling" tendencies.

7. Orwell, *Collected Essays*, vol. 3, p. 166.

8. Orwell, ibid., vol. 4, p. 564.

9. George Kateb, "The Road to *1984*," *Political Science Quarterly*, no. 81 (Dec. 1966), pp. 568-9. The quotation from Orwell is from *Collected Essays*, vol. 3, p. 411.

10. Orwell, *Homage to Catalonia* (Harmondsworth: Penguin Books, 1962), p. 102.

11. Kateb, "Road to *1984*," p. 568.

12. George Woodcock, *The Crystal Spirit: A Study of George Orwell* (Boston: Little, Brown, 1966), pp. 29-30.

13. Woodcock, *Crystal Spirit*, p. 57.

14. Kateb, "Road to *1984*," p. 577.

15. Orwell, *The Road to Wigan Pier* (London: Victor Gollancz, Left Book Club edition, 1937), pp. 236-64. On Orwell's politics, see Alex Zwerdling, *Orwell and the Left* (New Haven, CT: Yale University Press, 1974) for rather too unspecific a view, and Bernard Crick, *George Orwell: A Life* (Harmondsworth: Penguin Books, 1982), for far too specific a view. Crick is much more familiar than Zwerdling with an often labyrinthine left within which he is concerned to locate Orwell, but he is also so familiar with the minutiae of Orwell's life that general statements about his politics emerge only with difficulty.

16. Orwell, *Wigan Pier*, p. 182.

17. Woodcock, *Crystal Spirit*, pp. 24-5, 81-2, 32.

18. Woodcock, p. 343-6.

19. Zwerdling, *Orwell*, pp. 188-190.

20. Orwell, "Why I Write," *Collected Essays*, vol. 1, p. 30.

21. Orwell, "Politics and the English Language," *Collected Essays*, vol. 4, pp. 167-8.

22. Orwell, *Collected Essays*, vol. 2, p. 266.

23. Williams, *Orwell*, pp. 54-5.

24. Orwell, *Wigan Pier*, p. 158.

25. Williams, *Orwell*, p. 91.

26. Ibid., p. 50.

27. Williams, *Politics and Letters: Interviews with New Left Review* (London: New Left Books, 1979), pp. 388, 390.

28. Williams, *Writing in Society* (London: New Left Books; Verso edition, n.d.), pp. 249-50.

29. Samuel Hynes, *The Auden Generation: Literature and Politics in England in the Thirties* (London: The Bodley Head, 1976), pp. 272-8.

30. Williams, *Politics and Letters*, p. 388.

31. Williams, *Culture and Society, 1780-1950* (New York: Columbia University Press, 1983), p. 280.

32. See Williams, *Politics and Letters*, pp. 384-92.

33. Podhoretz's tendentious article, "If Orwell were Alive Today," appeared in *Harper's*, no. 266 (Jan. 1983), pp. 30-2, 34-7.

34. Francis Mulhern, *The Moment of Scrutiny* (London: New Left Books, 1979), pp. 35, 306-7, 330-9.

35. Richard Hoggart, *The Uses of Literacy* (Harmondsworth: Pelican Books, 1958). Hoggart acknowledged his debt to Orwell in an Introduction to a 1965 Heinemann edition of *The Road to Wigan Pier*, to which *The Uses of Literacy* (which was subtitled *Aspects of Working Class Life With Special Reference to Publications and Entertainment*) was often compared in the late 1950s and early 1960s.

36. Thompson, *Making of the English Working Class* (New York: Vintage, 1966).

37. See, e.g. Paul E. Willis, *Profane Culture* (London: Routledge and Kegan Paul, 1978), and *Learning to Labor* (London: Routledge and Kegan Paul, 1979), *passim*.

38. Williams, *Orwell*, p. 61.

39. Orwell to Cyril Connolly, 8 June 1937, *Collected Essays*, vol. 1, p. 30.

40. Orwell, *Homage*, p. 8.

41. Ibid., pp. 102-103.

42. Ibid., p. 221.

43. Williams, *Orwell*, p. 47. Cf. Orwell, *Collected Essays*, vol. 1, p. 437; Fyvel, *George Orwell*, pp. 81-2; and Hynes, *Auden Generation*, pp. 373-6.

44. Woodcock, *Crystal Spirit*, pp. 241-2.

45. Williams, *Politics and Letters*, p. 296.

46. Eagleton, "Mutations of Critical Ideology," in *Criticism and Ideology: A Study in Marxist Literary Theory* (London: New Left Books/Verso, 1978), pp. 11-43.

47. Eagleton, *Literary Theory* (Oxford: Blackwell, 1983). See also the review by John Bayley, *Times Literary Supplement*, London (10 June 1983).

48. *Henry IV*, Part 1, Act 111, Scene 2.

Appendix I
The State and Education, 1818–1870

1818 *Report of Parliamentary Select Committee on the Education of the Lower Orders of Society:* showed that only 1/4 of the child population was receiving any education at all.

1820 *Brougham's Parish Schools Bill:* envisioned a national system of elementary education based on the provisions of buildings by the manufacturing class. Did not pass.

1833 *Roebuck's Education Bill:* a plan for the "universal and national education of the whole people." Did not pass, but stimulated Parliament's interested and led to grant of £20, 000 for erection of elementary schools. Also helped passage of Factory Act of 1833, which provided for first effective regulation and limitation of child labor.

1839 Establishment of *Committee of the Privy Council for Education.*

1839 Dr. Kay (later, Sir James Kay-Shuttleworth) appointed first Secretary of Committee of the Privy Council for Education: responsible for creation of the Education Department in 1856

1858–1861 *Newcastle Commission* created and authorized "to inquire into the present state of popular education in England, and to consider and report what measures, if any, are required for the extension of sound and cheap elementary instruction to all classes of the people."

    (i) spotlighted inadequacy of provisions in poorer areas. However, Commission rejected the idea of state provision and control in favor of continuance of voluntary initiative and self-help. Condemned any attempt to introduce compulsory attendance or fee elementary education.

(ii) based positive recommendations on two essential criteria:
  — need for more financial assistance for voluntary bodies and extension of aid for previously unassisted schools. Proposed block capitation grants to be supplemented by local rate aid channeled through new network of County and Municipal Education Boards
  — grant assistance should be tied to minimal attendance requirements for capitation allowance and annual examination requirements for receipt of rate aid

1862 *Revised Code.* Introduced by Robert Lowe, Vice President of the Privy Council of Education and Head of Education Department 1859–1864. Revised Code emphasized need to ensure value for money, introducing new set of regulations which subjected grant-aided elementary schools to strict "payment-by-results" system

1870 *Elementary Education Act*: declared purpose was to "cover the country with good schools" and so enable all parent to secure elementary education for their children.

Appendix II
The Principal Factory Acts
1802–1901

1802 *The Health and Morals of Apprentices Act.* Repealed 1878.

1819 *An Act for the Regulation of Cotton Mills and Factories.* Repealed 1831.

1833 *An Act to Regulate the Labour of Children and Young Persons in Mills and Factories.* Repealed 1878.

1844 *An Act to Amend the Laws Relating to Labour in Factories.* Repealed 1878.

1847 *An Act to Limit the Hours of Labour of Young Persons and Females in Factories.* Repealed 1874.

1864 *The Factory Acts Extension Act.* Repealed 1878.

1867 *The Factory Acts Extension Act.*
       The Factory Acts Extension Act.

1874 *An Act to Make Better Provision for Improving the Health of Women, Young Persons and Children Employed in Manufactures.* Repealed 1878.

1878 *An Act to Consolidate and Amend the Law Relating to Factories and Workshops.* Repealed 1901.

1891 *An Act to Amend the Law Relating to Factories and Workshops.* Repealed 1901.

1895 *An Act to Amend and Extend the Law Relating to Factories and Workshops.* Repealed 1901.

1901 *Factory and Workshop Consolidation Act.*

Bibliography

PRIMARY (NON-ARCHIVAL) AND SECONDARY SOURCES

Adamson, Walter A. *Hegemony and Revolution: A Study of Antonio Gramsci's Political and Cultural Theory*. Berkeley and Los Angeles: University of California, 1980.

Adorno, Theodor W. *Aesthetic Theory*. Trans. C. Lenhardt. Ed. Gretel Adorno and Rolf Tiedeman. New York: Routledge and Kegan Paul, 1984.

———. "On the Fetish-Character in Music and the Regression of Listening." *The Essential Frankfurt School Reader*. Eds. Andrew Arato and Eike Gebhardt. New York: Urizen, 1978, pp. 270–99.

Akenson, D. H. *The Irish Education Experiment: The National System of Education in the Nineteenth Century*. London: Routledge and Kegan Paul, 1970.

Althusser, Louis. *Lenin and Philosophy and Other Essays*. Trans. Ben Brewster. New York: Monthly Review Press, 1971.

Anderson, Benedict. *Imagined Communities: Reflections on the Origin and Spread of Nationalism*. Rev. and extended ed. London: Verso, 1991.

Anderson, Perry. "The Antinomies of Antonio Gramsci." *New Left Review*. No. 100. (Nov. 1976–Jan. 1977), pp. 5–78.

Arendt, Hannah. *Lectures on Kant's Political Philosophy*. Ed. Ronald Beiner. Chicago: University of Chicago Press, 1982.

Arnold, Matthew. *Culture and Anarchy, with Friendship's Garland and some Literary Essays*. Ed. R. H. Super. Vol. 5 of *The Complete Prose Works of Matthew Arnold*. Ann Arbor: Michigan University Press, 1965.

———. *The Popular Education of France. Democratic Education*. Ed. R. H. Super. Vol. 2 of *The Complete Prose Works of Matthew Arnold*. Ann Arbor: University of Michigan Press, 1962.

Asad, Talal, ed. *Anthropology and the Colonial Encounter*. New York: Humanities Press, 1973.

Ashcraft, Richard. "Liberal Political Theory and Working Class Radicalism in Nineteenth-Century England." *Political Theory*. Vol. 21, no. 2 (May 1993), pp. 249–72.

Aspinall, A. *Politics and the Press, c. 1780–1850*. London: Home & Van Thal, 1949.

Babington, Thomas (Lord Macaulay) "Education." *Selected Writings*. Ed. John Clive and Thomas Pinney. Chicago: University of Chicago Press, 1972.

Baczko, Bronislaw. *Utopian Lights*. Trans. Judith N. Greenberg. New York: Paragon House, 1989.

212

Bakhtin, M. M. "Discourse in the Novel." *The Dialogic Imagination: Four Essays.* Trans. Michael Holquist and Caryl Emerson. Ed. Michael Holquist. Austin: University of Texas Press, 1981.

Barrow, Clyde W. *Universities and the Capitalist State: Corporate Liberalism and the Reconstruction of American Higher Education, 1894–1928.* Madison: University of Wisconsin Press, 1990.

Bayley, John. Review, of Terry Eagleton, *Literary Theory. Times Literary Supplement.* London. 10 June 1983.

Belchem, John C. "Radical Language and Ideology in Early Nineteenth-Century England: The Challenge of the Platform." *Albion.* No. 20 (Summer 1988), pp. 247–59.

Benjamin, Walter. *Illuminations: Essays and Reflections.* Trans. Harry Zohn. Ed. Hannah Arendt. New York: Schocken, 1968.

Bhaba, Homi K. "DissemiNation: Time, Narrative and the Margins of the Modern Nation." *The Location of Culture.* London: Routledge, 1994.

Bowles, Samuel, and Herbert Gintis. *Schooling in Capitalist America: Educational Reform and the Contradictions of Economic Life.* New York: Basic Books, 1976.

Brantlinger, Patrick. *Bread and Circuses: Theories of Mass Culture as Social Decay.* Ithaca, NY: Cornell University Press, 1983.

Brenkman, John. *Culture and Domination.* Ithaca, NY: Cornell University Press, 1987.

Briggs, Asa, ed. *Chartist Studies.* London: Macmillan, 1960.

Brougham, Henry. *Practical Observations upon the Education of the People, Addressed to the Working Classes and their Employers.* London, 1825.

Burger, Christa, Peter Burger und Jochen Schulte-Sasse, eds. *Zur Dichotomisierung von hoher und niederer Literatur.* Frankfurt-am-Main: Suhrkamp, 1982.

Burke, Edmund. *Reflections on the Revolution in France.* 1790. Ed. L. G. Mitchell. Oxford: Oxford University Press, 1993.

Butler, Marilyn, ed. *Burke, Paine, Godwin and the Revolution Controversy.* Cambridge: Cambridge University Press, 1984.

Claeys, Gregory. *Citizens and Saints: Politics and Anti-Politics in Early British Socialism.* Cambridge: Cambridge University Press, 1989.

Clifford, James, and George Marcus, eds. *Writing Culture: The Poetics and Politics of Ethnography.* Berkeley and Los Angeles: University of California Press, 1986.

Coleridge, Samuel Taylor. *Biographia Literaria.* 2 vols. Eds. James Engell and W. Jackson Bate. Princeton, NJ: Princeton University Press, 1983.

———. *On the Constitution of the Church and State.* Ed. John Colmer. Princetor., NJ: Princeton University Press, 1976.

Crick, Bernard. *George Orwell: A Life.* Harmondsworth: Penguin Books, 1982.

Deutscher, Isaac. "*1984*—the Mysticism Of Cruelty." *Heretics and Renegades.* New York: Bobbs-Merrill, 1969, pp. 35–50.

Debord, Guy. *Society of the Spectacle.* 1967. Detroit, MI: Red and Black Books, 1983.

Dickens, Charles. *The Speeches of Charles Dickens.* Ed. K. J. Fielding. Oxford: Clarendon Press, 1960.

Dobbs, A. E. *Education and Social Movements, 1700–1850.* London: Longmans, Green and Co., 1919.

Eagleton, Terry. *Literary Theory.* Oxford: Basil Blackwell, 1983.

———. "Mutations of Critical Ideology." *Criticism and Ideology: A Study in Marxist Literary Theory.* London: New Left Books/Verso, 1978, pp. 11–43.

———. *The Ideology of the Aesthetic.* Oxford: Blackwell, 1990.

Ellison, Mary. *Support for Secession: Lancashire and the American Civil War.* Chicago: University of Chicago Press, 1972.

Escobar, Arturo. *Encountering Development: The Making and Unmaking of the Third World.* Princeton, NJ: Princeton University Press, 1995.

Fanon, Frantz. *The Wretched of the Earth.* Trans. Constance Farrington. New York: Grove Press, 1965.

Foner, Eric. *Tom Paine and Revolutionary America*. Oxford: Oxford University Press, 1976.

Foster, John. *Class Struggle and the Industrial Revolution; Early Industrial Capitalism in Three English Towns*. New York: St. Martin's Press, 1974.

Foucault, Michel. *Discipline and Punish: The Birth of the Prison*. Trans. Alan Sheridan. New York: Vintage, 1979.

———. "Governmentality." *The Foucault Effect: Studies in Governmentality*. Ed. Graham Burchell, Colin Gordon, and Peter Miller. Chicago: University of Chicago Press, 1991.

Fyvel, T. R. *George Orwell: A Personal Memoir*. London: Weidenfeld and Nicholson, 1982.

Gilroy, Paul *'There Ain't No Black in the Union Jack': The Cultural Politics of Race and Nation*, foreword by Houston A. Baker, Jr. Chicago, IL: University of Chicago Press, 1988.

Gitlin, Todd. *The Twilight of Common Dreams: Why America Is Wracked by Culture Wars*. New York: Metropolitan Books, 1995.

Godstrom, J. M. "The Content of Education and the Socialisation of the Working Class Child, 1830–1860." *Popular Education and Socialisation in the Nineteenth Century*. Ed. Philip McCann. London: Methuen, 1977, pp. 93–109.

Goldberg, David Theo. *Racist Culture: Philosophy and the Politics of Meaning*. Oxford: Blackwell, 1993.

Goldsmith, Stephen. *Unbuilding Themselves: Apocalypse and Romantic Representation*. Ithaca, NY: Cornell University Press, 1993.

Gramsci, Antonio. *Selections from the Prison Notebooks*. Trans. and ed. Quintin Hoare and Geoffrey Nowell-Smith. New York: International Publishers, 1971.

Green, Martin. *The Children of the Sun*. New York: Basic Books, 1976.

Grey, Robert. "The Deconstruction of the English Working Class." *Social History*. No. 11 (Oct. 1986), pp. 363–73.

Hall, Catherine. "Rethinking Imperial Histories: The Reform Act of 1867. *New Left Review*. No. 208 (Nov./Dec. 1994), pp. 3–29.

Hall, Stuart. *The Hard Road to Renewal*. London: Verso, 1988.

Herbert, Christopher. *Culture and Anomie: Ethnographic Imagination in the Nineteenth Century*. Chicago: University of Chicago Press, 1991.

Hirschmann, Albert. *The Passions and the Interests: Political Arguments for Capitalism before its Triumph*. Princeton, NJ: Princeton University Press, 1977.

Hobsbawm, Eric, and George Rudé. *Captain Swing: A Social History of the Great English Agricultural Uprising of 1830*. New York: Pantheon, 1968.

Hoggart, Richard. *The Uses of Literacy*. Harmondsworth: Pelican Books, 1958.

Holub, Renate. *Antonio Gramsci: Beyond Marxism and Postmodernism*. New York: Routledge, 1992.

Howe, Anthony. *The Cotton Masters, 1830–1860*. Oxford: Clarendon Press, 1984.

Humboldt, Wilhelm von. *Individuum und Staatsgewalt*. 1792. Leipzig: Reclam, 1985.

Hunter, Ian. *Culture and Government: The Emergence of Literary Education*. London: Macmillan, 1988.

Hynes, Samuel. *The Auden Generation: Literature and Politics in England in the Thirties*. London: The Bodley Head, 1976.

JanMohamed, Abdul, and David Lloyd. Introduction. *The Nature and Context of Minority Discourse*. Oxford: Oxford University Press, 1990.

Johnson, Richard. "'Really Useful Knowledge': Radical Education and Working Class Culture, 1790–1848." *Working Class Culture: Studies in History and Theory*. Eds. John Clarke, Chas Critcher and Richard Johnson. Centre for Contemporary Cultural Studies, University of Birmingham. London: Hutchinson, 1979.

———. "Educational Policy and Social Control in Early Victorian England." *Past and Present.* No. 49 (Nov. 1970).

Kant, Immanuel. *Critique of Judgement.* 1790. Trans. James Creed Meredith. Oxford: Oxford University Press, 1952.

———. *The Conflict of the Faculties.* 1798. Trans. and ed. Mary T. Gregor. New York: Abaris, 1979.

Kateb, George. "The Road to *1984.*" *Political Science Quarterly.* No. 81 (Dec. 1966), pp. 568–9.

Kay, James. *The Moral and Physical Condition of the Working Class as Employed in the Cotton Manufacture in Manchester in 1832.* Repr. in *Four Periods of Public Education, As Reviewed in 1832, 1839, 1846, 1862.* London: Longman, Green, Longman, and Roberts, 1862.

Kirk, Neville. "In Defence of Class." *International Review of Social History.* Number 32 (1987), pp. 2–47.

Knight, Charles. *Passages of a Working Life During Half a Century: With a Prelude of Early Reminiscences.* 2 vols. London: Bradbury & Evans, 1864.

Koselleck, Reinhart. *Critique and Crisis: Enlightenment and the Pathogenesis of Modern Society.* Cambridge, MA: MIT Press, 1988. Trans. of *Kritik und Krise: Ein Beitrag zur Pathogenese der bürgerlichen Welt.* Freiburg und München: Alber, 1959.

Laclau, Ernesto, and Chantal Mouffe. *Hegemony and Socialist Strategy: Towards a Radical Democratic Politics.* London: Verso, 1985.

Lawson, John, and Harold Silver. *A Social History of Education in England.* London: Methuen, 1973.

Leavis, F. R., ed. *Mill on Bentham and Coleridge.* London, 1950.

Lloyd, David. "Analogies of the Aesthetic: The Politics of Culture and the Limits of Materialist Aesthetics." *New Formations,* No 10, (Spring, 1990), pp. 109–26.

———. "Genet's Genealogy: European Minorities and the Ends of the Canon." *The Nature and Context of Minority Discourse.* Eds. Abdul JanMohamed and David Lloyd. Oxford: Oxford University Press, 1991.

———. "Kant's Examples." *Unruly Examples: On the Rhetoric of Exemplarity.* Ed. Alexander Gelley. Stanford, CA: Stanford University Press, 1995, pp. 255–76.

———. "Race under Representation." *Culture/Contexture: Explorations in Anthropology and Literary Study.* Eds. E. Valentine Daniel and Jeffrey M. Peck. Berkeley: University of California Press, 1996.

Loewy, Michael. *Marxisme et romantisme révolutionnaire.* Paris: Sycomore, 1980.

Loewy, Michael, and Robert Sayre. *Révolte et mélancholie: le romantisme à contre-courant de la modernité.* Paris: Payot, 1992.

Longmate, Norman. *The Hungry Mills.* London: Temple Smith, 1978.

Lovett, William. *The Life and Struggles of William Lovett, in His Pursuit of Bread, Knowledge, and Freedom.* 1876. 2 vols. New York: Knopf, 1920.

Lovett, William, and John Collins. *Chartism: a New Organization of the People.* 1840. New York: Humanities Press, 1969.

Lowe, Donald. *History of Bourgeois Perception.* Chicago: University of Chicago Press, 1982.

Lowe, Lisa. *Immigrant Acts: On Asian-American Cultural Politics.* Durham, NC: Duke University Press, 1996.

Lowe, Lisa, and David Lloyd, eds. *The Politics of Culture in the Shadow of Capital.* Durham, NC: Duke University Press, 1997.

Mah, Harold. "The French Revolution and the Problem of German Modernity: Hegel, Heine and Marx." *New German Critique.* No. 50 (Spring–Summer 1990), pp. 3–20.

Malthus, Thomas Robert. *An Essay on the Principle of Population.* Ed. Antony Flew. Harmondsworth: Penguin Books, 1970.

Mao Zedong. "Speech to the Yenan Forum." *Selected Works of Mao Tse-Tung*. Peking: Foreign Languages Press, 1965, Vol III. pp. 69–88.

Marcuse, Herbert. *The Aesthetic Dimension: Toward a Critique of Marxist Aesthetics*. Trans. and rev. Herbert Marcuse and Erica Sherover. Boston: Beacon Press, 1978.

Marx, Karl. *Capital: A Critical Analysis of Capitalist Production*. Vol. 1. 1867. Trans. Samuel Moore and Edward Aveling. Ed. Frederick Engels. With a Supplement, ed. & trans. Dona Torr. New York: International Publishers, 1947.

———. "Contribution to the Critique of Hegel's *Philosophy of Law*." 1843. In Karl Marx and Friedrich Engels, *Collected Works*. Vol. 3. New York: International Publishers, 1975, pp. 5–129.

———. "Contribution to a Critique of Hegel's Philosophy of Law. Introduction." 1844. In Karl Marx and Frederick Engels, *Collected Works*. Vol. 3, pp. 175–87.

———. *Critique of the Gotha Program*. 1875. *The Marx–Engels Reader*. Ed. Robert Tucker. 2nd ed. New York: Norton, 1978, pp. 525–41.

———. *The Eighteenth Brumaire of Louis Bonaparte*. 3rd ed. Moscow: Progress Publishers, 1954.

———. "On the Jewish Question." 1843. In Karl Marx and Friedrich Engels. *Collected Works*. Vol. 3, pp. 146–74.

Marx, Karl, and Friedrich Engels, *The Communist Manifesto*. 1847. Harmondsworth: Penguin Books, 1967.

Miliband, Ralph. *Parliamentary Socialism*. London: Merlin, 1972.

Mill, John Stuart. "Civilization." 1836. *Essays on Politics and Society*, I. Ed. John M. Robson. Intro. Alexander Brady. Vol. 18 of the *Collected Works of John Stuart Mill*. Toronto: University of Toronto Press, 1977.

———. "Coleridge." *Essays on Ethics, Religion and Society*. Ed. John M. Robson. Intro. F. E. L. Priestley. Vol. 10 of the *Collected Works of John Stuart Mill*. Toronto: University of Toronto Press, 1969.

———. *Considerations on Representative Government*. 1861. *Essays on Politics and Society*, II. Ed. John M. Robson. Intro. Alexander Brady. Vol. 19 of the *Collected Works of John Stuart Mill*. Toronto: University of Toronto Press, 1977.

———. *On Liberty*. *Essays on Politics and Society*, I. Ed. John M. Robson. Intro. Alexander Brady. Vol. 18 of the *Collected Works of John Stuart Mill*. Toronto: University Toronto Press, 1977.

———. *Public and Parliamentary Speeches, November 1850–November 1868*. Vol. 28 of the *Collected Works of John Stuart Mill*. Eds. John M. Robson and Bruce L. Kinzer. Toronto: University of Toronto Press, 1988.

Montmorency, J. E. G. de *State Intervention in English Education: A Short History from Earliest Times Down to 1833*. Cambridge: University Press, 1902.

Moretti, Franco. *The Way of the World*. London: Verso, 1987.

Morris, William. *The Collected Works of William Morris*. 24 vols. London: Longmans, 1910–1915.

———. *The Letters of William Morris to His Family and Friends*. Ed. Philip Henderson. Longmans, Green & Co., 1950.

———. *News from Nowhere*. 1890. *News from Nowhere and Selected Writings and Designs*. Harmondsworth: Penguin Books, 1984.

Morris, William, and Belfort Bax. *Socialism: Its Growth and Outcome*. London: Swann Sonnenshein, 1893.

Mulhern, Francis. *The Moment of Scrutiny*. London: New Left Books, 1979.

Negt, Oskar, and Alexander Kluge. *Public Sphere and Experience: Toward an Analysis of the Bourgeois and Proletarian Public Sphere*. Trans. Peter Labanyi, Jamie Owen Daniel, and Assenka Oskiloff. Foreword by Miriam Hansen. Theory and History of Literature, vol. 85. Minneapolis: University of Minnesota Press, 1993.

Ngugi, Wa Thiong'o. *Decolonizing the Mind: The Politics of Language in African Literature*. London: J. Currey, 1986.

Omi, Michael, and Howard Winant. *Racial Formation in the United States: From the 1960s to the 1980s*. New York: Routledge, 1986.

Orwell, George. *The Collected Essays, Journalism and Letters of George Orwell*. Eds. Sonia Orwell and Ian Angus. 4 vols. Harmondsworth: Penguin Books, 1970.

———. "Burnham's View of the Contemporary World Struggle." *Collected Essays*. Vol. 4, pp. 360–74.

———. *Homage to Catalonia*. 1938. Harmondsworth: Penguin Books, 1962.

———. Letter to Cyril Connolly. 8 June 1937. *Collected Essays*. Vol. 1, p. 301.

———. "Politics and the English Language." 1946. *Collected Essays*. Vol. 4, pp. 156–170.

———. *The Road to Wigan Pier*. London: Victor Gollancz, Left Book Club Edition, 1937.

———. "Why I Write." 1946. *Collected Essays*. Vol. 1, pp. 23–30.

Ozouf, Mona. *Festivals and the French Revolution*. Trans. Alan Sheridan. Cambridge, MA: Harvard University Press, 1988.

Podhoretz, Norman. "If Orwell were Alive Today." *Harper's*. No. 266 (Jan. 1983), pp. 30–2, 34–7.

Pope, Alexander. *An Essay on Man*. 1733–4. *Alexander Pope: A Critical Edition of the Major Works*. Ed. Pat Rodgers. Oxford: Oxford University Press, 1993, pp. 270–308.

Richards, Paul. "State Formation and Class Struggle, 1832–48." *Capitalism, State Formation and Marxist Theory: Historical Investigations*. Ed. Philip Corrigan. London: Quartet Books, 1980.

Rousseau, Jean-Jacques. *Emile, or On Education*. 1762. Trans. Allan Bloom. New York: Basic Books, 1979.

———. "Essay on the Origin of Languages." 1755. In *The First and Second Discourses, together with the replies to critics and the Essay on the Origin of Languages*, trans. and annotated by Victor Gourevitch. New York: Harper and Row, Perennial Library, 1986. pp. 239–95.

———. "First Discourse." 1750. *The First and Second Discourses*. Trans. Roger D. Masters. New York: St. Martin's Press, 1964.

———. *Politics and the Arts: Letter to M. D'Alembert on the Theater*. 1758. Trans. Allan Bloom. Ithaca, NY: Cornell University Press, 1960.

———. *The Social Contract*. 1762. Trans. Maurice Cranston. Harmondsworth: Penguin Books, 1971.

Sanderson, Michael. *Education, Economic Change and Society in England, 1780–1870*. London: Macmillan, 1983.

Schiller, Friedrich. *On the Aesthetic Education of Man, In a Series of Letters*. 1795. Trans. and ed. Elizabeth M. Wilkinson and L. A. Willoughby. Oxford: Clarendon Press, 1967.

———. "On the Stage as Moral Institution." 1784. *Essays Aesthetical and Philosophical*. London: George Bell & Sons, 1879.

Scott, Joan Wallach. *Gender and the Politics of History*. New York: Columbia University Press, 1988.

Silver, Harold. "Ideology and the Factory Child: Attitudes to Half-time Education." *Popular Education and Socialisation in the Nineteenth Century*. Ed. Philip McCann. London: Methuen, 1977.

Simon, Brian. *The Two Nations and the Educational Structure, 1780–1870*. London: Lawrence and Wishart, 1974.

Sinfield, Alan. *Literature, Politics and Culture in Postwar Britain*. Berkeley: University of California Press, 1989.

Stallybrass, Peter and Allon White. *The Politics and Poetics of Transgression*. Ithaca, NY: Cornell University Press, 1986.

Starobinski, Jean. *Jean-Jacques Rousseau: Transparency and Obstruction*. Trans. Arthur Goldhammer. Chicago: University of Chicago Press, 1988.

Stedman Jones, Gareth. *Languages of Class: Studies in Working Class History 1832–1982*. Cambridge: Cambridge University Press, 1983.

Stocking, George W., Jr., ed. *Colonial Situations: Essays on the Contextualization of Ethnographic Knowledge*. Madison: University of Wisconsin Press, 1991.

Sykes, Robert. "Early Chartism and Trade Unionism." *The Chartist Experience: Studies in Working-Class Radicalism and Culture*. Eds. James Epstein and Dorothy Thompson. London: Macmillan, 1982.

Tholfson, Trygve R. *Working Class Radicalism in Mid-Victorian England*. New York: Columbia University Press, 1977.

Thomas, Paul. *Alien Politics: Marxist State Theory Retrieved*. New York and London: Routledge, 1994.

———. "Critical Reception: Marx Then and Now." *The Cambridge Companion to Marx*. Ed. Terrell Carver. Cambridge: Cambridge University Press, 1991, pp. 23–54.

Thompson, Dorothy. *The Chartists: Popular Politics in the Industrial Revolution*. New York: Pantheon, 1984.

Thompson, E. P. *The Making of the English Working Class*. New York: Vintage, 1966.

———. "The Moral Economy of the English Crowd in the Eighteenth Century." *Past and Present*. No. 50 (Feb. 1971), pp. 76–136.

———. "Outside the Whale." *Out of Apathy*. London: Stevens and Sons, 1960, pp. 158–65.

———. "The Peculiarities of the English." *The Poverty of Theory and Other Essays*. London: Merlin Press, 1979, pp. 35–91.

———. *Whigs and Hunters*. New York: Pantheon, 1975.

———. *William Morris: From Romantic to Revolutionary*. London: Merlin Press 1977.

Vernès, Paule-Monique. *La ville, la fête, la démocratie: Rousseau et les illusions de la communauté*. Paris: Payot, 1978.

Vester, Michael. *Die Entstehung des Proletariats als Lernprozess*. Frankfurt-am-Main: Europäische Verlagsanst, 1970.

Viswanathan, Gauri. *Masks of Conquest: Literary Study and British Rule in India*. New York: Columbia University Press, 1983.

Walton, John K. *Lancashire, a Social History, 1758–1939*. Manchester: Manchester University Press, 1987.

Webb, R. K., ed. *The British Working Class Reader, 1790–1848: Literacy and Social Tension*. London: Allen & Unwin, 1955.

Williams, Raymond. "Base and Superstructure in Marxist Cultural Theory." *Problems in Materialism and Culture*. London: Verso, 1980, pp. 31–49.

———. *Culture and Society, 1780–1950*. New York: Columbia University Press, 1983.

———. *George Orwell*. New York: Viking Press, Modern Masters Series, 1971.

———. *Marxism and Literature*. Oxford: Oxford University Press, 1977.

———. *Politics and Letters: Interviews with New Left Review*. London: New Left Books, 1979.

———. *Problems in Materialism and Culture*. London: Verso, 1980.

———. *Resources of Hope: Culture, Democracy, Socialism*. London: Verso, 1989.

———. *Writing in Society*. London: New Left Books, n.d.

Willis, Paul E. *Learning to Labor*. London: Routledge and Kegan Paul, 1979.

———. *Profane Culture*. London: Routledge and Kegan Paul, 1978.

Wilson, Benjamin. "The Struggles of Old Chartism." *Testaments of Radicalism*. Ed. David Vincent. Frankfurt: Europa, 1977.

Wokler, Robert. "Rousseau and Marx." *The Nature of Political Theory: Essays in Honour of John Plamenatz*. Eds. David Miller and Larry Siedentop. Oxford: Oxford University Press, 1983.

Wood, Ellen Meiksins. *The Retreat from Class*. London: Verso, 1986.

Woodcock, George. *The Crystal Spirit: A Study of George Orwell*. Boston: Little, Brown, 1966.

Wordsworth, William. *Poetical Works*. Ed. Thomas Hutchinson. Rev. Ernest de Selincourt. Oxford: Oxford University Press, 1969.

———. *The Prose Works of William Wordsworth*. Ed. W. J. B. Owen and Jayne Worthington Smyser. Vol 2. Oxford: Clarendon Press, 1974.

Wordsworth, William, and Samuel T. Coleridge. *Lyrical Ballads, 1798*. Ed. W. J. B. Owen. Oxford: Oxford University Press, 1969.

Yeo, Eileen. "Practices and Problems of Chartist Democracy." *The Chartist Experience*. Eds. James Epstein and Dorothy Thompson. London: Macmillan, 1982, pp. 345–80.

Zwerdling, Alex. *Orwell and the Left*. New Haven: Yale University Press, 1974.

PRIMARY ARCHIVAL SOURCES

"Address of the Democratic Chartist Association of Manchester to the Lovers of Truth and Liberty." *Poor Man's Guardian and Repealer's Friend*. No. 2.

Anderson, John. "Thoughts on Education." *The Workman's Friend*. Vol. 1, no. 1. 1 February 1862.

"Chartist Schools." *Chartist Circular*. 21 March 1841.

Form of Report for Her Majesty's Inspectors of Schools, Minutes of the Committee on Education, 1840–41.

Jones, Ernest. "Political Prisoners." Letter written at the Old Bailey, 10 July 1848, to Chief Justice Lord Truro. Reprinted in *Notes to the People*. Vol. I, no. 11. 1851.

"Letters from Lancashire, by a Lancashire Lad. I.—Something of Self-Education in Lancashire." *The Working Man*. 27 January 1866.

"Letters from Lancashire, II." *The Working Man*. 3 February 1866.

Linton, William. "The Right of Universal Suffrage: The Principle of the People's Charter, Part Two." *The Red Republican*. Vol. 1. 1848.

Mechanic's Magazine. No. 7. 11 October 1823.

———. No. 12. 15 November 1823.

———. No. 99. 16 July 1825.

———. (New Series). No. 7. 16 June 1827.

"Morality of the Working Classes." *Chartist Circular*. 2 November 1839.

"National Education." *Chartist Circular*. 28 September 1839.

New Moral World (Third Series). Vol. 1, no. 3, 18 July 1840.

———. Vol. 1, no. 17. 24 October 1840.

———. Vol. 1, no. 23. 5 December 1840.

Northern Star. 17 October 1840.

———. 11 July 1846.

———. 30 January 1847.

———. 29 January 1848.

Penny Papers . 18 March 1831.

———. 23 April 1831.

———. 26 March 1831.

"Political Intelligence." Editorial. *The Working Man*. 16 June 1866.

The Poor Man's Advocate and People's Library. 25 February 1832.

Poor Man's Guardian. 26 January 1833.

———. 28 February 1835.

"The Popular Education of the People." *Chartist Circular*. 21 December 1839.

"Popular Legislation—its Effects." *Chartist Circular*. 14 March 1840.

Proceedings of the Third Co-operative Congress. 23 April 1832. Ed. W. Carpenter.

"Progress of Democracy, Part Two." *Chartist Circular*. 1 October 1841.

"R. W. C. T." "The Education of the Young." *Sixpenny Magazine*. Vol. 9. 1 March 1865.

Republican, April 1832.

Rossiter, William. "History of the Working Men's College, I." *The Working Man*. 13 January 1866.

———. "History of the Working Men's College, II". *The Working Man*. 20 January 1866.

"Senex." On Associated Labour. Letter X. "On the Pretended Ignorance of the Working Classes." *The Pioneer: or, Trades Union Magazine*. Ed. James Morrison. 31 May 1834.

Solly, Rev. H. "The Working Men's Clubs and Institutes Movement. Their Origin and Progress." *The Working Man*. 30 January 1866.

Solly, Rev. H. Letter to Lord Lyttleton. 6 December 1866. *Occasional Papers of the Working Men's Club and Institute Union*. No. 9. February 1866.

Spence, Thomas. *The End of Oppression*, Cambridge University Library Rare Books.

The Times. 5 December 1866.

"The Value of Knowledge to Working Women." *The Working Man*. 28 April 1866.

Westminster Review. Vol. XIV, no. 28. April 1831.

"Working Men and the Art Treasures." *Art Treasures Examiner*. Manchester, 1857.

Index